Free At Last

Steven Rosen

About the author

Steven Rosen has been stalking the denizens of rock and roll for over twenty years. During that period he has written major features and cover stories for virtually every important music magazine including *Rolling Stone*, *Musician*, *Creem*, *Circus* and *Guitar Player* (including 16 cover stories), as well as *Playboy* and the *LA Times*.

He is also the author of rock books about Bruce Springsteen and Prince, as well as the highly acclaimed *Wheels of Confusion: The Story of Black Sabbath* and recently *The Beck Book* (a documentary on guitarist Jeff Beck).

This literary hunter has come face to face with the biggest animals in the musical kingdom. Confrontations include interviews with Led Zeppelin, Paul McCartney, Stevie Wonder, Frank Zappa, The Who and Michael Jackson. At times the pen-wielding writer has been called upon to accompany the likes of Led Zeppelin, ZZ Top, Deep Purple, Van Halen, Humble Pie and Aerosmith on safari to exotic locales.

Free At Last

The Story of Free and Bad Company

Steven Rosen

saf publishing

saf publishing

First published in 2001 by SAF Publishing Ltd

SAF Publishing
Unit 7, Shaftesbury Centre,
85 Barlby Road, London. W10 6BN
ENGLAND

www.safpublishing.com

ISBN 0 946719 37 3

Cover photographs: Paul Kossoff: Glen A. Baker / Redferns
                       Bad Company: Ian Dickson / Redferns

In some cases it has not proved possible to ascertain or trace original illustration copyright holders, and the publishers would be grateful to hear from the photographers concerned.

All lyrics quoted are for review, study or critical purposes.

The publishers would like to thank Paul Widger for additional editorial.

A CIP catalogue record for this book is available from the British Library.

Printed in England by The Cromwell Press, Trowbridge, Wiltshire.

CONTENTS

FOREWORD

Yes, dear reader, your esteemed author accompanied Bad Company on some of the West Coast shows on our first American tour. And pleasant company he was too, turning in a fine piece to *Rolling Stone* a bit later.

I like to think of myself as a literary buff and had an ongoing bet with Steven that the hapless hero in John Steinbeck's *Of Mice And Men* was named – Larry?

Steve swore it was Lenny. I said he was nuts and raised the bet to a dollar (money was tight back then). We upped it in increments of a quarter. When the book was produced and I read the name – Lenny – I, red-faced, handed over Steven's winnings.

He was gracious enough not to crow, "I told you so" and gave me a respectful shake of the hand.

You should've kept that tenner, Steven – what would it be worth now?

People ask me if I still have the fire? Absolutely. This is what I do and I do it bloody well. It is how I have made a living for nearly 35 years. Nothing can replace creating a good song, or playing a good gig. To be bathed in that applause is pretty special.

Like the astronauts who glimpse the planet Earth from deep space, we are never quite the same after that phenomenon.

I love my wife and family, my kids are very special to me – but a corner of me will always love performing live.

And I'll always love what I did with Free and Bad Company.

Simon Kirke
March 2001

INTRODUCTION & ACKNOWLEDGEMENTS

*It was the best of times, it was the worst of times
it was the age of wisdom, it was the age of foolishness
it was the epoch of belief, it was the epoch of incredulity,
it was the season of light, it was the winter of despair,
we had everything before us, we had nothing before us
we were all going direct to Heaven, we were all going direct the other way ....*

-from Charles Dickens' *A Tale of Two Cities*

Paul Kossoff, standing on stage at the Hollywood Palladium, wavered from side to side. Looking like some sort of buoy stuck in churning waters, the Free guitarist anchored himself by leaning against his massive stack of Marshall amplifiers. Reaching only around 5'3" in stature, he was dwarfed by these huge guitar cabinets and sought a way to hide behind them. Reluctantly standing in front of the amps, he looked most uncomfortable, as if something was chasing after him. Something was. Nightmares and demons triggered and fueled by too much alcohol and far too many drugs. The band, on this Thursday afternoon in 1972, was running through a soundcheck for the show they were scheduled to perform later that night.

The band – vocalist Paul Rodgers, drummer Simon Kirke, bassist Andy Fraser and guitarist Kossoff – ran through an afternoon set consisting of material from the group's then current album, *Free At Last*. Life ran in the wrong direction on this particular day. Though this should have been just a preamble for the main set, it ended up representing the entire show. It was impossible that someone as wrecked as Kossoff could have played with such passion, but he did. For the few people present at this afternoon tune-up, what they heard was music bordering on the aggressively angelic. Pre-show run-throughs are typically precursors to the Big Show and not the other way around. On this particular day, songs such as "My Brother Jake", "Sail On" and "Travelling Man" took on a character not present on the recorded versions. With head tilted and hair cascading down his back, the diminutive musician coaxed screaming and sensual notes from his Gibson Les Paul. Maybe it was because the venue was empty and there was nothing these four musicians had to prove. Maybe it was the Hollywood sunshine creeping in the side windows and washing the old dance hall in a shadows and light aura of some other world. Or maybe it was just that his guitar, perfect in tune and tone, a stunning partner to Rodgers' vocals, and supported by the rhythmic dialogue of Kirke and Fraser, combined to create a seamless performance. Sadly, only a handful of onlookers experienced the warm-up. Whatever it was, these four musicians conjured up a harmonic heaven if only for a few minutes. This was the best of Free.

Koss was in his own private mental room, a space inhabited by the personal muses he'd created. By 1972, he was drinking hard liquors and devouring an assortment of drugs virtually non-stop, giving him the edge he felt he needed. To some these were crutches, but for the guitarist they'd become necessities. Paul would die a few years later on a flight to New York on 19 March 1976. His passing would be devastating, finally marking the end of any possibility that Free might return.

Outside, cars rumbled east and west on Sunset Boulevard, the main artery of the machineries of the music business. All the record labels were situated up and down the boulevard including Atlantic, Columbia and Elektra, not to mention the high end recording studios such as Ocean Way and all the heavy entertainment law firms and publicity companies. Kossoff, after running through four or five songs, was barely able to stand upright and nearly dropped his guitar on the floor when he attempted to hand it to an attending roadie.

The band finished running through its set, placed guitars in stands, set amplifiers to standby and retired backstage. A few hours later, show time had arrived and the huge room, empty earlier in the day, was now stuffed sardine-like. Dr Hook and the Medicine Show opened the evening, running through a set of muscular pop tunes capped off with a frenzied version of their novelty-tinged hit single of the day, "The Cover of the *Rolling Stone*". Free took the stage after an hour's delay, apparently in an attempt to revive a stoned and drunken Kossoff. The effort failed and the quartet was reduced to a trio. Rodgers took the stage with his two remaining band mates and apologized for the late start. He told us Paul "wasn't feeling well" and made a heroic attempt at presenting a couple of songs. A justifiably angry audience hurled plastic cups as well as invectives at the threesome. They plowed through "My Brother Jake", Rodgers singing his heart and lungs out, but without Kossoff's guitar they sounded like a bad bar band doing third-rate cover versions. They left the stage, ignominiously diminished by the experience. Paul Rodgers was obviously embarrassed and even when he announced the band would return for a make-up show a few months later, the hostile crowd made no secret of their disdain. West, Bruce & Laing headlined that Friday evening debacle and by the close of their inferior Cream-influenced set, Free became a fleeting and swiftly forgotten memory. This was the worst of Free.

But for all the disappointment, sadness and anger experienced by these ticket buyers, this was really a remarkable moment – if unbeknownst to most of them. All the sadness and glory of rock 'n' roll had been revealed that day. On the one hand, this band had blown through a blistering pre-show warm-up, revealing the magic they possessed when everything fired properly, when the guitarist, even in an altered state, was able to reach inside himself and hurl out chilling notes of stunning intensity; when the singer, arguably one of the finest and most emotional to ever grab a microphone, tapped into that last hidden reserve of adrenaline. It was a living, breathing example of why the band had generated, if not overwhelming support, at least fanatical sustenance. Nobody did what these musicians did and nobody sounded like them.

And on the other hand, this guitarist so wonderfully possessed of digital legerdemain couldn't even get himself straight enough to appear at his own performance.

And that is in large part what this book is about. We take for granted that musicians simply unite, find a common ground and bash out a sound. But so many elements fall in the way – personality conflicts, power plays and the ubiquitous problems, which are always ever present. Whose name appears first on publicity releases? Who will be the main songwriter? Which member will handle the bulk of the interviews? Who gets the hot blond and who is stuck with the dumpy brunette? Who will be the one to fall under the nasty influence of drugs? The list is never-ending, and always reads the same.

Free was faced with all these stepping-blocks, but somehow managed to rise above them. And on that day, so many memories ago, they hurdled the obstacles and ran headlong into them. This book is an attempt at presenting in words the uphill climb they faced. The only way to truly understand the present is to inspect the past. How someone grows up, what they experience and don't experience, is what shapes character, and this biography will make every effort at exploring roads taken and roads left behind. The creation of music, at best, is a fragile proposition where the slightest nod or softly spoken comment might rend the whole process asunder. So we will listen carefully to those spoken words.

On that Hollywood afternoon, only a few diehards witnessed Kossoff swaying between creation and unconsciousness. His fragile skeleton was barely able to support the creative flesh. Maybe music is composed of just such moments, the silences scattered amongst the played notes. One word, one nod, one broken guitar string, one pill too many and the fire burns out, artistic ashes are scattered and the room grows cold. Had he taken one less drink that night, maybe he would have been able to perform. We'll never know.

Who knows how a band outdistances its own devils and demons? Bad management, bad decisions, drugs, egos and facing down the corporate monsters are just a few of the evil little things nipping at the heels. The simple coming together of four people with a common vision seems insurmountable. Most marriages never last and that is just the union of two people. So, when four people marry themselves to the notion of a higher cause, to the pursuit of imagination, and attempt to mold and fashion sounds, timbres and cadences into joyous, explosive, resonating strains, the odds against success seem infinite.

Though Paul Kossoff never played that night for Free's main set, he would recover enough in the following years to record albums, find the strength to undertake other tours, and even establish a solo career of his own.

This is a book about Free and Bad Company and Paul Kossoff and all the notes he, unfortunately, will never play. These pages will focus on Free, that band of blues brothers and Bad Company, the troupe organized by Paul Rodgers when his dear friend was melting before his eyes. This is not a book devoted to the drug-induced demise of Paul Kossoff, but in many respects these pages revolve around that senseless death. Rodgers focused on a new horizon prompted by the guitarist's earthly exit. The singer has confessed many times that if Paul had never passed he would have absolutely gone on to work with the guitarist in his next incarnation. These words will address that horrific event but the focus here will be far broader. Those were dark days and terrible times and no amount of words could resurrect his memory more truly than a single listen to his music. That was, however, a pivotal moment in the life of the band and it just seemed natural to open this volume with that long-gone day. Kossoff's passing was a cruel blow and greatly affected the momentum and future of these musicians, as well as the careers of countless other guitarists who hold his repertoire in the highest regard.

If you view that incident so many years ago as a whim, a happenstance, a bad juju, you might come away with a better sense of just how remarkable this band called Free really was. Stepping around landmines, looking past inflated egos and shrugging off the ever-present insult, they bonded and built a sound that some three decades later can still move the listener to tears. They reached inside you, tore your heart into yearning pieces and stunned you with an amalgamation of blues, soul and even folk, weaved into a unique style and sound unmatched by other bands.

This is the story of a musical journey, of survivors and those left behind, of paths crossed and paths never taken. The history of Free and the many legacies it spawned – Back Street Crawler, Kossoff, Kirke, Tetsu and Rabbit, Bad Company, The Firm, The Law, the splintering and reassembling of

Bad Company and various solo projects – is what I'll talk about here and try to understand.

I was a diehard fan of Free so when I heard Paul Rodgers and crew were playing at the Hollywood Palladium, I had to be there. As a journalist immersed in his first years of trying to get published, I had to sneak into that mid-afternoon soundcheck and hope I wasn't kicked out before the real show later that night. I didn't have the $6 price of admission so I pried open a side door and tried to appear as if I belonged there, as if watching a Free pre-concert rehearsal was just another day in the life.

How many times had I played "All Right Now" with various cover bands but never quite hearing it the right way? I experimented with different chord forms and listened to Kossoff's solos on a thousand different nights, slowing down my portable record player to 33 in the hope of catching the exact note. I never did. That song was one bitch of a tune to figure out.

Years later I had the supreme honor of sitting and talking with Paul Kossoff and he actually showed me how he played the chords on his very own Gibson Sunburst Les Paul guitar. That episode made me feel as if I could walk on water, walk through fire, or at the very least now play the song I had wrestled with for a virtual eternity. That interview would appear as a feature in the July 1976 issue of *Guitar Player Magazine*. I was so psyched when Koss showed me the magic chord forms that I made a point of including diagrams in my article showing the exact fingerings of the chords.

What made Free so compelling was the apparent simplicity of their music. At first blush, copping a Free tune seemed a breeze but on second and third and tenth listening, you realized how wonderfully the guitar weaved in and around Andy Fraser's melodic bass figures. And how Paul came up with the most twisted and tantalizing chord figures and how seemingly impossible they were to recreate.

The bulk of this book is based on dozens of interviews I conducted over a period of nearly 25 years. These include multiple recorded conversations with the principals: Paul Rodgers, Paul Kossoff, Simon Kirke, Mick Ralphs, and Boz Burrell. Andy Fraser was not available for comment. I also spoke with many auxiliary players including Geoff Whitehorn, Tony Braunagel, Terry Wilson, Terry Slesser and many others. Again, special thanks must be passed on to Paul Rodgers and Simon Kirke for taking time out of crazy schedules to pass on recalled memories. In early 1974, I spent several days with Bad Company when they were in Los Angeles, traveling with them on their private bus to several local shows and just generally hanging out. I even convinced *Rolling Stone* to run a story on the band before their album had even been released, and in writing this first major report on the band was able to establish a long-term relationship with them. And all those historic moments are represented here.

I went through hundreds of magazines (*Creem, Circus, Musician, Sounds, Melody Maker, Guitar Player, Guitar World* and many others) in an attempt to find out something I didn't already know. I perused dozens of music encyclopedias and source books; anthologies on the culture of the sixties and seventies and eighties; and a potpourri of peripheral periodicals that may have shed some light on the subject. I listened to every track on every Free and Bad Company album as well as a handful of bootlegs and also tracks from the various solo offshoots from two main bands.

But I could not have written this without the selfless help of the principals and so I bestow undying thanks and bend in supplication to Paul Kossoff and Paul Rodgers and Mick and Simon and Boz for the giving of their time. And an extra nod to Simon for his wonderfully insightful e-mails worthy of a book in their own right.

To Mick and Dave from SAF Publishing who saw the merit in this project and gave me the green light.

Cynthia Michelle and Laura Kramer helped connect the dots and got me from here to there. Sean Dennison (for trying to make the dream come true) and Bobby Jackson (the greatest fan in the world). Danny Goldberg put me on the road with Led Zeppelin for nine days and gave me tales I will tell my grandchildren.

In trying to create a more fully realized picture of their music, I contacted a number of other persons who were critical in the evolution of the band. They include Rabbit Bundrick, a longtime friend and auxiliary band member during the waning days of Free. This Texas keyboardist deserves special thanks for providing me with the introduction to many other musicians. Rabbit made a special request that his web site address be displayed and that is the least I can do. The keyboardist can be reached at: www.johnbundrick.freeserve.co.uk. Others include: Sandhe Chard (whose memories of Kossoff brought him into clearer focus), David Kossoff, Tetsu Yamauchi, Johnny Glover, Richard Digby Smith, Bob Pridden, Snuffy Walden and Todd Jensen. I also spoke at length with Jimmy Page and had the unique experience of talking with Alexis Korner and also John Mayall. Ritchie Blackmore for confessing to the fact that Paul Rodgers was the noblest singer to ever draw a breath (as if I didn't know that already). Producers/engineers Eddie Kramer, Ron Nevison and Andy Johns for spreading the magic on tape and telling me what it was like working in the studio with these musical giants.

I would also like to thank my father Hal for putting up with me, and my younger brother Mick for believing in me. Nods are also in order to my sweet sister-in-law Nancy, my best friend and music writing partner

Jimmy Waldo and his obliging wife JoAnn, and to Howard and Dana at Sunset Records. I owe a bow to Toby Mamis, David Clayton (a true keeper of the Free flame), Brad Gregory, Rose (from the Record Plant), Tim Young and to Pete Frame for his magic music trees and David Evans for supplying a missing piece.

And to my mom who isn't here to read these pages but would smile if she could.

Lest I forget, Michael Cecilia, Mark Spiro, Sven Gusevik and Richard Ellis for the giving of their time – when I really needed it.

And to the legions of the Free and companions of Bad Company, I thank you. You've kept the band alive with your never ending interest, your web sites and fanzines. I hope after you digest these pages that you come away from the experience with a feeling that *"you were there"*. I want you to understand, in as real a sense as possible, what it was like spending time with these brothers of invention. This book is culled from over twenty years of writing about and spending time with these creative creatures. My greatest wish is at the end of the day, or more precisely at the end of this book, you take a deep breath and say, "I know this band. I know what they think about, I know what they feel about the music they've made and I know how they view the world around them." I want you to feel a part of the pages you now hold in your hands and my greatest wish is that I haven't disappointed you.

Anyone who would like to contact me may do so through my email, srosen11@netzero.net

Steven Rosen

BAND ON THE BUS

Roll along, roll along,
O'er the deep blue sea
Yes, life woulda been
a mistake without music"
                    -from Jack Kerouac's *Mexico City Blues 53rd Chorus*

A highly customized tour bus pulled up in front of the Sunset Strip's Continental Hyatt House, the home away from home for traveling musicians, minstrels and entertainers of all varieties. This was the safe house, the neutral zone turned into a den of sins when Led Zeppelin, several years earlier, reserved entire floors and transformed them into 24-hour orgy fests. They would ride motorcycles the length and breadth of entire hallways; they would rip television sets from hotel rooms. The Who indulged in their own unique brand of hotel trashing. Jeff Beck had his moments as well. The establishment flew under a new banner when musicians were in residence: The Riot House. Inside this palace of chrome and glass and $5 cups of coffee, Paul Rodgers, Simon Kirke, Boz Burrell and Mick Ralphs are making last-minute checks of personal inventory. Bags are given a final once over, zippered, drinks hastily swallowed, and the troupe makes its way to an awaiting elevator. Older guests feign nonchalance, stealing glances when they think no one is looking, but the teenagers and sons and daughters of these parents stare unabashedly and can't believe Bad Company are here in *their* hotel. They run up to the English quartet, pens and pads at the ready, hoping against all odds that they'll score an autograph or at the very least manage a handshake or hello. This is a moment, a space in time these diehard devotees will never forget and would never forgive themselves for a missed opportunity. Books are signed, hands are shaken and the troupe makes its way down to the bus.

The waiting vehicle is a motorized boudoir, entertainment complex and culinary convoy. There are berths for anyone in need of privacy, individual sleeping quarters isolated by heavy soundproof curtains, easily unrolled to cover the hibernating areas. Color televisions and audio centers with enough decibel disseminating features to blow out windows are at hand. A fully stocked refrigerator with a gourmet selection of edible delicacies and high-end beverages – from imported beers and *sommelier*-chosen wines to top-label whiskies, vodkas and brandies. Enough food and drink to feed an army and then get it too drunk to fight.

This was 1974 when success was measured by excess and Bad Company sat firmly atop the fatted calf. Journalist Tom Wolfe called the seventies the "Me Decade". Indeed. Record labels couldn't do enough to pamper their artists and this rolling chariot represented a mechanized example of this overboard syndrome. Too much was never too much. Bad Company had just been signed to Led Zeppelin's private boutique label, Swan Song Records, were being managed by Zeppelin's own power broker, Peter Grant, and already had a Top Five hit single in "Can't Get Enough" (from their eponymously titled first album). All the elements were there. Mick Ralphs sat on a custom lounge, delicately sipping some exotic concoction from an expensively cut crystal beaker and seemingly oblivious to the impending gig. Paul Rodgers wandered about the bus, singing softly to himself. Boz eyeballed some cable music video on one of the numerous mounted monitors. And Simon was deluged with a virtual library of John Steinbeck paperbacks. He was, and remains, a serious fan of the master storywriter and reading provided a literary tranquilizer.

What made this hour-and-a-half carriage ride to the city of San Bernardino so surreal was the feeling of being on the edge of big changes. Looking from the outside, this was just another band on the run, boys on a bus ride to an out-of-town gig. But if you peeled back the layers and had a chance to see beneath the surface, you'd realize this was no ordinary expedition and, for these four young men, no ordinary times. They were on the road leading to the gilded castle – they were the new conquering kings. Bad Company, four young English boys from working class families, had traveled long highways to arrive at this moment. San Berdoo, as the city was jocularly referred to, a place best known for rotten air, bikers and meth labs, was one of many dates on this 1974 US tour. And while it may not have been the defining moment in the development and emergence of this band from the ashes of Free, King Crimson and Mott the Hoople, it was a perfect example of the empire they had created.

The Swing Auditorium was a large old hall previously used for rodeos and monster truck rallies. On this Saturday night the floors were covered not with sawdust but with people, legions of fans who had bought the first Bad Company record and catapulted the band from new risers into headliners almost overnight. These were the rabid ones, the Free followers waiting to see where Paul Rodgers would surface. Wearing Bad Company t-shirts and hats, these were boys and girls out for a night of real rock without the embroidery. This crowd was ready to be sonically reassembled and the band would not disappoint. For these 6,000-plus diehards, realization would be far heavier than the anticipation.

Many people – critics, media, industry honchos – saw the seventies, and particularly these middle years, in less than glorious terms. It was a period when rock became big business dependent on how many tickets you could sell and how many bodies could you cram into a hall. Gargantuan sellers such as Pink Floyd's *Dark Side of the Moon* and Peter Frampton's *Frampton Comes Alive!* became the benchmarks. The intimacy of performances in smaller venues and clubs dissolved into lost notions. Revenues ruled and artistry fell by the wayside. Thankfully, heartfelt and insightful artists such as Jackson Browne and Joni Mitchell brought balance back to the playing field by demonstrating that songs possessing melodic content and lyrical weight could still find a home in this overblown decade.

Bad Company crossed all the boundaries by marrying bluesy and pop-oriented rock/arena anthems with incisive and wonderfully constructed melodies and lyrics. Their music was at once intimate and universal, a product of the unique talents of all four members. Paul Rodgers was a singer capable of bringing the individual listener into his own private vocal world, seducing them with a voice variously striated with R&B inflections and blues leanings. At the same time, he could fill a void such as the Swing Auditorium with sung utterances of Godlike proportions, taking 6,000 separate souls on a journey to the end of the musical night. Guitarist Mick Ralphs had a keen ear for composing and his slimy, swampy guitar licks were essential in weaving the musical magic carpet upon which Paul would lay his golden vocal cords. Boz Burrell brought an arty approach to the bass, climbing inside the music with textured and symphonic four-string lines fingered on his fretless instrument. And drummer Simon Kirke was the timekeeper, the metronome, the kid behind the kit who long ago left the fast feet and fills to players such as Bonham and Moon.

The show was an important harbinger of things to come for Bad Company. The dedicated hordes screamed themselves hoarse, fists raised in air in exuberant communal harmony. Bodies swayed in a single orgiastic motion. On this night, and for years to come, the band would fill halls, return for encores and exit auditoriums in extensively outfitted buses that would take the English foursome back to expensive and lavishly appointed hotel rooms. On the ride back to the Continental Hyatt House, the band was finally able to unwind, sipping on cold imported beers and breathing in the heady air of success. But it was not always like this, nor would it stay like this forever.

For now, the years of playing in warm-up bands, school bands, bands that really didn't appreciate you, and bands you didn't really want to be in, were over. All the hardships encountered in trying to bring Free to international acclaim had vanished, and were now replaced by huge tours, fast cars and the best looking girls.

But to fully understand how the band had arrived at this lofty perch in 1974, you have to travel back through the corridors of their personal experiences, back to those defining moments of human emotion and interaction. When the concept of strapping on guitars and making records and performing in front of people became more than just passing whims; when these acts became as important as breathing. When creating music started out as a ritual experienced second-hand by listening to old-time Victrolas, playing vinyl albums on small portable tabletop record players, and by watching other bands step onstage. Viewing The Beatles and Elvis Presley on the Ed Sullivan Show; those universal encounters everyone experiences. A time arrives, however, not for everyone but for the select few, when the adduction becomes too great, when the attraction to the art draws you to it like sailors to the siren's call. When watching the show or listening to a broadcast is not enough – participation becomes priority number one. For Paul Rodgers, Paul Kossoff, Simon Kirke and Andy Fraser, the transition from onlookers to zombie-like zealots swiftly became reality. Then follows a journey down the road littered with the bodies and broken hearts of all those would-be musicians who never quite got it right. The ones who fell prey to bad decisions, monstrous managers, the killing allure of drugs and alcohol and the most terrible plague of all – the refusal to accept their own weaknesses as singers, guitarists, bassists or drummers. And then begins the baby steps of learning an instrument, asking parents for that guitar in the shop window, the one with strings so high off the neck that fingers are bloodied and hands terribly cramped as a result of attempting to master the beast. Pots and pans are bashed to hell in trying to recreate a drum set and microphones are fashioned from rolled-up newspapers. These are the early episodes every musician recognizes.

But these musicians had the gift of creation, of vision, of tenacity built on sheer determination of will. These pages will reveal the brutal realities these artists still had to endure and at the end of it all, how they succeeded in conceptualizing and ultimately realizing a sound, a singular vision.

IF GOD CARRIED A TUNE

Paul Rodgers is easily one of the best
singers in the Rock & Roll world!

-Mick Jagger

The names are famous landmarks immortalized as stopping points for the touring rock band. The Whisky in Los Angeles where Zeppelin played for $500 a night on their first journey to America; the heralded Fillmores East and West, owned by the now departed promoter extraordinaire Bill Graham; the Agoura Ballroom in Cleveland; the Fox Theater in Atlanta; and the Psychedelic Supermarket in Boston. These were the hallowed halls that bands, just beginning the journey, called home. Free performed at many of these venues but on 8 June 2000, Paul Rodgers assembled a band to play at the legendary Cavern Club in Liverpool, England. The Cavern Club – the king daddy of them all – a dank, sticky, underground lair which first opened its doors on 16 January 1957 as a jazz haven.

A few years later The Beatles would appear here more than 300 times between 1961 and 1963. Rodgers may not have known all the dates, but he did know that The Beatles had played here, created what we now know as the Merseybeat sound – that hybrid of rock 'n' roll, blues and sweetly sung pop – and altered for all time the way music sounded and how it could shake us from our tree. This was a place he'd heard about since he was a young boy, a sort of Shangri-la only imagined in his most distant dreams. No one was left untouched by The Beatles and certainly for a young boy growing up in England during the reign of the Fab Quartet, their influence was overwhelming.

On this summer evening, in the town that gave the group to the world, the singer tagged "Rock 'n' Roll Fantasy" with a mini-Beatles tribute, covering such classics as "I Feel Fine" and "A Hard Day's Night". Ghosts inhabited this hallowed hall, the memories of music history swirling around the basement room. These were the same voices that had spoken to him many years earlier when John Lennon and Paul McCartney revealed to him the secret of life. That a musician in quest of that Holy Grail is able to unlock any door in pursuit of his ultimate vision. At once inspired, awed and perhaps slightly intimidated by performing here, Rodgers is only able to talk in superlatives in describing the event.

"I played in the Cavern recently; it was a fantasy thing. The spirit was really strong; I could feel those guys all around me. We hadn't really planned to go there. But a couple of years ago I visited as a tourist while on tour and I thought, 'Oh, we're in Liverpool and I got to see the Cavern.' I went down and stood on the stage that they played on. There's two stages down there, one is under construction, and the one they used is slightly bigger but it's over on the side. It was awesome. Unfortunately, I never saw them live. I was thirteen when they were out there doing it. I was a school kid really.

"They really were a big influence in the sense of when I looked at them, and probably the other guys too, you felt, 'Well, if they can do that coming from the same background as me, I could quite possibly do it too.' Maybe not as grand but I too can escape what's in store for me if I stay here. Which was a job in the factories and the furnaces and the steel works.

"It's funny though. I saw a picture recently in one of the magazines, and I don't know where they get all these shots, but there's a shot of Lennon in McCartney's house making tea before they were famous. He's a young lad, probably eighteen. He's making tea in the background in this little old kitchen and all the pots and pans and the shape of the bottles and everything is exactly the way I was brought up. We were brought up in a similar area of the world just across the other side of England."

This 'other side' was Middlesbrough, where a young Paul was brought up in a typical working class family. The fourth of seven children, and the first boy, he was raised by a father working on the docks and a stay-at-home mother. Along with older sisters Tina, Doreen and Susan, and younger siblings Ian, Stella and Gerad, there was little to look forward to – you either went into shipbuilding, the steelworks, chemicals or heavy factory jobs. Paul's first baby scream echoed throughout the halls of Parkside Maternity Hospital in the early hours of 17 December 1949. He kept his mouth open and this became the vehicle that would cart him away from a future of blue-collar work. Only a few years later the ultimate decision was reached that a career as an iron forger or chemical worker was not on the cards. Music became his chosen chariot.

At the tender age of twelve, Paul's parents Bernard and Phyllis managed to scrape together a few extra pounds and bought him a guitar – life was changed forever. Immersing himself in the instrument was not an easy task. But these sounds moved him, these strings being strummed and these songs being sung. The Beatles proved to be a major influence along with the Rolling Stones. When he saw other bands at school playing music, the Lorelei's call drew him hither. A band was joined with schoolmates and they rehearsed in a friend's kitchen, Paul strumming wildly on a dreadful six-string while the pseudo-drummer assaulted a set of pots and pans. But the guitar didn't come easy and proved to be more frustrating than fulfilling. He turned his attention to the bass, figuring that this would be an easier instrument to master since it had two fewer strings than a normal guitar. This, too, was a losing prospect and he "put that down and tried singing and was getting away with the singing pretty good."

His voice was a piece of machinery he could control and after rehearsing in food preparation areas for some months, he started to feel as if headway was being made. But if truth be told, he really didn't feel they were any good.

"Various people heard us and thought, 'That's not bad.' Yards of confidence from a little compliment like that and eventually we did our first gig and people actually danced. This was quite good. My first gig I played bass and sang on one song; I think it was 'Louie Louie' or the Searchers 'What Have They Done To the Rain' (originally recorded by Malvina Reynolds). This was a group called the Titans "because that was the name on the drum kit" comprising vocalist and rhythm guitarist Colin Bradley, drummer Malcolm Cairns and guitarist Mick Moody (a schoolmate chum from St. Thomas Secondary Modern in Grove Hill; he would later be aligned with Tramline, Juicy Lucy, SNAFU, David Coverdale's Whitesnake and the Moody Marsden Band).

Still playing cover material, Rodgers started his dues paying by doing odd club dates around his hometown. The Titans first outing was a less than stellar performance as a beat band in November 1964 at St. Mary's Cathedral Youth Club on Sussex Street. Drawing on blues and pop, the Titans metamorphosed into the Roadrunners (the name appropriated from the Jr Walker track). Paul was still on bass, another instrument his parents sacrificed to purchase, but gravitated more towards the position of vocalist when Colin made the decision to depart. Bruce Thomas (later to become an Attraction with Elvis Costello) was brought in on bass. Right after leaving school, around the spring of 1967, Paul made the decision to forgo the chemical or dock work of Middlesbrough to venture south to London. The former lead singer had felt the move was "too risky". A new drummer was brought in by the name of Dave Usher, a "guy with wild flaming, ginger hair".

In preparation for the journey south, the band gigged as much as possible in local clubs and dives.

"We had guitar, bass, singer and a drummer and we did a lot of shows. We had a good following and were making quite a splash. We weren't writing our own songs, we were doing our own arrangements of the stuff we liked. Blues and pop and everything."

The Roadrunners, in short order, transformed into The Wildflowers, a moniker adopted to embrace the growing Mod and psychedelic strains swiftly changing the landscape of music, fashion and culture both in England and America.

The trek to London was made in a van that broke down en-route to the big city – would history have it any other way? Moody, Rodgers, Thomas and Usher lived communally, sharing an upstairs room in Finsbury Park. They did manage to sign with a musical employment agency but gigs only numbered about one or two per week. Eventually forced to sell everything not breathing, including clothes, stage props and even Paul's prized PA columns, band life had become almost unbearable.

Whoever said life only hands us as much as we can take was either insane or dreaming. London life tossed a brick load of worries on these youths such as their van's last gasp on the way to a show at Floral Hall in Great Yarmouth. The infamous date was 3 June 1967 – a very black Saturday. Moody and Thomas hitched back to London; Usher tossed in the towel and returned to the Northeast of England.

They found a replacement through the music weeklies, but this proved a mere stop-gap. The Wildflowers were wilting. Venturing into Selmer's Music Shop, a visit they made regularly, the band ran into a little gnome-like sales assistant named Paul Kossoff. He suggested Andy Borenius, a drummer pal. Rodgers and band snapped him up and continued playing dates, using Andy as not only a drummer but also a source of food and housing. They ate him out of house and home. Kossoff, living just around the corner, came by one afternoon with Simon Kirke, the drummer in his own band, Black Cat Bones.

Borenius was only a Band-Aid on a bloodied body and Moody, fed up with London and Rodgers, followed Usher in making the long sorrowful journey back to Middlesbrough.

The Wildflowers, for all their preparation and club gigging, didn't fare very well. Rodgers, without a band and short of money, made a brief attempt at continuing his education. This didn't work out and desperately in need of funds he decided to sell his two Marshall 4x12 block cabinets, since blown out, and bought a more streamlined Selmer 100-watt amplifier. Paul joined a blues band seeking a singer and since they didn't have a name, Rodgers suggested Brown Sugar. He did some dates with them, but the other members saw the project as a 'fun' thing while Paul was determined to turn the band into a professional unit. Approaching Brown Sugar as a stepping-stone, he sought out something much grander. He wanted to keep his hand on the tiller, being out there and doing shows. At the core, he wanted to create a band along the lines of the Beatles, Cream and Hendrix.

"We were pretty creative. Then Hendrix came out and sort of blew everybody's mind totally. He was the next phase of rock 'n' roll but it was still the blues. And we were listening to the blues as well. We listened to a wide range of music. I listened to Otis Redding and it was all great music and I didn't categorize it so much. So we mixed pop with whatever was in the charts. There were so many Beatles look-alikes; I mean if you look back at the Searchers and Gerry and the Pacemakers and all those bands. But God bless them. They were great bands and all very Beatleish and all in a certain vein and this whole Hendrix thing really put it all together: the psychedelic stuff, the hair, the image, the guitar, the blues. Because 'Hey Joe' was the first song we heard in England (Jimi turned it all around with the release of this 45 in the UK in early 1967 resulting in the first of his many Top 10 singles) and that was really a slow blues."

The next phase was a particularly critical juncture for Rodgers. During the mid and late sixties, London found itself awash with blues. A revival of this American art form had found its way across the Atlantic in the guise of stalwarts such as Muddy Waters and had inspired the indigenous population. Paul actually saw the legendary one perform at the Marquee Club and was instantly fixated.

London during this period was the hatching lab and stomping ground for all that was new and unusual. At the heart of this were London-living musicians who intercepted this new-found art form and morphed it into a sound of their own. Cream was the supreme interpreter. They too arose from the heady wake of the Beatles and had appropriated simple blues changes and shuffled the pieces to give birth to a sound no one had ever heard. Like Rodgers, the trio – guitarist Eric Clapton, bassist Jack Bruce and drummer Ginger Baker – resurrected long-forgotten tracks by the blues masters and lobotomized these songs into a sound often far removed from the originals. Muddy Waters' "Rollin' and Tumblin'", Robert Johnson's "I'm So Glad" and Willie Dixon's "Spoonful" were administered amplified shock treatment and so entranced an audience that the threesome, some three-plus decades later, still remains the final word on the Anglicizing of American blues.

"I'd seen Cream in my hometown. During their fledgling years they played at a lot of small clubs and I was at one of them, in front of the stage which was only knee-high. They didn't have the equipment we have now; it was the big Marshall stacks, a kit that wasn't miked, and two PA columns off to the side. It was a great sound. I sat through Ginger Baker's solo ("Toad") and Jack Bruce's harmonica solo ("Traintime"). They dressed in these sailor trousers – flared trousers – and the next morning we were down buying these sailor trousers made out of canvas stuff. We were so hip."

Rodgers experienced not only the blues-directed sounds of Cream but the more arty twists and turns of groups such as Procol Harum and the

Moody Blues. With their classic composition, "A Whiter Shade Of Pale," the former, fronted by Gary Brooker, a gifted vocalist/writer/keyboardist, synthesized pop with the dirge-like rhythms English smart art bands would continue to create for years. Procol, named after a feline belonging to one of the members, had borrowed a melody from classical composer JS Bach and stitched it to cryptic verses penned by lyricist Keith Reid. Lyrically, the listener either becomes part of an acid trip gone terribly wrong or is simply a participant in a wordsmith's elegant exercise. Reid would later pronounce "obscurity means profundity".

The Moody Blues began life as a Beatles clone but soon began adopting strains that had drifted over the Big Pond from San Francisco's Haight-Ashbury area. Their sound was crafted not so much on obscure wordplay – though they too ventured into lyrical realms unknown – but rather on the strength of noble instrumentation. Much like Brooker's troupe, the Moody Blues blended classical with pop but enhanced this by utilizing a then new primitive keyboard called a Mellotron. This pre-synth synth used rows of actual cassette-type tapes to reproduce the sounds of cellos, flutes and horns.

All of this Paul took in and, no maybes, he was a man amazed.

"Yes, London was quite eye-opening. 1968 was a big turning point; there was a lot happening. Twiggy and the whole thing, fashion and music, and I haunted all the areas, King's Road and places like that; there was music in every shop and every window. It was a great thing."

Brown Sugar, playing mostly covers with Rodgers honking it out on harmonica, were playing a show at The Fickle Pickle, a pub in Finsbury Park. Kossoff stopped by and would join them on stage to run through BB King's "Four O'Clock In the Morning", "Stormy Monday Blues", "Everyday I Have the Blues" and additional material making up two 45-minute sets. Kossoff and Rodgers connected immediately. Paul remembers the experience.

"I was looking for like-minded people and it's funny because when you put that out there, it seems to draw those kinds of people. Paul Kossoff turned up for a jam at one of the Brown Sugar gigs and that proved the advantage of being out there on the lookout."

Though this wasn't their initial meeting – having bumped into one another at Selmer's and Andy's Music shop in Denmark Street – it was their true first musical interaction. In his mind, Paul was now certain that making the trek to London had been the right choice. Paul details the memories of his first jam with Kossoff.

"There was this instant spark – even the audience felt it. You could hear a pin drop when we played something like 'Stormy Monday Blues' during the quiet passage. And he was as intense and emotional as I was about the music, about doing it. We were very passionate. As soon as we got off stage it was, 'Yeah, we've got to put a band together.' He actually suggested I come and join Black Cat Bones, which was his current band, but I felt if I was going to join another band and not start something new, I might as well stay where I was. I was all for starting something brand new. I had started to write songs and I could see the potential there. I had written 'Walk In My Shadow' which appeared on the first Free album. And I also wrote 'Over the Green Hills'. So we were of the same mind; we were not going to do day jobs where someone would say, 'Oh, I can't do that gig, man, I have to be at work.' We were going to be totally dedicated to doing shows."

Kossoff, together with Simon Kirke, left the remaining Black Cat Bones to fend for themselves. But not completely. Always one to hedge bets and cover his bases, the guitarist remained with the band while rehearsing with this new singer. Simon did the same. In this way, if the new union did not work, both Koss and Kirke would still have employment.

The future Free were three – a bassist had to be uncovered.

BAND OF ANGELS

After silence that which comes nearest to
expressing the inexpressible is music.

-Aldous Huxley

Unlike Paul Rodgers, who had grown up in a working class home in an industrial town, Paul Francis Kossoff was raised in an upper class household in London. Paul's father, David, was the master of the house, a dominant yet loving parent who had made a name for himself as a mainstay of English television and stage (appearing with Peter Sellers, Jean Seberg, William Hartnell, and Leo McKern in the 1959 satire *The Mouse That Roared* and many other productions). Jennie, David's wife, was the family caregiver, always the protective and proud mother, and Paul, her baby. Even in his early youth, he exhibited the driven approach that would remain for the rest of his life. In sports, for instance, he took it to the edge, fearlessly pursuing skiing and high board diving with no thought for life or limb. His diving exploits earned him the nickname "the flying rockcake". As a young boy of seven or eight, he was entranced by horses and the day would often find him galloping at breakneck speeds on animals he could barely control.

But sport was not where the youthful Kossoff was headed. Music blew his way when he was still a lad in shorts and he followed his nose. Born 14 September 1950, the youngest of two sons (brother Simon was two years his senior), he quickly abandoned sports and as a boy began studying classical guitar with teacher Blanche Monroe, a one-time student of a local professional who had tutored under the legendary Segovia. Even in serious moments he combined mischievousness with an insightful sense of humor, in contrast to brother Simon. The older member gave no quarter when it came to scholastic pursuits while the last-born breezed through school with hardly a care. His time was spent toiling with a cheap acoustic guitar, a pursuit that consumed six years of his young life.

During this period he attended private schools (until age fourteen), then his father, a strict Jewish man of principle, moved him to the neighborhood state school in Golders Green. Though neither son was ever *barmitzvahed*, they were required to attend Hebrew School – after a fashion. But Koss was already spreading his wings, flashing that energy which would become almost impossible to corral, and began experimenting with various pep and diet pills. This new school did little to curb his appetites and so father decided to take his son on the road with him where Paul would play guitar and actually act as assistant stage manager.

Though Paul abandoned his classical training, he retained a love for the instrument. His heart would beat like a Bonham bass drum upon seeing Tommy Steele play the London Palladium. During one performance, the slightly rotund adolescent made his way backstage to meet this larger-than-life idol and it was not long after this that his first guitar, a Steele knockoff, made of compressed plastic and virtually impossible to play, was in his hands. He would be electrified when listening to his father's collection of Big Bill Broonzy and Ray Charles albums. But nothing could compare to the night he witnessed Eric Clapton performing with John Mayall's Bluesbreakers at The Refectory in Golders Green. This was the winter of 1965.

And this was the magical London of the mid to late sixties, the London that Paul Rodgers would find when he migrated south. Though the two future band members would take extraordinarily different paths to this place, they both found themselves transfixed by what they saw and heard. This was fast becoming the focus of the music world, where Clapton and later Jimi Hendrix would take the blues, electrify it and smash it down the eardrums of awestruck teenagers. Where Jimmy Page would soon redevelop the art of studio recording with his Keith Moon-monikered Led Zeppelin band; where Jeff Beck would take up the challenge by twisting the blues into even more unrecognizable forms, aided by a then virtually unknown vocalist named Rod Stewart. This is the mythical kingdom where Peter Green, Mick Taylor and Mick Abrahams would travel new roads armed with little more than Les Pauls and Stratocasters. This was the nexus – it all began here.

What was that moment like for hundreds of young boys, like Kossoff, seeing a baby-faced Clapton create the sound and technique that would be forever etched into the vocabulary of blues/rock guitar? In that club, on that evening, Paul Kossoff found himself.

"The first real inspiration I had to get back into playing was seeing Eric Clapton with John Mayall (the Bluesbreakers included Hughie Flint on drums and John McVie, who would ultimately join Mick Fleetwood in Fleetwood Mac, on bass) at a small club. I didn't know who he was or what had gone down, but here's all these people yelling, 'God, God!' He really caught my attention and then I wanted to play. I found that my classical training had no bearing on that sort of music, other than dexterity. After Clapton, my interest grew. I went from him to Peter Green (Fleetwood Mac's Jewish guitarist), to BB King and Freddie King, and then I got into soul – Otis Redding and Ray Charles (the same vocalists Paul Rodgers admired). Green and Clapton were very dexterous and powerful at the same time. Clapton is everything I'd like to be. I also liked [keyboardist] Long John Baldry, and Rod Stewart was good in those days too. I saw the Jeff Beck band with Stewart and was very impressed."

Kossoff was smitten. The sound that Clapton created with his Gibson Les Paul and Marshall amplifier (now recognized as a classic combination) lit him up like a muzzle blast. Forming his own band was all he could think of and in between low rent jobs as a factory robot and bike messenger, he spent all his waking hours working on finding other musicians. A group of like-minded thinkers was assembled and practiced in an abandoned garage in close proximity to the Kossoff household. Father David banged nails and cut planks in order to provide his son with a rehearsal space. Around age sixteen, the young Kossoff landed a job as a sales person in Selmer's musical instrument shop on Charing Cross Road in London. The Goddess Fortune was smiling. He educated himself about gear, learning the simple workings of amplifiers and the differences between various types of guitars. But he turned deaf, dumb and blind when, a scant two weeks after beginning work, a frizzy-haired black man with hands the size of Christmas hams walked in the door. Pulling down a right-handed instrument from the wall, this bizarre figure reversed the guitar, flipping it over to play it in a left-handed fashion. Paul was at once stupefied and intimidated.

"When I was fifteen or sixteen, Hendrix first came to Britain with Chas Chandler (ex-Animals bassist turned manager) and he was going around to the music shops and I was working in one. In that shop, if there were a colored person buying something, they'd put a 'C' on the top of the sales sheet. Chas came in with Jimi one day and, honestly, Hendrix looked freaky and he really did smell! When he first walked in, all the salesmen were going, 'Oh, my God!' There weren't any guitars strung left-handed so he took this right-handed (Fender) Strat and turned it over, so that the low *E* was on the bottom. He started playing some chord stuff like in 'Little Wing' and the salesmen looked at him and couldn't believe it. They wouldn't own up to it afterwards, but they were all hanging around him, putting up with the smell and everything. He didn't buy anything, but just seeing him really freaked me; I just loved him to death. He was my hero and still remains my hero."

Several months later this pungent, freaked-out character who played guitar upside down, would release "Hey Joe," his first single, and that instant would represent another life-altering experience for the struggling musician.

By 1968, London was in the inescapable grip of the blues Renaissance; Clapton, Green, Taylor and a host of others were on their way to legendary status. What America had wrought, England had bought. John Mayall and Alexis Korner were the Godfathers of the movement, assembling bands on the fly, shifting members around like so many puzzle-pieces. They would be pivotal in the eventual formation of the band known as Free.

Paul had been practicing, working with the instrument to develop his own identity, his own set of string-prints. He was more than aware that no one sounded like Clapton and no one approached the blues like Peter Green and that in order to become a significant player he would have to develop his own style. This woodshedding reaped rewards when he came to the attention of a local R&B septet called Black Cat Bones. They had already ensconced themselves as a mainstay around the London club circuit and had appeared at various pubs and clubs including the flagship Marquee on Wardour Street in Soho. They were essentially hired as openers for bigger artists like Mayall and his Bluesbreakers. Revenues were, well, less than stellar – as a support band they split £15 amongst the five of them while the headliners pocketed sums in the range of £250.

Black Cat Bones was steeped in the Chicago blues idiom, a virtual music revolution that began brewing in the 1940s, mixing up urban, northern and electric translations of the Delta blues. Seminal figures such as Muddy Waters, Big Bill Broonzy (the blues icon Kossoff heard on his father's vinyl collection), Washboard Sam and Willie Dixon were arbiters of the movement. Dixon, in particular, and perhaps more than any other figure of the time, defined the sound. His compositions now stand as classics and include "Hoochie Coochie Man" (interpreted by everyone from Muddy Waters to Steppenwolf), "Just Make Love To Me", "I'm Ready", "Little Red Rooster" (covered by the Rolling Stones and Howlin' Wolf) and "Spoonful" (the elongated jam made famous as Cream's closing number).

These Chicago blues pickers provided the essential fodder for all the English bands circulating in London during this sixties guitar explosion. Led Zeppelin literally stole Dixon's "You Need Love" and transformed it into "Whole Lotta Love" on the *Led Zeppelin II* album. Jimmy Page's quartet had already covered Willie's "You Shook Me" and "I Can't Quit You Baby" on their debut and had accredited the Chicago blues king with his rightful compositional dues. However, Page, John Paul Jones, John Bonham and Robert Plant were involved in litigation when they "interpreted" "Bring It On Home" and did a surface rewrite of his "Killing Floor," turning it into "The Lemon Song".

This was the sound Black Cat Bones was brewing, assisted in large part by appropriating and borrowing these traditional Chicago elements. Paul was instantly drawn to the five-piece, comprised of Stuart Brookes and brother Derek on bass and rhythm guitars respectively, vocalist Paul Tiller and drummer Frank Perry. The group, in kind, was attracted to the waiflike player because he owned a Gibson Les Paul – only "serious" devotees owned instruments of this caliber. Feeling assimilated, Kossoff was given his first real opportunity to display the sinewy blues lines he had been developing, enlisting techniques from Clapton and Peter Green.

"I was about sixteen when I got my first electric; it was an EKO or something like that with a gold finish and a billion knobs. Soon after that, I got myself a Gibson Les Paul Junior which was the cheapest Gibson around at the time. Then I had this obsession about getting a real Les Paul; it was from seeing Beck and Clapton using them. I wanted the very same thing – they were very basic influences on me."

Koss elevated the group's musicianship and notoriety, though at one point early on he toyed with the idea of changing his name to Heath Stonefield. Thinking that the Kossoff surname brought too much baggage with it – the penance of having a famous father – he was determined not to ride on his coattails. Thankfully, he kept his birth appellation. The band began attracting attention and secured a regular weekly spot at the Marquee club in Soho (later, Free would land a similar weekly appearance). In November 1967, Alvin Lee, riding the tiger with Ten Years After, requested Black Cat Bones to open for them. Other dates followed with John Mayall, Aynsley Dunbar, The Nice and Jethro Tull. Even Fleetwood Mac tapped them and it was here Kossoff's relationship with the masterful Peter Green began.

Black Cat Bones also caught the eyes of American blues bands coming to England. Eddie Boyd was one of these original black blues champions. Then they were hired to support New Orleans pianist Champion Jack Dupree at the Nag's Head in Battersea. This was a major coup for these up-and-comers and perhaps it was the importance of the show that brought to a boil the inadequacies of drummer Frank Perry.

"This happened around February 1968 when I saw the band asking me to leave because I couldn't pare my drumming down enough to what they wanted," Frank described in an on-line interview. "I think this might have been to do with Mike Vernon (manager) who probably saw the band benefiting from the blues boom if one or two changes could be made. Paul came around to see me and I told him that he'd be next. This is because of the singer Paul Tiller who was jealous of anyone stealing his thunder. Tiller asked me to cut back on my drumming during the number 'Rock Me Baby' during his harmonica solo, and he was always on at Paul to cut down his playing too."

Frank became a close friend of Paul's and would often talk to the guitarist about the band's limited set list. Paul commiserated but decided to hang in there – at least for a while longer. The drummer remembers Paul as "bright and quick-witted, discriminating and discerning." All this was undoubtedly true but the percussionist was also seized of the guitar player's "heightened awareness of suffering" due to his sensitivity. "Drugs, alcohol and smoking were ways of reducing this emotional burden," he recalls, but seeing with eyes open or closed, Paul had already embarked on a path of self-destruction.

Part of this may have had its roots in his father's censorious nature. Though Perry describes David Kossoff as "just one of the fathers showing an interest in his son's activities" there was a noticeable change in atmosphere when Kossoff senior came to a rehearsal.

"That's not to say that David Kossoff went throwing his weight around," Frank summarizes. "Far from it. I recall him dropping in on a rehearsal with a large box of Coca Colas and I never even noticed him entering [the room]."

This seemingly neutral relationship between father and son was experienced firsthand by the latter's longtime girlfriend, Sandhe Chard, and given a little different twist.

"It would break his father's heart if I told you what Paul felt. Paul had to live up to his dad's standards and his brother Simon, who looked just like Paul.

So Paul had to shoulder not only the burden of a distant relationship with his father but also the demoralizing emotional weight of a band that did not fulfill his deepest musical desires. Still, he did not abandon ship and in that strange and twisted way fate has in dealing with the human species, Simon Kirke surfaced. Simon was at the Nag's Head that evening when Black Cat Bones backed Dupree.

"I had been in London nearly a year and had had little success. I was doing various menial jobs – demolition worker, construction, car washing, plastic factory worker – and had gone to auditions. I had played in one group, Maton's Magic Mixture whose lead guitarist, Terry Thomas, would produce several Bad Company records some twenty years later.

"I was pretty despondent because time was running out and college was looming. One night I was skimming through *Melody Maker* when I saw an advert for a blues club, The Nag's Head, in Battersea, a suburb in southeast London featuring Black Cat Bones. Although it was quite a way from Twickenham where I was living, fate stepped in and I took the train across town."

Now, though not realizing it, three of the four puzzle-pieces had arrived at this place, this London of great expectations, and the merging of the trio and the ultimate addition of bassist Andy Fraser was drawing closer. A quartet that would in many ways re-define how blues and rock could come together in a seamless bond, was just an echo away.

Simon, like future bandmate Kossoff, was born in a post-war London on 28 July 1949, a place he describes quite succinctly as "depressing". The city had been decimated by enemy bombs and money was hard to come by. If Rodgers' background was working class, the Kirkes strived to attain even that lowly perch. His father, Vivian, had given his best years to the British armed forces and with the unholy strain of war crushing his emotional backbone, was unable to find, much less maintain, any sort of trade or profession. Making ends meet became a sorrowful challenge. His father bounced around between menial factory work, sales and the occasional trip over the waters as a merchant seaman.

In 1956, father Vivian and mother Olive May moved Simon and his two brothers, Nicholas (four years his senior) and Miles (fifteen months his junior) about 200 miles to the Welsh border. Just seven at the time, Simon looks back on that period with fond but realistic recall.

"We lived in a very remote cottage. I delight in telling my kids now that we had no electricity or running water for several years and our rent was £1 per week. School was two miles away and we walked there and back five days a week. We were definitely the family from the city; it was years before we were accepted as one of the locals. But oddly enough it was a good time in our lives. Looking back I did feel sorry for my parents. Here they were in their mid-30s in this remote backwater far away from London and the bright lights. I and my younger brother, however, did all the things that young boys did in the country – we built a tree house, chased sheep, worked on farms, hiked, stole apples, rode bicycles ... it was overall for us a great experience. Very character-building. We read by the light of gas lamps and I didn't even know of the existence of TV until I was thirteen.

This Shropshire village called Clun (the same hamlet where Ian Hunter hailed from) had no electricity and when it finally did come to this isolated spot, Simon's life would be forever changed. The Kirke house obtained a television when the middle son was about fourteen years of age. He readily admits being "glued to the set". Prior to the arrival of the tube in the Kirke domain, Simon had become mildly enamored with music when he was chosen to sing the lead verse from "A Christmas Carol" at the age of ten years old. This school activity didn't exactly ignite his love for melody, but it did give him a taste of performing before an audience. He turned to the recorder at the age of twelve and then by his thirteenth birthday the world tumbled sideways. A show called *All That Jazz* mesmerized him; he was riveted by the drummer of the house band and was starry-eyed by all of the "flashy" gear. Every waking moment would find him glued to the TV and to this day those memories remain as vividly inspiring as ever. Dreams of becoming a drummer etched themselves into the tissues of his soul. Mail order was about the only way to obtain exotic merchandise such as sticks and since this could take weeks and weeks, he made the decision to make his own. He cut and fashioned his first sticks – only five inches long because he didn't know any better – by chopping down garden hedges and banging away on books, biscuit and chocolate tins, and any other available sound-producing object. These he covered with old newspapers, magazines, and tape to create what he calls a "nice, solid sound". The local market town of Shrewsbury housed a small music shop and here he ordered his first real drum – complete with a splash cymbal. The future fanned out before him and nothing seemed out of reach.

The clan Kirke moved to a larger house a few miles away and call it fate, call it karma, call it coincidence, but the fledgling percussionist was about to experience his first encounter actually playing drums as an accompanist to his school bus driver. In one of the early fate-loaded twists that would be a constant companion of a band destined to be known as Free, Alexis Korner actually saw the drummer knocking it out at one of bus driver Mr Lane's disco nights.

"Our school bus driver asked me if I would like to play drums alongside his disco turntables in what I thought was, and still is, a unique situation. For three to four hours, he would play the hits of the day along with other staples such as Jim Reeves, Bill Haley, Bing Crosby and a variety of other styles. In the course of the evening on my little four-drum Gigster kit, I would play around 60 different songs. Obviously I had to keep in time otherwise it wouldn't have worked. And to this day I credit that period in my life with my pretty well-defined sense of timekeeping."

Simon would venture around to village halls and play to crowds who paid money – a pre-disco disco – playing along with waltzes and quick-steps and older, more traditional music. But he outgrew this and soon began looking around for a real band.

"I joined forces with some local lads and we formed The Maniacs (during which time he tried experimenting with a double bass kit for a short period) and we played all over the area. The guy who formed the band was an ex-Army guy. He'd been all over Germany and he came back with an amplifier with four inputs… no, *eight* inputs. So everything went through this one amp. We had three guitarists, a bass and a drummer, two micro-phones, and a spare input. They all went through this one amp. We won a talent contest with a cover of The Surfari's 'Wipe Out.' We did 'Satisfac-tion'. This was the time of the Beatles, the Beach Boys and the blues. We got a good following and must have played three or four nights a week. We had a great time. That was my first real, fully-fledged group and I thought, 'This is the life for me.' That lasted for a few months and then I teamed up with two guys and we formed The Heatwave; this was a great band. I suppose we modeled ourselves on Cream and it had me on vocals as well as playing drums. Overall, these late nights diminished my studies at school although I still managed to attain good grades. I knew that this was what I wanted to do from then on and when I was sixteen I made a deal with my parents that after high school I would pursue my career as a musician for two years. If after that time I hadn't really gone anywhere, I would pick up my studies and go to university."

He would never make it back to school, however. This was 1966, the year four young men from Liverpool would declare absolute supremacy over the kingdom of pop music. Simon recalls, two years earlier, when The Beatles dominated the charts with the top five records on the singles parade as well as crushing all album competition by securing the first three spots on the long player listings. Simon's fixation with the foursome was just another in the myriad similarities of taste he would share with future band-mate Rodgers. But this similar taste in music did not end here. In fact, it's almost eerie the way that both Pauls, Simon and even Andy Fraser all gravitated towards the same artists, finding in them a voice which would eventually be heard in the music of Free – and to a lesser extent, Bad Company.

"A little after The Beatles, I discovered Otis Redding and James Brown and Ray Charles. There was Chuck Berry and Marvin Gaye, The Stones and The Animals, and then the blues. John Mayall and the Bluesbreakers featuring Eric Clapton; I still remember to this day the staggering effect Eric's playing had on me when I heard 'Hideaway' from that album (*Bluesbreakers: John Mayall with Eric Clapton* released in July 1966 climbed its way to number six in the English charts). Then there was Muddy Waters and Robert Johnson and Sonny Boy Williamson. I was in the choir at school and our music teacher turned me on to some of the classics: Mozart and Bach and Beethoven. A few years later Paul Kossoff would turn me on to Segovia and Julian Bream. I still remember a quote from Miles Davis: 'There are two types of music in the world… good and bad.' And that's still my philosophy today."

Simon's elder sibling Nick was an Army recruit and as such had access to various gray market accessories. On one memorable day he brought back the Holy Grail itself – an electric guitar. Neighbors had been complaining about the drummer's non-stop banging and bashing and coupled with a court order stipulating he could only practice 45 minutes each day, he made the simple and obvious choice to vent his musical frustrations on the guitar. The Beatles – who else? – provided him with his main source of copy material and thrown into the mix was his fixation with the three Kings: BB, Freddie and Albert, Charlie Christian and Django Reinhardt (the first non-American jazzer to break into the ranks). Clapton and Beck rounded out his curriculum.

With his confidence growing and realizing Clun held little potential for a budding musician, Simon left home in July 1967 for the glamour and glitz of London. It was not a spontaneous decision but one he'd ruminated over for some time. Just after his eighteenth birthday, he, like Rodgers, made the pilgrimage.

"My plan was pretty vague; stay with some distant relatives and answer ads in the local music papers for drummers while doing odd jobs. I had some pretty decent grades in my pocket; good enough to earn me a place in college should this venture not pan out. I was under no illusion that this was going to be easy. I had hitchhiked to London several times previously and seen the quality of musicianship firsthand."

And the musicianship in this year of 1967 was bewildering. On the other side of the great blue pond, America was experiencing its own wondrous unfolding. The Summer of Love had arrived and the West Coast sound, defined in terms like psychedelic and acid rock, was expanding like an oil spill. Jefferson Airplane, The Doors, Frank Zappa's Mothers of Invention, Quicksilver Messenger Service and a host of others were busting through the gates and expanding the harmonic limits. In England, and primarily London, these textures had infiltrated the Anglo lexicon with such bands as The Moody Blues, Traffic, Procol Harum and Jethro Tull.

"The scene in England at that time was blossoming; there was so much talent. One of the best showcases was the Windsor Jazz and Blues Festival held each year. This was a three-day event and the lineup was just awesome. I remember one year seeing in one evening [conceivably referring to the 7th National Jazz and Blues Festival held at the Royal Windsor Racecourse on 13 August 1967] The Yardbirds (with Jeff Beck), The Small Faces, Fleetwood Mac (with Peter Green), Ten Years After and Cream's first big show. The standard of musicianship was staggering. Remember, I was from an incredibly remote area and was used to various small show bands as competition – these guys in London were the business.

"There was so much talent led naturally by The Beatles. Without the Beatles, I don't think any of us would be doing what we're doing now. Although they had ceased to perform now, they had stood the musical world on its ear with three albums: *Rubber Soul* (December 1965), *Revolver* (August 1966), and *Sgt. Pepper* (June 1967). Flower Power was everywhere – think *Austin Powers*, it was actually quite close to that! You had the sort of psychedelic era and from there it got into the folkie thing: Joan Baez and Joni Mitchell started happening. There was a big blues boom in evidence. The American giants who couldn't get arrested in their homeland were finding a new audience in Europe and their influence had spawned Ten Years After, the Yardbirds and Cream as well as a host of smaller groups around the country – one of which was Black Cat Bones featuring Paul Kossoff."

Black Cat Bones, a band he'd heard was one of the second-tier outfits running through the perfunctory steps so many other groups were forced to follow, was playing at a distant club on this anonymous evening. This was the autumn of 1968 and his recollection of their appearance that night is vivid.

"They were a pretty average band playing blues standards but the guitarist stood out. He was a little bloke standing on the far right of the stage with a mane of long hair and he was playing incredibly well. He wasn't fast like Alvin Lee, more in the mold of Clapton and Green [as well he should have been, breathing in their styles for some time now]. But I could tell he was the star of the show. He was, of course, Paul Kossoff.

"During the break he came to the bar and ordered a drink. I sidled up to him and said that I thought he was a terrific player. He was self-assured and took the compliment well but not in a particularly bigheaded way. In a rare moment of pushiness, I said that I didn't think much of their drummer and offered my services. He said that actually this was the drummer's last night with them and they were auditioning new ones the next day. They were leaving the gear set up and prospective drummers were being asked to play on the outgoing man's kit. If I wanted, I should come along. So the next afternoon, with just a pair of sticks and a heart full of hope I did just that. We played a shuffle and a slow blues and I sat around while two other hopefuls did the same. I remember the band going into a huddle and the leader, Stuart Brookes, coming up to me and saying I had the job. I floated home."

Though he landed the audition, Simon did not allow himself to be starblinded. This was, after all, London in the late sixties and virtually every player around was a monster talent. Ginger Baker, John Bonham, Keith Moon, Clive Bunker, BJ Wilson, and a cadre of other percussion perfectionists could be found playing in clubs on any night of the week. Perhaps it was Kirke's early realization that he was not a chopsmeister but rather a solid timekeeper capable of laying down metronomically metered patterns that swung open the gates.

"The Who were awesome back then and Cream were just starting out; Zep were just around the corner although I did see Robert Plant's Band of Joy at the Marquee in 1968 with John Bonham on drums. He knocked me sideways then. You know … a nineteen-year old John B was mighty special. I was a bit awestruck by these guys but even then I knew my limitations. I wasn't going to emulate them, I was going to try and get my own style together. I was starting to be affected more by the Americans, in particular Al Jackson from Booker T and the MGs. They were the Stax house band and played mainly with Otis Redding, Sam & Dave, Rufus Thomas and people like that. Motown was happening and their legendary rhythm section was Benny Benjamin on drums and one of the best bass players ever, James Jamerson. I just loved the solid economy of these guys, in particular Al Jackson Jr who is still a big influence on me even 26 years after his death."

There was no surprise really that Simon earned the spot – his blues influences were almost a mirrored reflection of Kossoff's own tastes. His early work with Black Cat Bones revolved around learning the band's repertoire, classics such as "Four O'Clock In the Morning", Willie Dixon's "Killing Floor" and "Rock Me Baby". This was *de rigueur* stuff for the drummer. But the band, backing Champion Jack Dupree, set his blond shag cut swirling and bestowed upon him his first taste, the first sweet savoring, of the positive feedback from more seasoned players.

"We backed Champion Jack Dupree, an authentic barrel house piano player from New Orleans [born 4 July 1910, Dupree was a kingpin in introducing his particular style of piano work to Europe and before his death in 1992, had shared his vision with the likes of John Mayall, Alexis Korner and Eric Clapton]. He lived in Yorkshire and was riding the wave of the blues boom. Not only was he an original boogie-woogie New Orleans piano player but he was a black man living in the north of England. It's kind of the equivalent to a Jewish guy living right in the middle of Syria. It's unheard of. We traveled in our Ford Transit van, the mode of transport for any self-respecting band in those days, and he drove himself in his own gaudily painted Cadillac. The first time I played in the band with him, after the first number he rolled his eyes at me and said to the audience, 'This guy can play!' I flushed a deep shell-shocked red and grinned at the floor."

The band backed Dupree on his Blue Horizon album *When You Feel the Feeling You Was Feeling* , the session falling on 22 April 1968 at the CBS Studios in London. Within three or four hours, Black Cat Bones had cut their tracks; eight were completed and five made it as keepers: "Income Tax", "Roll On", "I've Been Mistreated", "A Racehorse Called Mae" and "My Home's In Hell". Blues traditionalist Duster Bennett sat in on harmonica while Stan Webb (of Chicken Shack fame) strummed guitar on "I've Been Mistreated".

Self-deprecating to a fault, the drummer was intoxicated with this, his first taste of the addicting flavors of acceptance and creative fulfillment. But Kossoff had already begun a search for a new vehicle since he was feeling the constraints of the essentially twelve-bar blues Black Cat Bones had been pounding out every evening. Within days of this session, the pair handed in their notice. An easy decision, really. Several days earlier the quartet that would become Free had convened at The Nag's Head and, for the first time in any of their short musical lives, had found magic.

Kossoff wasted no time in seeking out new connections and in befriending Fleetwood Mac's Peter Green, he forged a bond with the only other Anglo-Jewish *mensch* who was out and about. Peter was essential in opening up Paul's eyes to all the other musicians around town and how the blues could be taken to new levels.

Green, born into the world as Peter Greenbaum on 29 October 1949, was the focus of the Mac for several albums. An alumnus of John Mayall and the short-lived Shotgun Express, Green was a guitar potentate, borrowing from Clapton and Mick Taylor to envisage the blues outside of its traditional twelve-bar boundaries. "Black Magic Woman", "Oh Well" and "The Green Manalishi" have become mainstays in the set lists of cover bands everywhere and it's really no surprise that he and Kossoff would have found each other. Though neither were practicing Jews, they had this unspoken spiritual tie and it was probably Peter's input that inspired Paul to seek out larger grazing fields for his musical sheep.

Kossoff, now on the outlook for a new flock of musicians, found himself of a weekend at The Fickle Pickle, a pub/club located in Finsbury Park. The Pickle played host that evening to another blues-obsessed band called Brown Sugar. Immediately the guitar player took notice of the singer on stage, a dark-haired character he recognised instantly as the band's standout musician. Brown Sugar was running through its set of blues standards, a program that could have probably been switched with a Black Cat Bones set without anyone noticing. Nothing opens the reservations door more readily than a proffered drink and after Koss bought Rodgers a heady pint, he asked about sitting in on a tune. Paul invited him up and they blew through a rendition of T-Bone Walker's "Stormy Monday" and Memphis Slim's "Everyday I Have the Blues". The singer was overwhelmed by the guitarist's intensity and, never one to sit on the sidelines, suggested a merger in establishing a new ensemble. Simon was of a like mind and within hours they had three pieces of the jigsaw. And since they all had the blues in common, they decided on creating a blues band, as Paul Rodgers recalls.

"We were going to put a blues band together because that was what was happening and that's what we wanted to do. Kossoff said he had a drummer in his band, Simon Kirke, and so that was three. So all we needed was a bass player."

That bass player would appear in the person of Andy Fraser, the son of a Scottish plantation owner and an indentured servant in British Guyana. Andy entered the world, one that would both reward and punish him for his unique heritage, on 3 July 1952. The elder Fraser, John Edgar, had endured miseries at the hands of desperately narrow minded people and, no longer able to shoulder family obligations, abandoned his six-year old son and three other brothers and left them in the care of his wife. Andy's mother Barbara worked incessantly, holding down three jobs at a time in order to provide the Fraser children with some sort of reasonable life.

Growing up in Roehampton, West London, Andy became smitten early with music, taking piano lessons at five and continuing with classical training for over five years. Suffering from the three Bs (bored, befuddlement and bewilderment) the young boy began teaching himself six-string guitar and ultimately the four-string bass. Amidst racially hurled epithets, he created a name for himself around East End Caribbean clubs as that odd little white boy who could play everything from perfectly executed Wilson Pickett covers to calypso and reggae songs. These rat holes disguised as clubs provided him with a hands-on education and it was in these very dives that he would meet Binky McKenzie, a fellow bassist who would become his teacher and idol.

Around 1967, the same time when Rodgers, Kossoff, and Kirke were banging about London, Andy was kicked out of school, not because his grades weren't adequate (they were) but because his hair was longer than the rules allowed. Ending up at Hammersmith Art College, the future Bluesbreaker became friendly with Sappho Korner, daughter of Alexis, master and gentile overlord of the English blues scene at this time.

Korner was born in Paris, France on 19 April 1928. Brought up by a mother of Greek/Turkish descent and an Austrian father, he moved to London during the mid-thirties. By the late forties, this future developer of blues artists all over London was already playing live, teaming up with Chris Barber's jazz menageries and finding his way into the camp of Cyril Davies where they created Blues Incorporated. A man of many devices, Alexis opened his own club in March 1962. Called The Ealing Rhythm & Blues Club, this became ground zero for the tutoring and cultivating of musicians who would go on to, literally, change the course of music. Charlie Watts, Mick Jagger, Paul Jones, Long John Baldry and Eric Burdon were just a few of these future history-makers. Andy Fraser would be another one.

In the late sixties, Korner formed a company of players he dubbed Free At Last. Members Hughie Flint and Cliff Barton, the latter replaced by Fraser's shining beacon Binky McKenzie, released one single, "Rosie" b/w "Rock Me". They endured from September 1966 to mid-1967 when Flint skipped out to work with Georgie Fame and bassist Binky just upped and quit. Alexis attempted to resurrect the outfit by enlisting Marsha Hunt and Victor Brox but the project broke apart like a cheap wind-up toy.

For good reason, many music purists and historians place Korner side-by-side with John Mayall, another blues patriot who established and launched the careers of dozens of one-time hopefuls. Eric Clapton, Mick Taylor, Peter Green, Jack Bruce, Aynsley Dunbar, Mick Fleetwood and the pivotal character in our tale, Andy Fraser, to name but a few. Born 29 November 1933 in Macclesfield, England, Mayall early on orchestrated The Blues Syndicate. This gave way to the malleable machine known as The Bluesbreakers, an ever-changing company that bred and nurtured dozens of the most gifted players around today.

But Korner was quick to point out, and with some disdain, that he was not the archetypical figure people thought he was. He was the jumping off place for many musicians but the similarities stop here.

"No, I don't see myself as playing a similar role as John Mayall and I never have," Korner observed in a 1975 interview. "I had that thrust upon me. The main European question, for instance is, 'What does it feel like to be called the Godfather of the White Blues?' And the answer is, 'Shitty.' I cannot understand that; I mean I can understand it from outside. But feeling as I do about me, I cannot possibly understand that. Because all I have done is to do what I've wanted to do. I was the right person in the right place at the right time. Which is more a matter of luck than foresight or planning. A title like that implies two things: it implies deliberate planning which wasn't the case and it implies it's all over.

"I think I functioned as a ground base security for the musicians to springboard off of. I think John did function as a springboard certainly but I think he was more deliberate in the way he did it than I was. I think from that point of view he's better entitled to that title – if he wants it."

But Mayall is not sure the title belongs to him either.

"I did work with them, Clapton and Taylor and Andy. And there's a bond there somewhere, which is very important. At the same time, you know the inside stories on them so you have to make your own opinions about it. I would like to think that anybody who worked for me would do good with their own careers afterwards. Fortunately a lot of them have and the public thinks, 'Ah, they worked with Mayall and Mayall was responsible,' but that's not true. They were talented before they worked with me; it's just that I figured out the talent just from my own point of view and I wanted to work with them. That was it. Whether they were known or unknown. The measure of any musician is whether he can make it on whatever he does. So what if I was involved with a lot of people who did make it?"

Alexis became pseudo-father and illustrious guide to a young and fragile Fraser. Andy was doing renegade dates with a group called The Outlaws, and on occasion playing bass on Korner's gigs. This Alexis alliance would culminate with a phone call from John Mayall seeking a bass player for a new version of his ever-morphing blues combos.

Coupled with Alexis's daughter's recommendation, John embraced him in the bosom of the Bluesbreakers. For six months, the bassist played alongside future Rolling Stones guitarist Mick Taylor, drummer Keef Hartley, sax player Dick Heckstall-Smith and trumpeter Henry Lowther. Mayall was about to embark on a European tour and the teenager observed up close how business was conducted. But John, always one seeking new players and new twists on the blues idiom, gave his rhythm section the boot and enlisted Tony Reeves, bassist for The New Jazz Orchestra and Jon Hiseman, a session drummer previously working with Georgie Fame and Graham Bond. The Bluesbreakers captain wanted to mix jazz with his blues and felt the current players weren't right.

Andy, out on the tiles once again, found solace and a paycheck by working the odd date with Alexis. But the future was bright. Label chief, club owner, and producer Mike Vernon was a selective musical detective, constantly scouring clubs and pubs for original players. His Blue Horizon label proffered such names as the Aynsley Dunbar Retaliation (a barbed reference at being tossed from Mayall's menagerie), Tony TS McPhee (later one of the Groundhogs), Savoy Brown, Champion Jack Dupree and Chicken Shack (including one Christine Perfect, later Fleetwood Mac's Christine McVie). A musicologist and fanatical record collector, he would find a home for blues principals Louie Jordan, Howlin' Wolf, Sonny Boy Williamson, Little Walter, Bo Diddley and Fats Domino.

For a time he had been keeping a close eye on the bond developing amongst Kossoff, Rodgers and Kirke. Realizing they had no bassist, Mike approached Korner. Once again, Fraser was offered up as a candidate and in yet another stretching of coincidence, he was to perform with the elder blues champion that evening at the 51 Club supporting – who else? – John Mayall. Vernon took Kossoff to the event and the bass spot was filled.

This story becomes warped in some circles. Rodgers maintains he found Andy via a posted notice on a rehearsal room bulletin board. The three musketeers had plowed through fifteen or more potential applicants and had come up with nothing. Andy declares Vernon was the lynch pin in the connection. Kirke is adamant that after seeing the gifted one at the 51 Club, the triumvirate was signed, sealed, and delivered.

Whatever story holds the most water is inconsequential – their meeting was life changing. And so the story begins.

TO FREE OR NOT TO FREE

Alas for those that never sing,
But die with all their music in them.

-Oliver Wendell Holmes

On 19 April 1968, Paul Rodgers, Paul Kossoff, Simon Kirke and Andy Fraser played together for the first time at The Nag's Head, the same place Koss had gone to hear Paul's Brown Sugar Blues band. Coincidence? Fate? Who really knows? Somehow, these four had braved the journeys from home to migrate to London, had sustained themselves with grunge work, and were now in a place, at a time, where they'd either find magic or mayhem.

During the early afternoon, Blue Horizon honcho Vernon met Kossoff at the pub in Battersea. Doors were opened – geographically and emotionally.

To talk about the occasion would amount to a secondhand account, a tale interpreted by someone who was not there that auspicious day. Simon Kirke was there, of course, and the memories he retains some three decades plus later are insightful, witty and heartfelt.

"As I remember it Koss and me met Paul Rodgers at The Nag's Head some time in early 1968. We set our gear up and then got a shout from Andy who was downstairs. He had arrived in a taxi – very impressive – and wanted a hand with his bass gear. He asked for a receipt – something which would have escaped me and which was a portent for things to come.

"We climbed the stairs and he set up his gear… In terms of rock history it would go down as a momentous occasion. In fact we viewed it as a very successful beginning. Ideas were flowing between us. Koss and me were very pleased to be playing with such professionals. I remember Rodgers' voice sending chills up my spine. This guy sounded like Otis… like he was 40 years old. He also played exceptional harp – something he never really showed in Free.

"After a couple of hours we had written, 'Walk in my Shadow', 'I'm a Mover', 'Moonshine' and also run through some old standards. Here we were – an average age of 18 – sounding like we had been together for years.

"Alexis Korner came in and stood at the back of the room with a couple of friends. He was all smiles… When we had a break we got to chatting. He knew Andy, of course, and Koss – he was an on/off boyfriend of Sappho, Alexis' daughter, but I had never met him … neither, I think had Paul Rodgers.

"We needed a name for the band. No two ways. After several hours together we knew we were going to be a band. Alexis had played in a group with Graham Bond and Ginger Baker which was called Free at Last. He suggested the name Free.

"We sort of rolled it around our tongues and it stuck – we liked it. So Alexis took his involvement one step further. He was going on a short tour of England in a few weeks and suggested we open for him, then after he came on and did his solo bit we would come back on stage and back him for a few songs and close the show. We all nodded enthusiastically. After all, he was a well-known figure, steeped in the music we loved – blues – and thought we were good enough after hearing us for an hour to take us with him on the road. How could we refuse? I tell you how knocked out we were. I think we did it for nothing! (Maybe just expenses.)

"And that was the start really. We did our very first show in Chester sometime in early '68. From the beginning we were a hit. The chemistry was just right. Released from the restraints of our previous groups we forged ahead. We used Andy's mother's house in Roehampton as a base. Every week we met with favorite albums and had a listening session – hard to imagine now, but the four of us would lie around in Andy's bedroom and play Otis, *Revolver*, Isaac Hayes' *Hot Buttered Soul* and early Stones. We once sat up into the early hours and wrote dozens and dozens of letters to club promoters stating our case as a worthwhile booking. Quite a few wrote back and said the name Free was misleading and patrons were liable to come around expecting free admission … it was too 'arty' a name."

Paul Rodgers has his own memories of that brilliant day.

"We had a rehearsal for the first time in The Nag's Head in Battersea, which is still there. There was an upstairs room and they had gigs there; I saw Freddie King there, he was beautiful, wonderful. There were a lot of venues like that, these sweaty, smoky rooms they played blues in. We rehearsed there for the first time and it just did click together. The great thing about blues as well is that you can all jam on it and you find out how good everybody is because you've already got the structure, the twelve-bar thing. We did a lot of blues, we did 'Walk In My Shadow' and I was very pleased with that because I heard my song played by a new band and Kossoff gave me an idea he had which turned out to be 'Moonshine' and he asked me if I could write some lyrics on that. I came back with lyrics for the following rehearsal and all of a sudden we were writing songs. And that was cool.

"You see, when Andy came along he brought the connection of Alexis Korner because I think Alexis had gotten him the job with John Mayall in the first place. Andy was kind of fired from John Mayall and it left a bad taste in his mouth; a lot of people did actually get fired from John Mayall (laughs). I mean Aynsley Dunbar's Retaliation and all those bands. But they went on with fire in their belly and did great things. So who knows if we should criticize him? But Andy was very gung-ho to be successful and show everybody. He introduced us to Alexis Korner and Alexis was really, really helpful. He came along and by that time we decided, yes, we were a band, whatever it took we were gonna be a band. So we sat around and had a break and the thought of a name came up. Names are always difficult. Alexis said, 'I don't know if this helps you but I used to have a band together with Cyril Davies and a whole bunch of people and it was very short lived and we called it Free At Last.' And we all went, 'Wow, it's gotta be Free!' It was just so right."

WALKING ON FIRE AND WATER

Music people seem to be happy. It is the
engrossing pursuit .... Almost the only in-
nocent and unpunishable passion.

-Sydney Smith

Those early days when the band was stretching its wings, seeing how high they could fly, exploring areas virgin to them all, was a magic time. Though the blues was the glue, the common denominator that brought them together, they were off within hours conjuring up original material. "I'm A Mover" was given birth by a Fraser lick and "Walk In My Shadow" was a piece Rodgers had composed before meeting his three future compatriots. "Moonshine" was brought from standstill to animation by chords from Kossoff and though the piece was bursting with passion and panache, it represented one of the very few collaborations between the singer and guitarist. This may have helped fuel the nasty fire in which Kossoff would eventually burn himself out. From the beginning he may have felt an essential cog in the creative machinery but he'd soon realize that the singer and bassist would supply the bulk of the songwriting. Kossoff was a quiet one who never really made comments that cut against the grain – but he was not happy with this early arrangement.

"I wish Paul and I had done more of that," confesses Rodgers, referring to the infrequent co-writes between himself and guitar player. "We didn't actually end up writing too many songs, Paul and I. When you look back, what happened was Andy was very keen to write songs and we threw ideas back and forth. We became the sort of Lennon and McCartney of the band in a way. We became the writing team. It evolved because we just had so many ideas to throw at each other. There were so many ideas that I think dear Koss got left out of the mix a little bit. It's sad because I wish he was around today, I could redress that, we could sit and work some things out. Because he did have great ideas."

Even Simon recognized early on that the Rodgers/Fraser axis was the prolific songwriting entity of this baby stepping four-piece.

"From the start, Paul Rodgers and Andy took over the songwriting. It seemed to come to them naturally. Koss and myself were content to play. My songwriting was sporadic at best, although I like to think in terms of quality, not quantity. And to this day with 30 years of experience in the business, I have maybe 90 songs written or co-written."

Andy played an essential role in fashioning the Free sound and also became the band's unspoken leader. His youth elevated him to some sort of Boy King status and as an alumnus of John Mayall's band, was perceived as someone with all the answers – all the right answers. Alexis, the man who had become the group's pseudo-patron saint, tracked down one Bryan Morrison and told the band he would be a suitable and efficient manager. Mike Vernon was understandably upset with the loss but held no grudge. Several months later he contacted Kossoff to play on an album by Martha Velez titled *Fiends & Angels*. Koss was in the high country, picking alongside such luminaries to be as Jack Bruce, Jim Capaldi, Gary Thain, Chris Wood (who'd later work with Free) and Eric Clapton. Paul even put in an appearance on Mike's own solo album, *Bring It Back Home*.

Andy worked hand-in-hand with the Bryan Morrison Agency taking care of all financial and business matters. From that first day of asking the taxi driver for a receipt, Andy was essential in booking gigs, keeping the books and parceling out weekly draws.

"He just seemed to have a natural bent for it," says Kirke, pointing to Fraser's almost effortless ability in tackling the matters of commerce. "Andy handled the business of the band. In terms of musical leadership Free were a pretty democratic band and I know both Pauls would take umbrage to any suggestion that Andy was the musical leader. Other than receiving my weekly wage, I had no inclination for group business. I always have been that way. I prefer to hire professionals to look after that end of things. Sure it means less money for me at the end but I just can't be bothered with it. So Bryan did book us in and around London and paid us a wage while keeping money aside for us, and his commission of course. I never really liked him; we seemed to be just an asset to him."

For the next few months, with a manager and an agent, and a "decent" Transit van, the band performed everywhere and anywhere a club would have them. They secured the service of a bona fide roadie named Graham Whyte who would prove to be indispensable.

There was a feeling of us against them; anything was possible and nothing out of reach. Under the watchful eye of Andy, the band played everywhere. The manager, Morrison, laid out some money for demos and then a month later complained about the band's expenses. Such pedestrian thinking struck the bassist as fundamentally wrong and, in a concerted effort with the singer, they would ultimately give him the boot.

Still, overall, it was a time of wonder and possibilities.

"They say there is nothing like the first of everything and this was true with Free," philosophizes Kirke. "Sure, I had been in bands before but this was the real deal. Everything clicked. We all seemed to be united in our cause and that was to be a top-notch band. I hung out a lot with Koss. He was definitely the man about town. He had a certain confidence about him now. I remember how he used to drag me around the music shops in London's West End and try out guitars. He would say that he was interested in a certain amp, plug in their finest Gibson and proceed to rattle everything in the place with a few bursts of the blues. Sales assistants would rush in to tell him to quit but inevitably would wait a bit while Koss would sit there, head thrown back, acting as if he was on stage in some hall somewhere. These were the Selmers shops, where he was once a junior assistant. And the other shop was Orange who specialized in amps – they were once all the rage in London about 1968 to 1969 and were all colored bright... orange."

KOSSOFF SOUNDS OFF

Perhaps it was because music resonated out of every doorway. Maybe there was something in the water. Whatever it was, London during the late sixties was the home of the Guitar God. Clapton, Page, Beck, Hendrix, Townshend, Trower and Fripp were just a few of the players developing their sound, coaxing melodies like angels singing from a plank of wood and six wires.

Paul Kossoff had the gift. His playing during these early shows was breathtaking with solos screaming and groaning in subtly constructed cadences.

His gear then was simple: a (circa) 1957 Gibson Les Paul Standard with a sunburst finish and a very old Marshall top with a homemade bottom. In an interview just months before his passing, Paul talked about his playing and his love of music.

"My father helped me build that cabinet which had four 12" speakers. I used this setup for about a year-and-a-half and then I got a regular 100-watt stack. Andy was using two Marshall Major stacks and we used a Marshall PA.

"The Les Paul is very sensible on gigs; it will not let you down tuning-wise or if I treat it roughly.

"I think my sound, especially my vibrato, has taken a long time to sound mature, and it's taken a long time to reach the speed of vibrato that I now have [there was no other player around who could match Kossoff for his rapid use of finger vibrato; his solo on "All Right Now" from the *Fire And Water* album is a textbook example of this technique]. I trill with my first, middle and ring fingers and bend chiefly with my small finger. I'll use my index finger when I'm using vibrato.

"I like to move people; I don't like to show off. I like to make sounds as I remember sounds that move me. My style is very primitive but at the same time it has developed in its own sense. I do my best to express myself and move people at the same time.

"I think there's still more room to develop in the way I'm playing. My vibrato is finally starting to grow up. Playing with Paul Rodgers helped me grow; he was my best teacher as to how to enhance a voice, blues-wise. I hate to play just solos; I prefer to hear his voice and back it up or rip it around or push it – without covering it over. My style and his grew up together."

ISLAND OF THE FREE

Where words leave off music begins.

-Heinrich Heine

While Korner helped shape the band's musical destiny, and Fraser took care of business and bookings, Kossoff became a sort of group chaperone. Growing up in London, he knew the hip clubs and places to be seen, and actually took drummer Simon under his little wing. Paul already had his own apartment in town *and* a girlfriend. Kirke used to stay over at Paul's flat in Covent Garden and he recalls one evening in particular.

"I remember watching an Elvis special (on television) in '68 with both of them and we were all on a sofa. Elvis made this one move with his whole body and Barbara (girlfriend) almost shot out of the seat in ecstasy. I think she had a partial orgasm. I thought, 'Fuck me. If Elvis can do that from across the Atlantic he must be on to something.' I tried getting that move down in front of a mirror one night... maybe it would come in handy on stage. Of course it was redundant – I sat behind a drum kit for most of my career!"

Elevating themselves from opening act to small-hall headliners, the band soon realized that in manager Bryan Morrison – who would later be immortalized in a 1969 B-side titled "Sugar For Mr Morrison" – they had more of an anchor than an asset. A "west end whiz kid," according to Simon, he smoked the potent, yard-long stogies, drove an expensive ride and in the end, really did not have much of an interest in the group. Morrison did find work for them and put them on a weekly wage of twenty pounds, but it was Free's live performances that were bringing them notice. Wherever they played, the club asked them back. A monumental step was taken when they landed a Monday night residency at the Marquee Club on Wardour Street.

Free had sent a tape to manager John Gee who invited the quartet down for an audition. They landed the coveted weekday assignment but it may not have been purely due to musical excellence. Kirke explains:

"When John saw us his eyes must have popped out; he was outrageously gay and the sight of four pretty boys belting out the blues in a sheen of sweat must have sent him frothing at the mouth. He gave us a three-month residency."

During this period, Chris Blackwell, then president of the eclectically driven Island Records entered their lives. Blackwell, another Korner contact, would become an essential component in the Free chemistry. He began by operating a shoestring record company in Jamaica in 1959 but just five years later moved the operation to London and began distributing reggae music. In 1964, he produced the infectious pabulum of Millie's "My Boy Lollipop". Many significant signings were made during the late sixties and early seventies that culminated in a roster including Cat Stevens, King Crimson, Jethro Tull, Roxy Music, Fairport Convention and Free. Bob Marley later found a home here and owing to the success of these prestigious signings, Chris opened an American office in 1975 and continued the bringing in of serious dollars by launching the likes of Joe South, War, Sparks, Stevie Winwood, Frankie Goes To Hollywood (on a subsidiary ZTT label), U2, Pulp and The Cranberries. Blackwell cashed out in 1989 by selling the company to Polygram for $275 million. He remained Chairman until 1997.

There are conflicting stories regarding how the band actually came to the attention of the label. One faction maintains that Alexis introduced them but Simon insists that it was Island that made the first move.

"I think someone from Island Records had been to the Marquee [Johnny Glover] and gotten in touch with Bryan Morrison. I think Mr M was only too glad to get rid of us; our contract had only been for six months and that was up. Anyway the four of us made our way to 155 Oxford Street one day and were ushered into Chris' office. CB, as he was known to his loyal staff, was a class act. He was in his early thirties then, very handsome and permanently tanned from his regular trips to Jamaica. He was a white Jamaican and could speak their dialect (patois) with ease. His family had an estate on the island and he had endeared himself to the local population by championing their music. He was introducing ska and blue beat to the UK but also had designs on the burgeoning British music scene. He managed Traffic and Joe Cocker and along with Spooky Tooth headed the most eclectic company of its time – and he was interested in us. So with a mixture of trepidation and cockiness we sat down in his office."

Blackwood could not hide his enthusiasm for the band as both personalities and musicians. Muff Winwood (Stevie's brother), Alec Leslie and Johnny Glover attended this initial meeting (representing the label's management and agency department) and they too were bowled over by the unadulterated focus of the foursome.

Morrison's management contract was bought out at this point and the band negotiated an advance for new gear, recording of the first album and monies for publishing. They subsequently signed an American deal with A&M Records.

One small, ever so inconsequential matter remained – Blackwell hated the name Free. His suggestion? The Heavy Metal Kids.

"There was no way on God's earth that I would contemplate that," chimes Rodgers, still trying to figure out, several decades later, what the label was thinking. "I must admit the rest of the band did consider it because we were looking at the difference between having a record contract and not having one. It's a heavy, heavy thing. You either change your name and you get a record contract or you don't and you don't get that record contract. And that was everything to us. But I stuck out for it and I'm glad I did really. Years later Island Records did have a band called The Heavy Metal Kids. *They* succumbed!"

"I thought that was such a cliché – heavy metal, the Heavy Metal Kids! Duh. I didn't want to put a label on it to that extent because I was interested in so many different kinds of music. And Free covered such a wide spectrum of directions we could go in. That's why it was so perfect."

Though Paul remembers being the sole member to defend the band name, Simon shakes up that memory.

"I remember Muff Winwood was there and he really started the proceedings. Roughly the conversation centered around his having been at the Marquee. He said he liked the band and would like to give us a management and recording contract. There was one snag, however. The name would have to go; it was too ethereal, too nebulous. Promoters were having a hard time with punters who thought that admission was free and so on. He suggested The Heavy Metal Kids.

"We collectively bristled. We said it was a fucking awful name. Andy spoke up to the effect that Free was our name, we liked it and if you took us on you took the name as well. Chris looked at us – he must have been impressed by our moxie but didn't let on – and then said, 'Well, that's it then, I guess there's no point in continuing,' or words to that effect. We left the office with a sinking feeling. What had we done? We went to our different homes in a depression. Andy called each one of us later that evening to say that Chris Blackwell had phoned him and said, 'OK, you can keep the name. I will give you a six-month contract with our option at the end to extend. Also a recording contract.' We were elated. We had stuck to our guns and had won against one of the most respected managers in the business. It was the start, to paraphrase (Humphrey) Bogart, 'of a beautiful relationship'."

TWO THOUSAND POUND TEARS

I've never heard Paul sing a wrong note.

-Jimmy Page

The band, now officially recognized as Free, forged ahead in creating a sound of their own. While the blues had provided them with a stockpile of songs from which to choose, they began to transform these standards into compositions stamped with their own unique brand. And they realized that it was imperative to write original music, a vision Rodgers was crucial in bringing to the forefront. All the bands around them, everyone from Cream to Jethro Tull, were defining themselves by cultivating novel songs and they knew, with a recording session looming before them, that they had to be prepared with self-written material.

In the meantime, they gigged on average five or six nights a week, newly guided by Island management executive Johnny Glover. Andy remained relentless in his participation in the business side, and following each show would meet with the promoter to pick up the earnings.

This brigade-like routine caught the attention of radio emissary John Peel, host of the *Top Gear* show. On 15 July 1968, Free were invited to tape a Wednesday session for the BBC broadcast that following Sunday. The band performed "Moonshine", "Free Me", Walk In My Shadow" and "Waiting On You".

This endless meandering around the club circuit did, however, take its toll and resulted in Paul Kossoff increasing his intake of those mean little pills – which isn't to say that the band didn't inhale more spliff smoke than a busload of Rastafarians whenever possible. Still, it was Kossoff's easy wit and storytelling prowess that made these journeys tolerable. He'd inherited the gift of the gab from his father and would regale the band for hours with tales and monologues. Kirke was the diplomat and his flexible mentality made him the sort of go-between when marathon trips in a battered Morris 1800 van might have turned ugly. Rodgers was the heavy hammer, ready to turn on that Northern aggression when a club owner may have been less than forthcoming in paying the band's fee.

Though the boys may have been more toasted than burnt bread, they always arrived early for shows and played as if Armageddon was but a day away. A typical set in those embryonic days included a clutch of blues standbys, classics such as "Every Day I Have the Blues" and Robert Johnson's "Crossroads" (Cream would later scream life into this old chestnut and on it Clapton would execute one of the best live solos ever). They continued to work on originals and when Rodgers fell ill, Fraser's mother allowed him to bed down on her living room sofa for two months. Here, thrown together, Paul and Andy really concentrated on composing and these new songs became the mainstays, much more than the revamped blues tunes, of their live set. During Paul's convalescence, he partnered with Andy in shaping "I'll Be Creeping", "Mourning Sad Morning" and even "Fire And Water" (which would remain unrecorded for two years).

Andy described to journalist Phil Sutcliffe how the partnership evolved.

"It came naturally. I think initially Paul was strongest on the lyrics. His songs were very vocal-based and I'd try to supplement that with some kind of arrangement. Mine started with arrangements, then we'd put a melody to it."

The band worked tirelessly to orchestrate the Free sound. In between bouts of non-stop writing sessions, they burned shoe leather by playing in clubs and attempting to crystallize their live show. Having been signed to Island, they were given a boost up the ladder in terms of live perform-ance and audience profile. Finding themselves in a stable of world class acts including Spooky Tooth, Joe Cocker, Fairport Convention and Traf-fic, they were given heavy incentive to hone live performance skills. Black-well, the overseer of the operation, was infinitely supportive – one of those larger than life figures imbued with gallons of charm and persuasion. In these formative days, he was labeled as the "baby-faced killer", alluding to a business acumen and prowess that did not understand the word "no".

After years of slogging through the sludge of dues paying, the foursome entered Morgan Studios in northwest London to begin work on their debut album. Though they all shared an unequivocally single vision, they nonetheless found their initiation into the world of album making some-thing less than idyllic.

The singer, in particular, found the studio a mind-bending experience.

"No, actually, I kind of hated the studio really because I always felt it took away [from the live side]. It was so hygienic and antiseptic and I found it very difficult to be very creative in such an environment. I don't know, the idea of a studio almost seemed to wipe away any kind of atmos-phere. There were all these bright lights and I tried to get a little mood going by turning the lights down. I'd close my eyes and imagine I was on stage and that was the only way I could really get a feel for it.

"You'd be surprised where they put the vocalists in those days – little air-less cupboards. I think now, 'No wonder I was inhibited.' It was so unat-mospheric. So it was a struggle for me at first."

Producer Guy Stevens was enlisted to organize the torrent of ideas rushing from these Free brains and transform them into proper album tracks. Stevens was a maverick and an enigma and had figured prominently in the careers of some of the most artistically driven bands around including Procol Harum, the Rolling Stones, the Paramounts, Spooky Tooth, Mott the Hoople, Hapshash and the Coloured Coat and Art. A record collecting junkie, he had assembled a library of vinyl that would dwarf the stock of most music stores. He was a fan of the Arsenal football team, married, signed to Island in 1963 and died in 1980, shortly after producing *London Calling* for the Clash. But he was a seminal figure on this first Free album and his role as catalyst is described by Simon.

"He (Blackwell) wanted us to do an album pretty well right away and suggested Guy Stevens. Here were four young guys who were possessed of amazing talent and energy; we lived for playing and wanted nothing more than to be a world-class band. Guy was amazing. He was a sort of mad professor who put elements together and then sat back and watched the results. Actually, he didn't exactly sit back so much as hurl himself around the place, interjecting ideas and observations. He suggested that all we should do was basically our stage set in the studio while the tape was rolling. There would be the minimum of overdubs; it would just be an evening's work. We did the album, I think, in two or three days. It was a pretty good showcase of where we were at that time. We were essentially a blues band with more adventurous leanings."

Andy Johns was enlisted as engineer, a teenager himself who was introduced to studio work by brother Glyn. The Baby Johns was on the house staff at Morgan and would work with every artist entering the doors, capturing crushing guitar tones and the true acoustic nature of drums on tape, an ability he'd later share with The Rolling Stones, Led Zeppelin, Van Halen, Humble Pie and even Mott the Hoople.

"Back then there weren't such things as independent engineers; my brother was one but he was the only guy. So obviously I made it my ambition to become one as quickly as I could." [*Note:* Andy and Glyn have had a love/hate relationship from the start. Though the elder Johns brought his brother into the den of the studio dogs, Andy has always been a bit jealous and angry about the situation. At one time, Andy was working on Jethro Tull's classic album *Benefit* and asked brother Glyn, working next door, to come in and hear some tracks. Glyn nodded amicably and then asked him to walk over to the adjoining studio where he was putting the finishing touches to one of the masterpieces of all time, *Who's Next*. Andy was silenced. They rarely spoke after that and on the rare occasion when they do get together, fistfights have been known to break out.]

"I was the only person at Morgan and the owner had made a deal with Chris Blackwell where he got a really great rate because he would start bringing in stuff from Island. So the Free project was really the first thing I did beginning to end, all the way through. By this time I kind of had it sussed out and knew what I was doing. I listened to some of that stuff last year [2000] and it sounds pretty good, you know? So it was just me and them and Guy Stevens was sort of the titular producer. Guy was mad, actually mad – very entertainingly, sometimes dangerously. He had no theory, he didn't know an *E* string from a teapot but he really liked rock 'n' roll music. Chris Blackwell really liked him because he was this really bizarre fellow."

Paul Rodgers agreed to some extent with Johns' observation, but felt that Guy didn't truly understand the underlying essence of the band. But he does give kudos when Stevens suggested they cut the sole acoustic track, "Over the Green Hills" into two sections and thus imbue the hard-edged R&B flavor of the album with a more serene ambiance.

Andy Johns maintains this arrangement was *his* doing. Regardless, Andy made overtures about abandoning a Fraser/Rodgers collaboration called "Visions of Hell" and replacing it with a rendition of Booker T & The MGs "The Hunter", a song that would become the band's show stopping anthem until it was eventually usurped by "All Right Now".

Paul Rodgers was both enamored and frustrated by the process of recording. *Tons of Sobs,* the debut Free album released in November 1968, was a blues hybrid, taking the identity of this American property and stretching it and bending it. On the one hand, the singer was forced to work in a recording studio that had about as much character and energy as a cadaver. That part he didn't care for. But upon returning home with the finished acetate – the vinyl master of the album – he began to feel the lovely tingle of completion.

"It brought it home to me when I brought an acetate home to Middlesbrough under my arm. A test pressing. I was coming home on the train and then I got the perspective of it. 'Here I am. I've been to London, formed a band, and I've got the record here to prove it.'"

The record did challenge the limits of blues-based bands at the time but somewhere *Tons of Sobs* missed. There were moments, however, and under the tutelage of Guy Stevens the quartet did flex its musical muscles on several tracks.

"The way 'Over the Green Hills' segued into 'Worry' was Guy's idea, that cross fade," recalls Simon (although Andy Johns claims these treatments originated with him). "The lilting guitar was me, by the way, with Koss playing lead and the reverse happening at the end on side two.

"I shall never forget that session; the energy was amazing. We were let loose. Overdubs were minimal – the odd vocal and lead solo here and there. Steve Miller, an English keyboard player, was on a couple of tracks and Guy sported an ear to ear grin."

The album was a pretty accurate rendering of the band's live stage set at that time. Unfortunately, they could not translate the immediacy and emotion of their club dates onto vinyl and the album would eventually undergo a silent death (barely breaking the Top 200 album charts). No one in the band knew about studio trickery – separation, overdubbing, doubling – and this may have contributed to the album's loose ends feeling. A lack of cohesiveness left listeners with empty ears. But they did understand how to play in ensemble fashion as a band, and even at this early juncture the listener can perceive the innate dynamics trying to scramble to the surface.

"We played as a band and let them record it," says Rodgers. "We did play live but we found out you could overdub and I said, 'Oh, you can do the vocal again? OK.' I can't even remember, maybe I did, maybe I didn't. I know Kossoff overdubbed quite a bit on 'The Hunter', the solo, brilliant stuff. We just piled it on because we could.

"Those recordings were very rough and ready but had a beautiful energy of a band in the studio for the first time. But they were a bit like pulling teeth in some respects because we now know it's best to lock out the time and keep the studio for yourself for three weeks or a month. But in those days there'd be a door with a glass window in it and the next band would be peering in going (imitates knocking on a window) – 'Hey, you guys gonna be long?'"

Still, Paul has the same buzz when he hears a record on the radio today as he did when he first recorded it. He was responsible for writing half the material: "Worry", "Over the Green Hills", "Walk In My Shadow" and "Sweet Tooth"; Andy shared half-credit for "I'm A Mover" and "Wild Indian Woman" and Kossoff soloed on "Moonshine". Homage was paid to their blues roots in covers of Howlin' Wolf's "Goin' Down Slow" and the seductive power of Albert King's "The Hunter".

Stevens not only titled the album – some twist of a phrase about money – but also had strange yet moving visions about how the record should be packaged. The album cover was shot in a graveyard in the Barnes area of London. All those Bosch-like images – Mickey Mouse in a coffin – were Stevens' twisted ideas. He was actually worried that the authorities would shut down the shoot because they were shooting in a graveyard and he constantly prodded and urged the photographer to nail the shot before the light faded.

Though Simon recalls the album being recorded in a frantic two-day burst, history places the chronology as spanning a three-week period including dates on 8, 11, 17, 22 and 31 October.

"That was my first big album and obviously very exhilarating to do – even though they got my name wrong [spelled Kirk instead of Kirke]. I think just about every track was done live. Yeah, great, I loved it."

Stevens once recalled that the album was pieced together for a whopping £800 and if you take that into consideration, it's difficult to imagine how they created genuinely unique textures on such a small budget. Fades from one track to the next, acoustic guitars, vocal performances that sounded as if they had been cut with golden microphones and diamond-studded sound boards. *Tons of Sobs* was a jumping off point for these Islanders and just a month after completing final overdubs and mastering, the group headed out on yet another road trip, this time with a new 35cwt Ford Transit van and improved gear.

Sole roadie Graham Whyte, having replaced a short-lived humper named Clive Carlson, doubled as driver and lookout. They did the normal circuit, Fraser keeping an eye on the finances that always seemed to be swallowed up in expenses.

Finally, in November 1968, after having appeared on sessions for BBC Radio One, including inevitable stops on the John Peel show, they had a real chance to ride the tiger of touring.

Simon says, "We were sent out on the road with a package tour, sort of swimming with the big fish as it were. Check out this lineup: The Who, The Small Faces, The Crazy World of Arthur Brown, Joe Cocker and Free. All on one bill.

"We traveled all over the country, about twelve gigs in all. Big venues – 2,000-seater theatres. We went in our car while the gear went ahead in a van – quite a step for us. I will *never* forget the first night, seeing The Who for the first time. Keith Moon, virtually untouched by drink and drugs... imagine! And hearing the Small Faces – Steve Marriott's voice, their total energy – we were humbled.

"While driving up to Bristol, we were dozing or reading and we heard this car blowing its horn. Looking to our left, we saw The Small Faces or rather three sets of buttocks belonging to them. Bless 'em."

Despite having an album completed, a major tour underway and the whole world before them, the band began experiencing the horrible clawing tension of matters unsettled. Paul Rodgers and Andy Fraser had settled themselves into the role as chief songwriters and while Kossoff may have remained silent about the situation, he was hurt. Add to this the distant relationship he shared with father David, the result was a recipe for disappointment and disillusionment.

FREEFALLING

They used to make fun of Kossoff a lot.

-Andy Johns

On the *Tons of Sobs* premier, Paul Kossoff had demonstrated an almost unearthly ability for an eighteen-year old guitar player. The album did not do well but the band had garnered, in large part due to Paul's magnetic stage presence, a large and loyal following.

This was Paul Kossoff, a boy possessed of talent and drive. A person of wit and charm, innocent and yet certain, he could be both leader and follower. A lion on stage and a lamb off.

But Paul was carrying a weight, a burden so heavy that not even his beloved music could ease the load. It's hard to say where it came from. His childhood was a relatively happy one and though his father provided a foundation for the musical challenges he would encounter, it's difficult to say how much parent/son bonding took place.

Even during the recording of the first album, a time that should have been full of hope and aspiration, Kossoff was unhappy. He was drinking and ingesting pills. It was a horrible waste.

Sandhe Chard, his longtime girlfriend and support system, tries to unravel the mystery – or at least provide a few clues.

"Paul's family, well... Jennie, his mom loved him, he was her baby. She used to be in the theater and that's how she met Paul's father. But then she became the 'famous actor's wife'. She had two children but Paul was her favorite. It was always OK if anything went wrong to contact mom, but if he contacted dad it was bad news."

Certainly the elder Kossoff must have been proud of Paul's success. After Paul actually landed a record deal, wouldn't his father have believed in him then?

"Yeah, his dad was proud, but after the success Paul went into the drugs and the booze. But he was beautiful and had a sense of humor, was witty. See, Simon, the brother, was more on a level with dad. Me and Paul were comfortable with his mother."

To better understand Paul, perhaps we need to better understand Sandhe. She moved to London (from America) and was living with another girl in a small flat. This roommate had a picture of Free (circa the *Tons of Sobs* period) on her stereo and it was actually through this friend that Sandhe had her first taste of Free.

"I looked at the picture and said, 'I want that man,' and it was Koss, right? With his hair hanging down. Within six months I was working for Keith Moon. A short time after that I'm at the Speakeasy, hanging out with Moon and Zeppelin and everybody, and these two guys come up and one of them is Simon Kirke. They bought me a drink, we sat and talked, and I went out with Simon. Simon and I were cool but then I introduced him to a German girlfriend of mine and he called me up one time and Keith Moon was out of town and I had his townhouse, and Simon goes, 'Sandhe, I want to cook dinner for your girlfriend? Is it OK if I use the house?' And I said, 'Fine.' I said, 'You get the food, you do everything, come over.' He did and he was cooking dinner and I was gonna leave and Simon says, 'No, my friend is coming over.'

"And this little man knocked on the door and he was in a long raincoat with a bunch of bootleg albums and he says, 'Is my friend Simon there?' And I said, 'Yeah, come on in,' and he played all his bootleg Jimi Hendrix and that was it. This little munchkin showed up; this is how it happened."

"The band had already recorded 'All Right Now' [May 1970] before I met him. I think it was around *Highway* [December 1970]." Sandhe had never heard of Free at this point though she had attended the Isle of Wight Festival where the band flew in via helicopter. That was the Jimi Hendrix Isle of Wight but she did not have any real knowledge of Free.

It was Paul's wry and sardonic sense of humor that attracted Sandhe to him. "He could knock you over in a second with his humor." When she eventually moved into Paul's tiny apartment, Simon occupied the spare bedroom and would practice his drum chops there.

Simon soon rented his own living quarters in the country and it was during this time that Andy Fraser "kidnapped" Kossoff and Simon returned the favor by allowing Sandhe to bed down at his place. According to Chard, one night upon returning home following an art lesson, Andy and a gaggle of roadies were sitting in the living room. After opening her portfolio and examining the work she'd created that evening, she sees Paul being carried out of the flat. Johnny Glover, manager, shut the house down, evicted Sandhe and the "thirteen cats me and Paul had" and that's when she moved in with Simon.

"That was not a happy night. They kidnapped him to try and clean him up. They thought I was doing drugs but I was going to art school."

A bit on the rambling side to be sure, but Sandhe does show that even early on Paul Kossoff's bent for self-destruction was already in full swing. These feelings of personal annihilation would grow steadily worse.

ONLY A VIRGIN ONCE

Tons of Sobs.*was a great success*
within their own special market.
                    -Bob Garcia (A&M Records label executive)

The spin-doctors were out in force, trying to resurrect hopelessly poor
sales of the first album by having the four-piece play virtually every waking
moment. Following this original release, Free toured non-stop, including
the extravaganza with The Who and Marriott's Small Faces.

By as early as January 1969, the band had returned to the studio to begin
scratching out ideas for a second album. *Tons of Sobs* had essentially come
and gone and with no time for asking questions or philosophizing as to
why the record had sunk, work began. Early in the month, basic tracks
were laid down for "Broad Daylight" and several days later they returned
to the studio to finish an idea called "Trouble On Double Time". "Broad
Daylight" was released as an advance single in July 1969 coupled with a
discarded *Tons Of Sobs* reject, "The Worm." The single flopped.

Paul Rodgers had assembled the troops early on in the process of beginning work on the follow-up, and while he did not have all the answers, he
realized they had to develop more of an original sound – and the only way
to do this was to write more of their own material. Gathered at Kossoff's
flat, the singer laid out the game plan.

"We were getting more into the writing but there came a point when we
had a band meeting. We had introduced about five songs into the set that
were our own and looking around there was bands like Cream and Jethro
Tull and one of the things they had in common was that they all wrote
their own songs. *All* of their own songs it seemed to me. And that was the
way to go. I said that we needed to phase out the blues and phase in all our
new material which was then something that we proceeded to do.

"Some of the blues songs survived like "The Hunter" and "Crossroads"
which we felt we had made our own and were really good live. But we did
phase out the blues."

For all his assurances made to the band that breaking out of the blues
cycle was the course to take, Paul, to this day, expresses some doubt.

"I've never been sure if that was the best thing to have done. Because I
missed them later on, I missed the blues. I think in a commercial way it

was the best because the band immediately then had an identity. 'Here was a band, it was Free, it was these new faces and they were doing songs.'"

Chris Blackwell well understood the importance of the second album. He became producer and referee.

Working in the studio during April and May of 1969, band tensions ran high. Andy Johns, mixer fixer on their debut, admits the band handled internal dynamics but sensed the foreshadowing of what might follow.

"Andy (Fraser) was the serious one and you could see he was the one in charge. In fact word had gone out that he had sort of nailed Chris Blackwell for a really heavy-duty deal. People used to say funny things about Chris which I never understood because he was always very, very fair with me. So I was aware of that. Plus his style, he would play around everything. And Koss, they used to make fun of because he'd pull a lot of faces; he never combed his hair or anything. And they would laugh and Koss was a pretty sensitive chap and I think it used to upset him a bit."

This may have been the first sign of dissension within the ranks. Previously you could not have slipped a knife blade between the group's communal armor. But rust, and insecurities, never sleep and the shielding was oh-so-slowly eroding. Rodgers and Fraser had emerged as the songwriting partnership. While Kossoff was normally given free reign to express his ideas and craft the songs as a guitarist should, he was shut out of the process almost entirely. This aspect of the project, tied to the guitarist's essential vulnerability – accentuated by the taking of pills – did not make for a healthy environment.

The situation grew so calamitous that guitarist and drummer spoke about forming their own duo while vocalist and bassist talked about leaving Free. Kossoff and Kirke made overtures to The Silence bassist (Overend Watts, later to join Ian Hunter's Mott the Hoople) about teaming up. Paul Kossoff even auditioned for the guitarist spot in Jethro Tull (created when Mick Abrahams departed) but the Ian Anderson band position ultimately went to Martin Barre, after a brief appearance by Earth's Tony Iommi.

Kossoff was deeply hurt by the situation and retreated even more heavily into his haven of alcohol and narcotics. Chris Blackwell, sensing disaster, stepped in and cooled out the situation. Guy Stevens, always a catalyst and perpetual volcanic personality about to blow, was removed and Blackwell himself took over the reigns as producer. The zany Stevens fell in line working with Mott the Hoople. Self-assured, quiet, and sensible, the Island entrepreneur guided the band through the June sessions.

Free became a far more introspective album than *Tons of Sobs*. Kossoff, once again given room to move, added to his guitar arsenal by strapping on a block neck 1960s Gibson ES-335 and traded the bombast and earsplitting Marshall amplifiers for the more stylishly resonant Fender Trem-olux units. Bassist Fraser continued with the same setup he used on the previous recording, his live arrangement which consisted of a Gibson EB series bass plugged into an old block logo Marshall stack.

"The reason the second album was different to the first was that we wrote for live on that one," states Rodgers about the process. "With the stage in mind. Andy Fraser and I used to discuss the way Lennon and McCartney did things or what we imagined their writing technique was anyway. There is a difference between sitting in your living room and play-ing your acoustic guitar and being out on stage in front of thousands of people with electric guitars; the whole thing is vamped up and geared up. You sing much differently when you're strumming around the campfire. People would probably think you're a lunatic if you got up and sang the way you sang on stage around a campfire. So we understood the difference between the two things and so we wrote things like 'Woman' and 'I'll Be Creeping' specifically for stage."

"Woman" was an ideal vehicle for Paul's voice and on "I'll Be Creep-ing", Andy demonstrated the potent bass lines he had been developing over recent months. Simon even went so far as to reveal his feelings about the bassist being the most talented player amongst them. He likened Andy to John Paul Jones, a musician capable of playing multiple instruments and at the same time an instrumentalist who spoke softly yet exerted a demonstrable influence.

The intention on this second release was to create a more eclectic sound collage, identified in large part by more sophisticated arrangements. To flesh out the vision, Kossoff was required to play more rhythm guitar, not his strongest point, and many times Andy had to physically sit down with him and teach him the parts. Kossoff hated acting the student. Keyboards became a more integral element; this time Fraser plunked out the ivory chords, deciding against bringing in an outside player as they had with *Tons Of Sobs*.

This was evident on "Mourning Sad Morning", a melancholic ode that borrowed from folk quarters, as well as "Mouthful Of Grass" and "Lying In the Sunshine", eerily atmospheric songs in which Rodgers pulled back his pipes to create ethereal effects. "Free Me", originally cut for the first record, was re-vamped in up-tempo fashion, enhanced by a Kossoff solo that winds, dives and spills guitar grease throughout the entire piece.

Says Kirke, "This was a much more sedate affair. Most of the songs were written by Paul and Andy. 'Songs of Yesterday' was a great favorite to play; I particularly like the tempo change in the middle. It always went down well at gigs. Chris Wood played flute on 'Mourning Sad Morning' because Chris Blackwell was a firm believer in his groups interacting. Later Steve

Winwood and myself played on Amazing Blondel's album as well as Claire Hamill's debut album."

In a second attempt to generate interest, Island released a new single – "I'll Be Creeping" (an abbreviated version of the album track) with B-side "Sugar For Mr Morrison". The 45 wiggled silently into obscurity. Blackwell, a man not easily dissuaded, began packaging his artists in samplers and on the first Island compilation titled *You Can All Join In* included "I'm A Mover."

In support of the *Free* album, plans were drawn up to caravan the band to America. But this would not be a club tour, visiting small venues with bad sound and the odors of unwashed bodies and unflushed toilets permeating the air. They would be opening for Blind Faith, ostensibly on the recommendation of Stevie Winwood. The band, made up of Eric Clapton and Ginger Baker both newly paroled from Cream (the guitarist couldn't wait to break away from the trio), ex-Traffic *wunderkind* Winwood and former Family bassist Ric Grech, had brought to pass a piquant and passionate first record revealing avenues never taken before. They would self-destruct after this single studio experience.

THAT DEAF, DUMB & BLIND FAITH TOUR

It was the first time I ever saw a gun on a hip.

-Simon Kirke (upon arriving at John F Kennedy Airport)

This is what every band in the world ultimately shoots for – striking at the seemingly impenetrable foundations of the big-time. Kicking down the doors of international popularity. Chris Blackwell thought his group was ready. What he didn't take into account was whether America was ready for them. In hindsight, he would later confess that his calculations backfired – it was too much, too soon. Though neither of the band's first two albums had even charted in America, the group was straining at the leash. So, in the summer of 1969, having completed the second album, they flew 3,000 miles westward, and prepared to conquer the world as the opening act for both Delaney & Bonnie and Blind Faith.

In the year 1969, the United States was a land undergoing turmoil and revolution, a place of infinite possibilities coming together in sometimes harmonious and sometimes horrific marriages. While there were those dancing in the streets, smoking Mother Nature and rubbing naked bodies one against the other, there were those fighting the dark fight in back alleys and avenues, burning draft cards and bombing buildings. The Vietnam War was escalating, the Woodstock Festival in upstate New York would attract over 400,000 people, and the Rolling Stones had the number one song on the charts with "Honky Tonk Women" (a composition, cynical critics would say, that would later be ripped off by Free in their *piece de resistance*, "All Right Now").

And against this crazy canvas of wide-eyed visionaries and farsighted wild men, a soundtrack was being created. Jimi Hendrix, the Who and the Stones were lighting up the night with electric rhythms; Bob Dylan, the Youngbloods and Creedence Clearwater Revival were stoking the fires with songs swirling with images of psychedelia and sexual rebellion.

Free was dropped into the middle of all of this. Their first show ever in America was at New York's Madison Square Garden, a huge 17,000-plus-seater hall in the Big Apple. Simon Kirke remembers it all as if it were yesterday.

"We had completed the *Free* album and were scheduled to tour in America. We arrived at JFK (airport) and it was a trip; there were hostile looks from authorities. We had long hair and the Vietnam War was in full swing.

"The first sound check at the Garden, our ever first American gig, I could not believe the size of the place. And the stage revolved. It was a nightmare; the place boomed like a rail terminal. The crowd had come to see only Blind Faith (who were selling out every concert on the tour). At one point through a miscommunication we were playing two different songs at the same time. I think Andy and I were playing 'I'm A Mover' while Koss and Paul were playing 'Walk In My Shadow'. After thirty minutes out of sheer frustration we left the stage. I walked through my drum kit; Koss trashed his amps. It was a mighty long way back to the dressing room."

Paul Rodgers shares his thoughts.

"It was terrible, it was awful. It did not work in the round [referring to the revolving stage], I don't even think the audience liked it. There would be the band playing away and the sound went round with them as well. So you'd get the back end of the amps and the front end of the amps. It was dreadful. And then of course the stage was supposed to turn and it broke down. And then security and everybody were pushing the stage around manually.

"Delaney fell off the stage and broke something, a leg or a hand. The cops were beating the kids up because it was that period of time, it was Vietnam, the establishment, and hippies, and whoosh [claps hands], we were in the front line of all of that. It was kind of chaos, we did not like it, we were not happy.

"One of the things we weren't accustomed to was the sound being out of our hands. Everything we played was put through this huge PA system and it was controlled by these people out front. In the past when I played in the clubs in England, if I needed more vocal I'd just turn around and turn it up. Get our own balance going. We weren't concerned with being louder than each other, we were concerned with the band's sound. And suddenly all of this was out the window and we didn't know what was going on."

Where Simon remembers the band playing two different songs at the same time, Paul brings back his own horrific memories.

"At one point, all four of us were at a different point in the song. Kossoff was playing something and I was singing something and wow!"

Flying like birds, the band had anticipated the opening of the heavens the first time they played in America. It was, however, not a pretty start. Free would continue the tour and in Los Angeles, where they opened for Blind Faith at the Inglewood Forum, they had found their footing and literally elevated a crowd, stone cold Clapton freaks, into the heady skies of their own music. Greatness was tapping, perhaps quietly, but knocking nonetheless, at their door. For now, though, Simon only remembers a beauty and a beast.

"I stood in the wings and watched Delaney and Bonnie, especially Bonnie, who was an absolute beauty with an astonishing voice. And Jim Keltner, a marvelous drummer who, in the sound check, did something I thought was physically impossible – a one-handed roll with his left-hand alternating with his bass drum.

"Then came Blind Faith and what a roar from the crowd. Luckily enough we would hear that for ourselves a few times in our own career. But tonight it was for them.

"Clapton's and Baker's work with Cream had made them thousands of fans over in the States and coupled with Stevie Winwood this was an awesome band. But tonight was not an auspicious debut; we watched from the wings for a bit but for some reason the crowd was getting out of hand. Threats were made by the security and staff and things quickly snowballed from there – the upshot being that Blind Faith played a shortened set and left the building quickly. We were advised to stay in our dressing room until things calmed down."

Apparently Baker, who had defined a style, also knew the meaning of mean. Rude, sarcastic and insolent, he has been known to throw tantrums – as well as drum sticks at the back of Jack Bruce's head – at the drop of a hat. Ginger spied a policeman trouncing on a fan attempting to retrieve one of his drumsticks and rising from his kit, knocked the officer in the back of the head. In America, this is not a wise move. A riot swiftly followed and an entire night of music fell on deaf and bleeding ears.

"One nice memory from that night: the four of us left a darkened and deserted MSG carrying our bags and a clutch of kids outside said we were better than Blind Faith. We smiled our thanks and with a spring back in our step, walked the few blocks to our hotel. Welcome to America …"

During down time, the band booked small gigs around New York and ended up playing several nights at a then-famous, now-defunct club called Ungano's. They opened for Dr John, the pianist who had just introduced the world to New Orleans-tinged voodoo funk. Still smarting from the Garden's sting, Free were entranced when, one evening, some special friends appeared.

"Dr John had me agog when he entered for his show dressed all in his robes and feathers and sprinkling incense and fairy dust everywhere. But on the second night, Clapton and Baker came into the club and that really had me and everyone else on their toes. Fancy them coming to see us on their night off; a band that they could see 30 times on the road if they wished. They came backstage after the set and Clapton astonished Koss by asking him to show how he did his vibrato.

"'You must be fucking joking!' Koss said with a smile, running a nervous hand through his mane of hair. But you could tell Eric had lit him up inside. I swear from that moment Koss' playing got better and better. What a compliment!"

Eric was so enamored with the young player that he even swapped his sunburst Les Paul (rumored to be the instrument responsible for recording "Sunshine Of Your Love" and the bulk of *Disraeli Gears*) for Koss' black three-pickup Les Paul Custom. Many years later, Slowhand auctioned that priceless antique at a Pop & Collectable Guitars benefit hosted by Christies. Offered at $68,338 (at that time an amount approximating £47,000) this unique relic was purchased and funds donated to the Isabel Hospice in Hertfordshire. David Kossoff attended the function and was "delighted" with the results.

That was a seminal moment. Here he was, supporting the man who had started it all for him, and here he was, Eric Clapton, actually speaking with him. Kossoff was someone constantly in need of affirmation and who better to deliver the compliment than St. Clapton, Paul's God of guitar playing.

"Several years later I saw Clapton whip up a storm [this was only months prior to Paul's passing]. There's no doubt about it; he could still play. When I saw him, he came on stage with an acoustic guitar and everybody thought he wasn't going to play – the band was doing all the playing. Then he went through a few songs and someone handed him a nice Gibson Firebird and he played 'Bell Bottom Blues', which is just a blues, but he whipped up such a storm. I thought, 'That guy's better than he ever was.' I was drawn out of my seat."

Ginger Baker, on the other hand, didn't play well with others and it was probably his infamous temper tantrums which broke Blind Faith up so quickly after forming. Simon Kirke remembers:

"Baker was quiet and morose. I understood later that he was pretty much strung out on heroin although how he managed to play the way he did boggled me. He was at his peak then, doing his lengthy drum solos night after night behind his enormous kit. He was a great drummer but I didn't find him very likeable. Years later on one of Ringo's tours, we played in Denver. Because Jack Bruce was in the band, Ringo got Ginger up to play 'White Room.' After I retook my place behind the kit and rearranged everything, I kept glancing at Ginger who was in the wings. He stayed for the rest of the set seemingly locked into place, not moving a muscle, not even tapping his foot or nodding his head in time to the music. A very strange non-action for a drummer."

"We got on well with Delaney and Bonnie and their band; they were such down home people. White soul personified. Every guy fancied Bonnie

Bramlett: figure, face and a voice from heaven. She liked her uppers, too. She gave me a Black Bomber on a bus ride from Houston to L.A. and I talked the whole way!

"Stevie Winwood would sit in our hotel room saying how much he wished he was in a band like ours; he didn't like the vibe in Blind Faith, huge crowds every night. Remember, this was the first super group and people could not get enough of them. He loved Eric though, and Ric Grech was innocuous enough, but Ginger was proving a bit of a handful. They threw a party for Ginger on his birthday – everyone was there except the guest of honor. He didn't even bother to show up."

Fraser, too, has his recollections of that trial by fire performance at the Garden.

"That was the night we discovered Southern Comfort," reported Andy in the *Songs of Yesterday* booklet that accompanied the multi-CD box set. "Between us we drank about three bottles. We got on stage totally ripped." Impossible to forget, he still visualizes Kossoff making tinder of his amplifiers and Kirke pulling a Keith Moon destructo act on his kit.

For the next seven weeks, Free was involved in Argameddon-like gigs mixed in with shows bordering on the brilliant. Island employee Johnny Glover was brought in to road manage the seven-week escapade. Money was not exactly being thrown at them; in all, they earned about $11,000, pulling in $1,500 per week. Still, between shows, they found time to plant the seeds for their next album, beginning the writing process for what would evolve into the landmark *Fire And Water.* When they weren't involved in Dante-esque shows of hellish overtones, everyone did manage to find time to unwind. They went shopping, saw other bands perform, and had to ride herd over a twenty-foot long totem pole purchased by Clapton. You heard that right.

"I remember Clapton bought a totem pole and he put it on our tour bus which he wasn't even on, he was flying. It was the full length of the bus and I don't know how they got in there. They must have opened the back window and slid it in; it was all along the seats and it had these big noses and wings. We all had to sit opposite this great big totem pole for the whole tour."

"Yeah, Clapton's bloody totem pole," chimes in Kirke. "Apparently it was shipped over (to England) and duly took its place in his garden in Surrey. Where I assume it still is."

The tour trudged on and the band found its feet. Though the sets were still composed of material from the first and second albums, as well as blues standards, this non-stop ensemble performing honed their sound to perfection. They balanced the crunch of amplified guitars and stinging vocals with the dynamic of silence – this was where the music was headed.

Where they weren't headed was to a huge festival taking place in northern New York on 16, 17 and 18 August 1969. Simon remembers that the organizers were looking for unknown bands to perform there as opening act on the first or second day. But personal manager Johnny Glover, in a sentence that would resound in their ears for years, said "No, it's several hours upstate and the traffic's appalling."

Glover did attend this event of *Three Days of Peace and Music* with another Island signing, Joe Cocker. He claims having no memory of being asked about Free but this seems improbable when balancing the media network Blackwell had at his disposal. An international event that drew over 400,000 people would escape the notice of a mogul like Blackwell? Unlikely.

Before returning to England, the band shot the cover for the *Free* album. The photo of the naked young woman walking across the sky was taken by photographer Ron Raffaelli. The photos on the back were snapped in hotel rooms. This image of an unclad female body, an eighteen-year old girl named Linda Blair (not the *Exorcist* creature) seemingly dancing on clouds, the shading of her body speckled with stars and night-lights, became a mainstay of album sleeve collections.

THE KIDS ARE ALL RIGHT NOW

Yeah, I know it sounds like
"Honky Tonk Women"

-Ed Ward (record review editor for *Rolling Stone*
during summer/fall of 1970)

Having missed Woodstock, an insane mistake, the band was on home ground for just a few days when mention was made of a festival taking place on The Isle of Wight. Spanning three days, it had attracted a roster of artists almost as impressive as the American extravaganza, and this time they would certainly not be absent. Bands played day and night and, typical of most multi-day affairs, schedules ran late and organization was lax.

Free were surrounded by The Who, Bob Dylan and The Band, The Nice, Fat Mattress, Joe Cocker, Blonde On Blonde, Edgar Broughton Band, Battered Ornaments, Pretty Things, Gypsy, Blodwyn Pig, The Moody Blues, Family, Marsha Hunt and White Trash, Aynsley Dunbar's Retaliation and Ritchie Havens. Many here had appeared at Woodstock.

Free was given a fifteen-minute slot. Everything ran late but they decided to tough it out and played an extra ten minutes. With The Who set to follow, they were determined to give no quarter. It was a durable if not sensational performance (at their second Wight appearance, the earth would move).

Even with all the overseas touring, promotion and festival exposure, the *Free* album was a still life. But disappointing sales did not lower enthusiasm. This second release revealed an expanding creative universe populated by singer and bassist revealing to the members that they were absolutely on the right track. The Free sound was being defined and it was a heady realization.

"One of the things that Alexis had told us was, 'Sometimes it's what you don't play that's more important than what you play,' recalls Rodgers. We were like, 'What the hell does that mean?' We began to understand it because we created those spaces and they represented unlimited possibilities. So part of the Free sound was its gaps."

Not long after the *Free* record came out, Andy indulged in a handful of sessions with longtime friend Korner. Tracks included "Rosie", "You Don't Miss Your Water 'Til Your Well Runs Dry", "Mighty Mighty Spade", "Whitey" and "I See It".

Drawing from the energy generated during the Blind Faith tour, the boys played shows wherever offered, but all the time they maintained a Zen-like approach to the music they were piecing together.

Energy and enthusiasm were commodities available in abundance. Fraser noted, "It wasn't like a work commitment, it was a good life," a sentiment he expressed to Phil Sutcliffe. The workload was minimized when they scored a new assistant, Jim McCrary, and a second vehicle. Since Kossoff was the only member with a valid driver's license, he had become a *de facto* driver, conveying gear and personnel in a recently acquired 35cwt Ford Transit van, the classic form of conveyance for bands on a budget.

The singer was assigned the task of keeping Koss awake during those marathon drives and while nothing serious ever happened, there was the occasional skidding out of control, flat tire and close call.

"We were young and we wanted to be big and we seemed to have endless amounts of energy," Simon opined. "Koss was the driver in the group and Andy was next to get his license but his driving never really made me feel particularly confident. Koss, however, was a superb driver. We used to drive all over the place, play the gig and more than likely drive back to London that same night. But we weren't reckless; if there were several long hauls in a row we would stay in guest houses or hotel."

Lodging typically meant five to a room and if they arrived at a hotel after food serving hours, they'd shove Andy – the smallest of the crew – through serving doors in order to raid the refrigerators. Comic relief was a way to counter the rigors of life on the road and a tool to balance this almost unbridled desire to succeed. If a show was booked for 9:00 pm they would arrive two hours early in order to run through a set they already knew inside out. Manager Johnny Glover soon learned that you had to wait at least a half-hour before entering their dressing room following a gig – enter any earlier and the slightest mistake made during the earlier set would have mushroomed into a virtual mini-war.

Slowly, like a cup filling with water drop by drop, interest in the live performances grew. Outlying areas such as Sunderland, a town founded on shipbuilding, embraced the band with exceptional enthusiasm. In early 1969, Rodgers and crew did a set at the Bay Hotel and were paid the princely sum of £30. Within a year, they would perform in this Northern industrial outpost earning over ten times that amount and drawing over 2,500 people to the Sunderland Locarno.

Interspersed with roadtripping were scheduled live radio appearances. The BBC brought them back in November to lay down "I'll Be Creeping", "Mouthful Of Grass" and Fraser's bass drama, "Mr Big". The session was later sent out on Alexis Korner's show on 20 December 1969. Another session at Maida Vale Studio 5 found them recording "Mr Big",

"I'll Be Creeping", "Woman" and "The Hunter" aired on 28 December on BBC Radio 1. Again in early December, the Playhouse Theater was the site for a taping of "Trouble On Double Time", "Mr Big", "I'll Be Creeping", "Mouthful Of Grass" and "Woman". This segment was turned over to John Peel's *Top Gear* show.

Chris Blackwell was neither isolated nor immune to the interest his baby band was generating, both in print and on the air. A decision was made to take a trip up North with the Pye Mobile studio and capture some live performances for a live album. When he arrived at the Fillmore North, the renamed Locarno, lines were backed up all the way down Roker Avenue and across Wearmouth Bridge. Several shows were recorded here in January 1970 with some tracks later turning up on the *Free Live!* album released about a year-and-a-half later.

The opening night set included "All Right Now", "Remember", "I'll Be Creeping", "Free Me", "Woman", "I'm A Mover" and "Walk In My Shadow". Evening two consisted of "Mr Big", "Songs Of Yesterday", "Oh I Wept", "Trouble On Double Time", "Moonshine", "The Hunter", "All Right Now" and "Crossroads".

Tighter than a well drawn corset and with more adrenalin pumping than a rampant adolescent, they realized, as did Blackwell, that to truly break into the ranks of rock elite, they needed a single. A hit single – that three-and-a-half minute opus sought out by every musician who ever picked up a guitar.

The rumors surrounding the conceptualizing and composing of "All Right Now", the song that would catapult Free from transit vans to trans-Atlantic success, take many forms. This would be their *Mona Lisa*, their *Fifth Symphony*, their *Of Mice And Men*. Andy and Paul had been brainstorming ideas for the third album, writing in hotel rooms and backstage between shows. To truly understand how the song developed, it seems only rational to present the recollections of everyone involved.

Though the singer has been questioned about the track thousands of times, he recently reached deep inside himself and located a sliver of a memory long forgotten. This is the first time it has ever been revealed.

"It was pretty much a story I guess. I do remember the girl from *Hair* who married Mick Jagger [they did not actually marry]. What was her name, that black girl from *Hair*? [It was Marsha Hunt.] I used to live near Oxford Street and *Hair* was playing right there on the corner. And I remember seeing this girl standing there in the street and she may have triggered the idea for that. Because there she stood in the street and she seemed to be smiling from her head to her feet. Island Records used to have their offices on Oxford Street and we used to go down there once every week or two weeks. We'd have a band meeting and talk strategy and gigs and all this stuff. Oxford Street is a crowded, teeming street and I remember seeing her.

"Actually I've never really said this before. People often ask me if it was inspired by someone and I usually say, 'I don't think so. It just came into my head.' But I was struck by her standing on the corner of the street. She obviously had a presence; do you know what I mean? Because there were a lot of people around and she just stood there and I thought, 'Wow, look at her.' Something triggered in my head and I think it came from that."

This was Free's third single, following the November 1969 release of "I'll Be Creeping", the opening track from the second album. "All Right Now", this three-minute plus masterpiece was released in May 1970 and would rocket to the number two position, unable to dislodge Mungo Jerry's "In the Summertime". This transformed the band into a major commercial draw.

Simon Kirke saw the track as just another song in the arsenal and had absolutely no idea of the impact it would have. Requiring 24 takes, he admits to being "glad to get it out of the way." An edit, a seamless cutting of tape, necessitated multiple run throughs and, after two dozen attempts, the song was finally perfectly captured.

"Let your readers see if they can find out where it [the edit] is because it wasn't a very good one. 'Jumping Jack Flash' has that section where someone leaned on the tape and it goes all wobbly during the guitar solo and they had to do a lot of edits on that. But who gives a shit anyway?"

"Time has dulled all of our memories a bit but as I recall, it all started at a gig in Durham, a town in the North of England. We had a reasonable gig but the crowd were a little slow; we seemed to have a lot of medium tempo songs and we left the stage to the sound of our own footsteps. By the time we got back to the dressing room we were all a little pissed off and anxious. And I remember Andy or Paul saying that we needed an up-tempo song, 'Something the buggers can dance to.' And I do remember this clearly – Andy bopping around the room singing, 'All right now, baby, it's all right now.' Whether he and Paul had concocted this phrase before this mildly historical night, I don't know. But during the next few weeks the song was hatched and took form.

"We never really thought that much about the single after that [its completion]. I think we were at our best around this time. We all got on well, the four guys together. We were playing to packed houses everywhere we went. We held attendance records all over the North East – Middlesbrough, Newcastle, Leeds and Redcar. There's a little story about Redcar which will illustrate what I mean. The Jazz Club at the Coatham Arms in Redcar was one of the biggest gigs in that area. We played there on a Friday night (September 20) to a pretty full house but nothing special. We went down great and as we had a night off the next day we decided to stay in town – it was a five-hour drive home. Sometime the next afternoon we got a call from our management saying that Jethro Tull were playing that same gig that night and were unable to make it – could we fill in for them? Tull were huge at that time and every ticket was sold; the place would be bursting. Would we be able to satisfy that crowd especially as we had played there only the night before? Would people not show up at all once they knew the change? We said 'yes' to the gig but were all a little nervous. The announcement had gone out over the local radio. When we took the stage you could not move. Hardly anyone had given their tickets back. A lot of people had been there the night before and we played one of the sweatiest, hard rocking shows of our lives and were called back for three encores. A major triumph. Something was in the air all right.

"I got a call a couple of days later from Island Records about ten in the morning. Denise, our secretary, said, 'You have to come in for a photo shoot, like now!' I knew that none were scheduled. This was in fact a rare day off. There was also something in her voice so I said, 'What do you mean, now?'

"'Your single has gone from 30 to number four this week, you're on *Top of The Pops* tomorrow. I'm sending a car – get ready and look good.'

"Well my voice just lit up and I thought, 'Be careful what you wish for, it just may happen.' And that was the start of everything. Who knows where we would have gone had we not had that monster hit? The huge irony was that it was the beginning of the end for us – we would disband eighteen months later."

Again, in Paul Rodgers' reminiscing, other details appear. He insists everyone was in the band room and talking about the cover, "The Hunter," and conversation rested on the fact that it was a monumental piece for them but they'd never been able to follow it with a creation of their own. Wanting a song everyone could sing, he discussed this with his band mates and actually sang [croons the melody] "all right now, baby, it's all right now". This was the idea, he explained, and then realized he had hit upon the perfect catch phrase. Donning a guitar, Paul wrote the chorus then and there and Andy took this basic piece and returned shortly with the primal guitar riff. Later, Paul would find the verse motif when he saw the woman standing on the corner.

"It was just another song in the batch but it was a good one; but then again we did believe in all of the songs. One of the things I noticed was that other people reacted to that song very strongly from the word go. The very first time we played it on stage we were doing these two 45 minute sets – you'd go on and do a set and then have a break for about an hour, so they could sell more booze, I guess – and then you'd do another set.

When we opened the first set there were very few people in the crowd, a few diehards dancing away. We opened the set with that and it was very rough and the reaction was immediate, even for those few people. And then later on towards the very end of the evening, about three hours later, it was request time, I asked the audience if they had any requests, and they shouted for that first song. And no one had ever heard it before. That's amazing."

Rodgers utilizes many sources as a songwriter; sometimes he is a story-teller, sometimes the lyrical escapades are developed around moments of wishful thinking. He writes from the heart and soul, that place where the blues resides.

While Fraser may have instigated the guitar riff, Kossoff – who had been effectively shut out of the initial music developing sessions – envisaged and designed stunning rhythmic figures and devised a solo that remains a landmark to this day.

"Well, on 'All Right Now', the bass was put down then the rhythm guitar. And it was best if the solo was simple. It wasn't exactly worked out but at the time we were thinking more of effect than of virtuosity.

"I use a lot of open strings and the chords are neither major nor minor. I don't like to play a major chord unless it's necessary. I prefer to use a chord that rings, having neither major nor minor dominance.

"My playing is very primitive and was on that song. I work from a few chord shapes, but it's really pretty basic. I've never been able to get into the quick runs, the super-duper stuff that Alvin Lee or Rory Gallagher do. It's never really interested me. I do practice whenever I can. With Free, we worked so much there was only time for women and sleep."

The singer, in looking back at Kossoff's work on that song, is awed by the creation.

"One of the things I appreciate about Koss, more now than I did then, is that his solos were very thought out and structured. It started in one place and went to the next place and ended up in a climax and took you with him. Classic. All the guitarists I've ever met since then who have played that song have all tried to do it the exact way it was done."

The single was spawned during the *Fire and Water* sessions that began on 11 January 1970. The band opted for Trident Studios in West London, a legendary facility that has hosted such luminaries as King Crimson and Queen. Chris Blackwell remained on-campus but sensing growth in their songwriting, had left them more reliant on their own devices. Roy Thomas-Baker (then known as simply Roy Baker) was enlisted as engineer while the band and John Kelly shared production duties. Andy Johns was originally hailed but an overworked body prevented his participation. He was holding down the fort at Morgan.

"It wasn't like I had a nervous breakdown but I was completely freaked out. I was the only engineer there [at Morgan]; the place was booked all the time, and I was just at the point of absolute nervous exhaustion. There was just no way I could have done it. They got fed up with Guy and they came back. And of course it had 'All Right Now' on it and I'm still kicking myself about that."

Paul was developing an ever-widening love for soul music and insists he had Wilson Pickett in mind when recording "All Right Now." Soul, to Rodgers, was a more immediate sound, a personal quality that struck you across the face like an angry lover. With this concept in mind, he sought to take more control of the process and maligned Blackwell's approach on the *Free* album as appearing too clean. Chris, ever the diplomat, allowed the band to control their own destinies. They did.

Roy Baker, later the architect of Queen's magnum opus "Bohemian Rhapsody", attempted to sort out the sometimes friction-laden concepts being developed. Musical opinions were tossed about like miscellaneous hand grenades and though egos might have been wounded, the resulting music was explosive and expressive.

The extreme success of "All Right Now" would prove to be a caress and a curse. Rodgers says, of that almost overnight leap, "I don't think we were ready for it – and it was a shame."

Nonetheless, the songs being brought to the sessions pulsed with personality. "Oh I Wept", "Don't Say You Love Me" and the title track revealed a depth of songwriting talent the singer had never before revealed.

Paul sanctions these sentiments and couples this newfound compositional style to Andy's commitment in creating a unique band sound. Many of the songs the vocalist came in with were filtered through the obsessive and yet unequivocally creative mindset of the bassist. Even the album's signature song, which ended up sounding like a guitar riff-driven piece, was reassembled in the Fraser home lab.

"I really wrote that as a soul song because of my Wilson Pickett influence and he actually did it in later years without any prompting [the black soul singer released his version as a single in April 1971 and would later include it on his *Don't Knock My Love* album about eight months later] which was amazing. But Andy took the riff and turned it into a Free thing. So we were developing a writing style and a band style."

Whoever they borrowed or stole from, the band had synthesized all their varied influences and given birth to one of the most significant records they would ever make. And the process was simple: the song was rehearsed and then a rhythm track laid down by Andy, Koss and Simon. Once the magic of this basic track had been captured on tape, Paul would come in and overdub lead vocal and Kossoff would embellish with lead guitar, fills, and all the bells and whistles he was so adept at contributing.

Though this represented a substantial leap from the second album, Kossoff was still an outsider peering in and when called upon to supply the embroidered guitar parts, would sometimes hibernate in another part of the studio and more often than not, adopt an angry tone. Some people are born into this world without the safety mechanisms of self-defense – Paul was such a person.

"He would get upset when we said, 'Go on, Kossy, put some guitar on it,'" describes Kirke. "He was very proud of his playing but how else could we have said it? It was just the vernacular at the time. I would 'put some congas on' or Paul Rodgers would 'put a main vocal on.' But say to Koss, 'put some guitar on it' and he would go nuts.

"We all loved *Fire And Water*, it still sounds good to this day. I finally shrugged off my own influences and started to sound like me. Simple and solid, a style which has endured to this day. We got Blackwell, CB as we called him then, to come down and played him the tapes. He was amazed and uttered the immortal words, 'You should put out "All Right Now" as a single.' Sure, whatever, that's what we thought. We were so pleased with it that we wanted everyone to hear it."

Chris arranged for an edit that would surgically remove a hefty chunk that included many bars of Paul's solo and the entire third verse. Reluctantly, the elimination was agreed to since Blackwell was adamant in his stance that no radio play would be forthcoming for a song that measured over five minutes in length. Two minutes had to be severed.

The hatchet job accomplished, everyone griped and groused but in the end this decision made commercial sense. Kossoff, nonetheless, was incensed and his already fragile shell was littered with hairline cracks. A dark, brooding feel reigned over the album in stark contrast to the lighthearted appeal of "All Right Now". Shadows and light.

Emotions ran high but they sensed this recording defined an essential crossroads in their career and relented. What was a single edit when surrounded by six mind-grinding songs? As it turned out, nothing.

Within two months of its release, "All Right Now" had sold a million copies. More importantly, it shoved open the doors to the American charts and US recognition; the heady rocker landed at the number four position and some three decades-plus since is heard somewhere on radio stations approximately every twenty seconds of every day, of every year, around the world.

In a perverse way, this unthinkable success exacerbated the underlying tensions within the band. While it unveiled the precious and precocious in them, in the end it would prematurely destroy a combined destiny.

But on this third record even the darkness radiated light, as if there was some sort of innate understanding that the finale was not far off. Paul was Otis Redding incarnate, his phrasing and attack so gloriously commanding that you forgot this was just a 21-year old white blues crooner and not an elderly black blues wailer crying out against a world turned against him. Andy's bass playing had taken on the singularly astonishing melodic sensibility of Paul McCartney and the hip funkiness of Motown legend James Jamerson. Simon, as he earlier noted, had found himself, and in tandem with Fraser made up a rhythm section as delicately balanced as a house of cards. And Kossoff, displaying on the hit single how a solo should develop, beginning down at the bottom of his Les Paul guitar neck and winding up on the stratospheric frets at the very top, had secured for himself a seat at the top table in the pantheon of guitarists.

Free had arrived. This was their *Revolver*, their *Dark Side of the Moon*, their document spelling out in bold letters that they were far more than just a blues band. Unfortunately the proclamation was printed in blood and written with a poison pen. They loved each other as brothers – but so did Cain and Abel.

Every blessing has its bane and the coming rain washes every rainbow away. Here, in 1970, with the world opening up to them like a suppliant oyster, concert fees quadrupling within a week of the song entering the Top 10, from bottom-feeding figures to £1,000 per appearance, minor cracks in the wall were transformed into huge gaping chasms.

Two years later the kingdom would come tumbling down.

BROKEN

Koss was sort of super-natural ... not of this world.

-John 'Rabbit' Bundrick

Maybe Paul was not of this earth. His playing certainly wasn't. But he did succumb to the agonies and grief of life and in some strange reversal of fortune, the more Koss had, the more he needed. With each and every gig he played, new worlds opened up to him, new ears listening to a guitar sound and style they'd never quite heard before.

Kossoff was the heart and hope of Free. Rodgers was the voice and spirit. Andy was the muscle and mind. And Simon was the collective body that housed the different psyches, the different personalities, the different desires.

But with each new day, Kossoff disappeared a little more, falling into the oblivion of drugs and self-doubt. No body can exist without a heart. For the members, the beating was slowing down.

"It was everything that we aimed for," admits Rodgers about the band's success. "Here it was, but it was more success than we ever thought possible. And it really knocked us for six because we thought, 'You had a hit record and everything was great.' It's easy to look back with hindsight and say, 'We should have done this and we should have done that.' I think we probably could have used a proper manager; Chris Blackwell was great but he did run the record company. He did do a little bit of strategizing but we did manage ourselves. And it was kind of a mistake because you need someone to stand outside of what you're doing and give yourself perspective.

"That same passion and intensity that brought us together started to really work against us. Instead of imploding we began to explode away from each other. It would have been good now, looking back, to have someone say, 'OK, what you guys need is to take three months off and do whatever you want to do. Then come back together and talk about it.'

"But instead we went phoooossshhh [mimics explosion] and it was almost too late. It surprised everybody how it affected him [Kossoff] and how quickly he deteriorated. He just seemed to go. Part of the problem there was he moved into a place on Portobello Road which was just drug city. His door was right on the street and people would come up and say, 'Hey, man, try this, try this.'"

The band indeed had started to fragment. Factions started forming and sides were taken. Music history books are full of chapters with headings such as "*Great Rivalries*" and "*Now the Truth Be Told*". Maybe it's inherent in the very art of creating music that without problems nothing ever gets solved; without personality clashes music stands still.

The backlog is famous: Pete Townshend and Roger Daltrey shouting at each other in rage and doubt; John Lennon falling out with Paul McCartney; Mick Jagger and Keith Richards almost killing each other; Robert Fripp sidelining nearly everyone he worked with; Jimmy Page and Robert Plant just about disowning John Paul Jones towards the end of their magic ride.

Well, Free was no different. Here, Kirke lays out the psychology that drove and would eventually destroy them.

"The band dynamics were fairly complex. Initially there were two camps: Koss and myself, Paul and Andy. As time went by and they became established as the major songwriters, Paul and Andy drifted away. They were never really social people. Andy was pretty insular away from the stage. When he got his first house, I remember thinking it was nice but very cold; people rarely went there and I don't think that concerned Andy in the slightest.

"Andy wasn't so much tough as he had a tremendous amount of confidence. To hear him play you would think he was 30 years old. The way he handled promoters and agents was a revelation. Mind you, he always had Graham Whyte around when the money was collected at the end of a gig. So that helped.

"A lot of people will tell you Andy suffered from the racial thing, but I never heard anything untoward in the years I was with him. I'm not saying he didn't cross it at times. Being half white and half black meant that he must have been a target from both parties – but we never witnessed it.

"Koss and Paul were pretty close. Koss had tremendous respect for Paul and so did I. There was that strange love/hate thing that binds singers and guitarists. Witness Page and Plant, Jagger and Richards. But Rodgers had an ace in the hole – he could play very good lead guitar and mouth harp. He was pretty much a one-man band. As his fame and prowess grew, Paul became pretty independent. He was quick to anger and aggressive. He might have been slight back in those days – he's totally different now, all barrel chest and muscles – but his intensity made people think twice about crossing him.

"Koss and Andy didn't get on well. Andy was the organizer and financial brains behind the band. He was pretty sober, too, and was quite a taskmaster; although I must say all four of us shared the same work ethic when it came to recording – rehearse hard and get it done in no more than four takes.

"I was very much the diplomat. I got on well in varying degrees of 'wellness' with each of the guys. We were still a gang, really. No wives or steady girlfriends to get in the way. I loved Koss, I felt very protective towards him. He was small and pretty vulnerable at times; but he sure changed when he plugged in his guitar.

"At the end of the day, we never hung out much, after shows or anything. Although I remember one time we arrived at a town way early. The hall wasn't even open so we all went to the movies. We saw *Who's Afraid of Virginia Woolf?* with Elizabeth Taylor and Richard Burton. Funny how some things stick in your mind!"

And what about the intake of illegal substances?

"As for drugs we all smoked joints; it was a staple in those days. And we all drank. Usually pints of beer with the occasional slug of vodka. Hashish. We smoked a lot of dope in those days. It mellowed us out, sort of. It counteracted our youthful energy [average age around this period was nineteen/twenty]. Koss had had a history of pill popping in his early youth, around fifteen and sixteen, but he seemed to have that under control. We had a lot to live for, no point in jeopardizing it now. Cocaine was unheard of then – thank God."

THE WIGHT STUFF

*You can make music of a sort with white
keys only, but for true harmony you need
the black keys also.*

-James E. Kivegyir Aggrrey

These next months were heady ones. *Fire And Water* broke into the Top
Five in the UK and the Top Twenty in America. A critical show in Sunderland took place on 30 June 1970, when promoter Geoff Docherty invited
A-list music journalists from all the leading weeklies – *Melody Maker*, *Disc*
and others – to see/review the show. Chris Charlesworth, from *MM* likened the band's effect on fans to Beatlemania; *Disc* proclaimed that Free
were the successors to the Stones' crown.

Kirke describes this period as "the stuff of dreams". Shows were sold out
all over the country and they were causing near-riot conditions whenever
they played. Two years of grueling tours and recording sessions, coupled to
an otherworldly hit, had transformed these four musicians from an average
club band into a tough and tumble unit of cohesion, insight and seemingly
endless capabilities.

A media blitz accompanied the release of *Fire And Water*, running full
throttle. Full-page ads, maximum exposure at every discotheque, heavy
rotation radio play and general publication coverage resulted in the sales
of over 46,000 units in the first week alone, a figure almost exceeding the
sales figures of their first two albums combined. In all, this third project
would go on to eventually sell over a million albums. Free had made the
grade.

The press embraced them. Headlines read "*Freemania is sweeping Britain*" while another shouted, "*Free took another big step in establishing themselves as one of our top heavy* (a word that undoubtedly rankled Rodgers)
rock bands." Show attendance was out of control and hundreds of devotees
were regularly denied admission. Up-and-comers ran themselves ragged in
trying to land an opening slot on one of their shows; Bronco, Juicy Lucy
(Paul's one-time band mate Mick Moody tried to pull sway over his former
associate), Amazing Blondel and Skid Row (Gary Moore's launching pad)
bowed to these newly recognized rock royalty.

From the outside, all edges seemed smooth. Band politics took care of themselves, drinking and drugging were apparently under control and the future was limitless.

While Paul Rodgers expressed that, in the end, having a manager who also ran the record label was not a wise choice, at this point Chris Blackwell had made all the right moves. His relationship with the boys was so close that towards the end of 1970, after an offer came in from the Kinney Group to buy Island Records, he actually asked each of his groups if he should sell. He did not but would relinquish controlling interests some twenty years later when Polygram Records acquired Island.

Blackwell, still smarting from his band's absence at the Woodstock Festival, made damn certain they'd be present for the second Isle carnival. The prestigious Isle of Wight Festival was coming up and Chris engineered his internationally famed hit band into the 6.00 pm slot on Saturday evening, 30 August. But the best laid plans of mice and managers often go astray and the band almost didn't appear.

This time around festival organizers phoned Island offices regularly to ensure their appearance. A fifteen-minute set on the first festival was now extended threefold. Still, troubles beleaguered them.

"We were scheduled to go on Saturday evening and naturally there was chaos all around," reminisces Simon. "We were picked up by helicopter from the hotel, which was at the other end of the island. About ten minutes into the flight the pilot pointed down. We all looked through the Plexiglas and were astonished to see what appeared to be wave after wave of ants. It was a crowd of some 250,000 covering the valley and surrounding hillsides. At the far end was a postage stamp sized area – this was the stage. We landed and went out to the trailers. Everything was running late. Our spot was pushed further and further back. We were getting increasingly frustrated. Around ten o'clock, after some four hours of waiting, Blackwell told us no way would he let us go on. There was talk about maybe an early morning [Sunday] slot. Far better if we went back to the hotel and had a late morning slot on Sunday when the vibes were cooler. We were disappointed of course, but went along with it."

A little bit of background puts the situation more in focus. Saturday's bill began well after the stated 11:30 am start time with John Sebastian, the ex-Lovin' Spoonful singer, opening the festivities. He was followed, all playing time delayed sets, by: Shawn Phillips, Lighthouse, Mungo Jerry, Joni Mitchell, Miles Davis and Ten Years After. Emerson, Lake & Palmer made their debut in the late evening, followed by a midnight set from The Doors. Remaining entrants included Chicago, Family, Taste, Procol Harum, Voices Of East Harlem, Arrival, Tony Joe White, Jethro Tull, Joan Baez, Leonard Cohen & The Army, Richie Havens, The Moody Blues,

Pentangle and Ralph McTell, Cactus, The Jimi Hendrix Experience and Melanie. Sly & The Family Stone closed out the night/dawn on early Sunday morning. Last-minute additions brought in Tiny Tim, Donovan, Heaven, Kris Kristofferson and The Who (taking the stage at one in the morning and serving up a marathon and miraculous three-hour set).

Rested and refreshed, Free returned the next day.

"As it turned out, we got a great reception," enthuses Kirke. 'All Right Now' was the hit of the show of course. It was great to see these people emerging from their sleeping bags with sleepy expressions and have them up and dancing by the end of the set. They didn't even have monitors back then; just a few mikes strategically placed on the equipment. It was a frightening experience for me. Of course I couldn't play to all those people – I just picked the first few rows and played to them. But it was a good gig.

"Personally, one of the highlights was Pete Townshend coming to our car as we waited for the ferry. He leaned in the window and was saying what a great record 'All Right Now' was. We were gob smacked! Pete bloody Townshend! There was another festival we played and this bespectacled guy in a college scarf walked up to us just as we came off stage and said what a terrific group we were and 'All Right Now' was the best record he had heard this year. I never really took any notice of him until he climbed on stage and tore into an amazing performance. It was, of course, Elton John."

Their set itinerary embraced opener "Ride On Pony", "Woman", "The Stealer", "Be My Friend," "Mr Big", "Fire And Water", "I'm A Mover" and the traditional encore, "The Hunter". "All Right Now" was almost transcendent and the finale of "Crossroads" brought an estimated 400,000 sets of ears ringing and tingling.

The event in its entirety had been captured on film and in 1996 a two CD package was released, accompanied by the re-distributed Isle of Wight film, *Message To Love*. "Mr Big", "Be My Friend" and "All Right Now" made it to celluloid.

HIGHWAY UNDER CONSTRUCTION

I think all we needed was a break.

-Paul Rodgers

Trying to capitalize on the momentum created by the single and the festival appearance, the label rushed out a new single in January 1971. Titled "The Stealer", it would be the first track from the band's upcoming album called *Highway*. Rushing into newly designed Island Studios, they began working. Unlike the majestic predecessor, "All Right Now", neither the 45 nor the LP managed to succor the favor of Free's public. The single failed to chart at all in England. The pressure to follow up "All Right Now" was a virtual impossibility as Fraser described in an on-line interview.

"Everyone expected 'The Stealer' to do something for us and it didn't. There were pressures on us to record another single that would be a hit, which is always a pressure, and you don't like being asked shit like that. In the studio there was real tension – no blame to be put anywhere."

For *Highway*, writing sessions actually took place in the studio, a new twist. Though Andy confesses newfound weights being placed upon their creative necks, tracks were demoed and completed in a relatively swift fashion. New influences crept in and though the album fared poorly in the marketplace – and was by no means on a creative level with *Fire and Water* – it did reveal the group's growing command of composition and that Who-like quality of marrying, almost seamlessly, acoustic and electric tapestries.

Where *Fire And Water* demonstrated a sleek, stripped down version of the music, *Highway* revealed a host of accoutrements. Fraser increased the role of the keyboard by bringing in the Mellotron, that devilishly fickle instrument utilizing actual tapes for sound. And the jump from eight to sixteen-track allowed them a new experimental freedom.

Melody Maker journalist Roy Carr actually came into the studio during the mixing process to do a track-by-track review. That type of prestige reporting was normally left to rock's elite – Zeppelin and the Stones – but even with this sort of blow-by-blow reportage, the album made little noise.

As always, the bassist and vocalist brought in the bulk of the material. In some ways, the pair recreated those listening sessions of the early days when everyone would gather at Kossoff's place and listen to their favorite albums. Paul and Andy were stretching the limits – perhaps stretching them too far.

"We were having listening sessions again," remembers Kirke. "I lived in the same apartment block as Paul did in High Holborn, London. *Otis Blue* was our favorite (Otis Redding) and when Elton's *Tumbleweed Connection* came out, that was scrutinized as well.

"Paul Kossoff and me were diehard blues and soul fans; Paul Rodgers and Andy, perhaps with the license borne of poets and songwriters, were becoming enamored of groups like The Band. *Music From Big Pink* will probably go down in history as one of the most influential albums of all time. It certainly grabbed Andy and to a lesser extent Paul. I didn't get it immediately, I must confess. We had one of our listening sessions over at Andy's place and he played most of the album. I liked 'Chest Fever' straight off but wasn't particularly knocked out like the others. Over time I grew to love The Band, particularly Levon's drumming and Garth Hudson's keyboards. Whenever [our] harmonies were a big ragged, we always fobbed them off as 'Band-type' harmonies which really meant they were crap."

Even with the influx of these new influences, or perhaps because of them, the music was straying and certainly the attempt to design a worthy successor to "All Right Now" burned like a hot poker in the ribs. The success of that song unfolded in several ways. Firstly, the commercial aspect of it caused their staunch following to see them as a lighter 'pop' oriented group. And combined with the visual image of four baby-faced guys determined to play blues-based rock, music was lost in the translation. From the beginning they'd mixed in odd elements – flute (Chris Woods on "Mourning Sad Morning"), female backing vocals ("Broad Daylight") and acoustic treatments. But Andy and Paul were growing increasingly eclectic and according to Simon, "It became a bit much for Koss' taste and mine."

These new bumps and ripples in the sound rankled guitarist and drummer. More blues based, they found these new influences conflicting with the essential primitive and unadulterated sound they'd founded on earlier albums. Engineer/mixer Richard Digby-Smith, an Island associate who had worked with the band over the course of their career, saw the rift forming. Describing Kirke as "simplistic", Andy as "melodic", Kossoff as "powerful" and Rodgers as "that voice", he felt the guitar player's sympathetic pains as he was pushed and dragged further and further from the center of creative activity. Kossoff could never understand why there was a piano in a guitar band but he was dead loyal to his singer. Salt was poured into the wounds when Koss, ostensibly at a loss, toyed with the idea of working with Jeff Beck/Faces front man Rod Stewart. The spiky-haired one was a champion of his work and suggested they get together and kick around his lyric ideas and Paul's abundance of guitar licks. This never happened.

Simon managed to score his first co-write when he brought in the crumbs of an idea for a song called "Love You So", but this new wrinkle in the writing formula was far too little far too late. Fraser was expanding his production chores and consequently his already firm grip around the foursome's musical neck. Countless takes were required and insisted upon; arrangements became ever more elaborate; and his growing love for keyboards manifested itself in a plethora of piano tracks. Paul Rodgers was also growing as an artist and provided all lyrics. These creative explorations ran headlong into corporate considerations and strangely enough the artistic decision won out over the economic argument.

"Right here, we began to feel we were losing control. There was this whole series of record covers suggested for the *Highway* album, none of which we used and some of which we liked. This record cover that came out we hated; it was suddenly there and I was very disappointed in it. I remember going to a record store and looking in the window and trying to see our record and I couldn't see it – and then I saw it and it was right in front of me. That's how much impact we had. We had "The Stealer" and we had a very big argument between record company and band as to what was going to be the follow-up to 'All Right Now.' They wanted 'Ride On Pony' and we wanted 'The Stealer' because we really felt it represented the magic and musicality of the band. It was one of the few records at the time that we actually wrote in the studio. And it was so exciting for us and we were so behind it and it failed. And I think that sort of kicked us in the nuts."

Andy Johns was once again summoned to put this house in order. He welcomed the challenge. Here he reflects on the creation of Island Studios and mirrors Paul's judgment of album artwork.

"Blackwell had opened up offices in a place called Basing Street in an old church. And he built two happening studios there (newly conceived Island Studios where future label artists would do the bulk of their recording) and they were really happening rooms. They were great; I did lots of stuff there. They had the record company upstairs and the agency and management downstairs. So I would see them all the time. The record company was this wonderful arrangement whereby they had this one very big room with a round table where everybody sat. And they each had a phone. So it wasn't like you got shuffled from one office to another. When you went in there to talk about a project or complain or whatever it was, there's Chris Blackwell and all these other A&R people, and the whole record company sitting at this big table. It was a great way to get stuff done.

"And I remember when I did the *Highway* record and it came out, the album cover was kind of obscure and you couldn't really see who they were and it was very pastel and there were these very finely-spaced pixels. I remember reading one review in some rag that said, 'New band called Highway sounds just like Free.' So I went into the record company with the album cover and said, 'Who the fuckin' hell is responsible for this?' And Chris Blackwell looks up and says, 'I am.' And I go [in mock indignant tone], 'Hmmmpphh, nice job!'"

Recording schedules, as they had been since the "All Right Now" phenomenon, were littered with intrusions. The single was beginning to rattle around in Europe and in early September commercial pressure demanded the band's presence in West Germany and Sweden.

During mid-month, a day prior to Kossoff's birthday, more live recording was undertaken. On 13 September, two nights were captured at the Fairfield Hall in Croydon, follow up sessions to the dates in January. Some of this material would be profiled on *Free Live!* Andy Johns, the king of concert recording, was summoned. He brought along the Pye mobile truck, and in hindsight, would have probably been happier running over Guy Stevens with it rather than using it as a tool of the trade.

"Guy Stevens managed to get in on that somehow," sighs a disgusted engineer. "That just consisted of Guy actually throwing around a lot of furniture in the dressing room when I was recording. That was it; that was all Guy did. I think he drove me to the gig in Croydon and started throwing things around and smashing things up. And then was really pissed off when his name got left off the album. Because I think it said produced by me and them or something. And he called me up outraged. And I said, 'Guy, you didn't have anything to do with the record.' He really didn't."

Johns employed the mobile Pye unit, an eight-track recorder, to cut the live performances. Upon returning to the studio to do mixes and clean up the tracks, Andy found that all ambience was missing [the record amp malfunctioned in the player]. In its place, the engineer used crowd noise and atmosphere from a Sunderland show.

"The audience does sound kind of fake but who cares? You don't buy a bloody album to listen to the audience. I just piled on enough reverb and delay and stuff to make them sound like they were in a big room."

To this day Andy is approached by fans and curious alike about his experiences with Free. He is still quite stunned by the enormous sound created by a trio with vocalist. A feat, he maintains, all the more impressive due to their less than towering physical statures.

"I think they were an average of 5'5" or something. A lot of English geezers were small – look at The Small Faces."

PACIFIC BLUES

Free was, in some respects,
the British Creedence Clearwater Revival.

-Ken Emerson

Though *Highway* would pass with about as much fanfare as a squashed bug on a windscreen, Island Records maintained a strict touring schedule both before and after its release. In autumn 1970, Free once again ran the marathon gauntlet of a UK tour, culminating in a rigorous set at Sunderland Top Rank with Deep Purple, Principal Edward's Magic Theatre and Cochise. Some of the audience had seen them in clubs so many times that when a visit was made to certain areas, locals would approach the players as long lost friends.

All this touring, including a request from the Woodpecker cider organization to compose an original tag line for their product, could not elevate *Highway's* status.

"In spite of the relative lack of success of *Highway*, with one of the worst covers in history, our shows up in the Northeast of England, Rodgers' country, were incredible," recalls Kirke. "Somebody had an idea to do a live album. I remember Spooky Tooth were on the bill because my snare drum broke and I didn't have a spare and Mike Kellie lent me his.

"It was chaos but it captured the true feel of what a live Free gig was about. Koss' amp cut out a couple of times, a couple of the recording mikes were out but the atmosphere was electric. I think Andy's solo in 'Mr Big' was one of the best ever.

"It was our idea to fade the final track into Paul's 'Get Where I Belong' – to my mind one of his most beautiful songs. It was a portent, too, because this song was all him as opposed to Fraser/Rodgers. We attended the mixing and topping and tailing sessions, the running order of the album, and we cleaned up the endings and beginnings of the songs. We attended these sessions on every album we did, all of us. Shit, if we had been allowed to glue the cover, we would have done that, such was our dedication.

"When the final cheers had subsided from 'The Hunter' and the guitar intro rises up through them, I was moved to tears. It was an exquisite moment for me – don't ask my why but it is a moment I will never forget."

There is a slim line between light and shadow, that precise second when the sun dips beneath the horizon to plunge a bright world into darkness. So, too, the barometer measuring excess and success is difficult to read. By this time, the band was flying on fumes, although they did not completely realize it. Shows were sold out and money earned but the fire was dimming – in Kossoff's case, sputtering dangerously.

During a tour of Sweden and surrounding countries, an uprooted Texas keyboardist named John Rabbit Bundrick happened to see a set in a smoke-filled Stockholm club. He had first seen the band in Houston when they opened for Blind Faith but seeing them in a small room like this one was a true experience. Born of a father pounding out honky tonk, he delved into the rollicking rhythms of country and western but soon went perpendicular when exposed to rock 'n' roll. Two Texas buddies, Terry Wilson and Glen Gibson, invited him to join their stuttering-titled band, The The. But the keyboardist was not a sideliner, not an onlooker, and post haste renamed them Blackwell (coincidence notwithstanding). John was snatched up when soul singer Johnny Nash visited Houston to lay down tracks and ended up jamming with Blackwell. Bundrick was invited to assist Nash compositionally, assured the assignment would only take a couple of months; ten months living in the land of the blond was enough to convince him that returning to the land of cowboys and oil wells would be counter-productive. England became his new home.

This encounter would ring sweetly some time later when he tickled ivories on *Heartbreaker,* and subsequent Kossoff solo endeavors.

In the meantime, blueprints were drawn up for a second assault on America. This time it would be different. The entire month of January 1971 was devoted to wreaking havoc on US stages. Chris Blackwell was part of the traveling circus, ensuring maximum press coverage. The tour culminated with a prestigious coming-out at the famed Carnegie Hall.

Upon completing the tour on 25 January 1971, rapid plans were sketched out to bring them back to America where they'd tour with Mott the Hoople, another Island acquisition gnawing away at the chains of obscurity. Returning from the States, they embarked on a European tour, headlining over Amazing Blondel. Two weeks into the tour, gear was stolen following a stop at the Civic Hall in Guildford and less than a month later, on rented gear, the attendance record was broken at London's Lyceum Ballroom – a record formerly held by The Rolling Stones.

Still, there was blood on the *Highway* and "The Stealer" was criminal in its inactivity. No other single was released from this fourth album and, oddly, the sole 45 was almost never recorded.

"Kossoff was out in the studio playing the riff from 'The Stealer,'" details Johns about the *Highway* session. "We were sitting around and we didn't know what we were going to do because we only had eight songs. He was playing the riff, and it's a great riff, and I said, 'Well, let's do that' and he said, 'No, I don't want to do that.' I said, 'What do you mean you don't want to do that? There's a song, let's do that.' He said, 'Well, it's not mine' which was ridiculous. So we had a bit of a go 'round and of course he lost because it just wasn't logical."

"My Brother Jake" was recorded during sessions in late March of 1971 and was singled out for its simplicity and Rodgers' devastatingly understated approach. It did reach number four in England but brain-dead followers viewed the stripped down track as too pop-oriented. Several other artifacts never even saw light of day: "Only My Soul", "Blowin'," "Rain", "Dressed To Kill In My Caddie", "Only My Soul" and "Makin' Love" were tracked but destined for the vaults.

The band embarked on a tour of the Far East and Australia. Manager Johnny Glover claims that on the flight to Tokyo, Fraser revealed this would be the last gasp. Andy's relationship with Johnny was on a higher, much more personal level, than his fellow Freemen. The band was unofficially on its last legs. So intense was the divide by this time that Andy and Rodgers couldn't even sit next to each other. Simon Kirke remembers:

"Looking back on the schedule we kept, I'm amazed that we lasted as long as we did. We never stopped. And this had to catch up to us. Japan was a trip, though. We flew on Aeroflot, the Russian Airline. Thirteen hours from London to Tokyo. The seats didn't recline, only beer and vodka to drink, no cameras or binoculars allowed. The stewardesses looked like former champions at track and field. I will never forget waking from a sleep and seeing the Himalayas literally outside the window. Soldiers aiming their guns at us in Moscow at a refuel stopover. Long hair in those days in Russia? Asking for it!

"We played to several thousand Japanese and worried at the silence between the songs. Then being bombarded with gifts and well-wishing letters and the end of the show – apparently it is impolite to make a noise during a show."

Paul Rodgers remembers the tour with more somber thoughts.

"We had been touring, touring, touring, working, writing songs, making albums instead of getting any kind of break. We suddenly had all this success and it intensified everything. We went to Japan, we went to Australia, we did all these things. I don't think I was ready for another tour of America having experienced the Blind Faith thing, unless it was going to be well organized. I said we have to be much more organized before we even attempt such a thing because I didn't want all the same disasters happening again. The tour was put in regardless and I thought, 'Wow, I don't have any control of this, people are just doing whatever they want to do.'

"And I said, 'I want to step out' and I said that many, many times prior to them putting that whole tour in. But it just went ahead; it just rolled ahead. I just stood up and said, 'Hey, I am taking a break, I'm out right now.' And the next thing was the headlines read: *Free Split* and that seemed to put a finalization on it. Seeing it in print was so final it was difficult to go back."

Paul's inability to control his own fate simply beat him down. He had expressed in no uncertain terms that he, and the band, needed a break from each other, a respite. But no one listened, the machinery kept on rolling and the point of no return was passed.

American vocalist Alan Merrill (later forming The Arrows and co-writing ex-Runaways Joan Jett's single, "I Love Rock & Roll") saw the shows in Japan. He had been friendly with the Japanese bassist Tetsu Yamauchi, member of the progressive band Samurai (two albums released on Phillips). In 1969, Yamauchi, born in 1947, moved to Europe and first saw Free at The Black Cat, a small club in Geneva, Switzerland. He returned home several months later and saw the band in Tokyo. Following a show, he met Kossoff at his hotel and spoke with him about their gig in Geneva, the weather, nothing in particular. Tetsu said he was a bass player and the next day, with studio time booked, Kossoff met him and they jammed for about two hours. The following day Simon and Paul tagged along. There was talk about working together – but just talk.

Still, Kossoff and Kirke tried hard to avoid the inevitable. As if by sheer force of will, they attempted to re-weave the fabric of unity, but this didn't happen. Rodgers, by this point, was so disillusioned, that although he had met a poet/songwriter in Japan named Machi and fallen helplessly in love with her (marriage was contemplated), he never even told the band about his affair.

Andy had also announced his decision to leave, leaving Kirke in shock and Kossoff in utter depression. The exhausting work schedule piggybacked with Chris Blackwell's ever-decreasing involvement in group activities – he was spending more time with Traffic and Spooky Tooth – had left the band to their own devices. Destructive devices.

The Australian leg was nuclear and near fission. Glover had to deal not only with the animosities poisoning his band but also had to carefully sidestep a local thug named Sammy Lee. Armed with guns and money and power, Lee controlled all tour monies, ticket sales and even stage size. The manager, near exhaustion himself, returned home. He went alone. Kossoff and Rodgers headed back to Japan – on separate flights, Fraser returned to his newly purchased 400-year old country cottage in Worthing, and Kirke, relishing a bit of sunshine, wound up in California.

KIRKE AS CONVICT

We just sort of exploded
away from each other.

-Simon Kirke

Following the final Free date in Australia on 9 May 1971 at the Randwick Racecourse, Simon found himself in Los Angeles, home of A&M Records, Free's American label. Coiled, angry and ready to be sprung, he sought out – and found – recreational diversion. But it couldn't reduce the frustration that had built up inside him.

"Andy had become a little too overbearing and domineering. Paul Rodgers' reaction was pretty intense and from there it kind of filtered down to me and Koss. Initially I couldn't believe it was happening; everything was going well. OK, we'd had a couple of setbacks – *Highway* didn't sell like we had hoped but Andy and Paul thought it was the end of the world as they knew it. The vibes were bad between those two and coupled with the workload, it just spiraled. By the time we came to the final dates, I just couldn't wait to get away; there was actually talk of an American leg but we nixed that before we went to Australia. Things were that bad. There was no way we could go on; someone might have gotten hurt."

Well, someone almost did. In Los Angeles, Simon indulged, overindulged and pushed the limits. The cage door was opened and he was the key master. Borrowing a car from a friend at A&M Records, he drove up the coast to San Francisco, a surreal and serene stretch of coastline that ranks as one of the most breathtaking in the world. But Simon was not here to sightsee. He wanted to make serious time and burned the rubber from the tires. Stopped for speeding, Kirke and car were searched by the Highway Patrol. They unearthed one half-inch roach. In 1971 this was a serious offense and the vacationer found himself handcuffed and hauled off to Salinas County Jail in King City, California.

No, this is not a fictitious script from some dismal B movie. Simon ended up sharing a cell with seven other detainees for four days. Of course, the script calls for his bunkies to have done hard time and, sure enough, they had. Up on charges ranging from rape to robbery to car theft, they were menacing figures that saw an English-speaking musician busted for speeding as beneath their contempt. The cell king, however, heard that he was bedding down with a fellow drummer, and the pair used to bang rhythms together on the metal eating table.

Simon regales us with the rest of his conning tale.

"Ironically 'All Right Now' was played several times on the in-jail radio and that led to a lot of derision among the inmates. After four days I knew that my rights were being withheld and I demanded to see the governor. I used my one and only phone call to A&M in L.A. and they were relieved to hear from me. I had only gone out for a packet of fags and that was five days ago. They flew up a lawyer who, unbelievably, knew the judge from their law school days. He got the drug charge dropped – which could have seriously hampered any future tours in the US – and I pleaded guilty to reckless driving and incurred a $100 fine.

"I was released that same afternoon with an incredibly healthy respect for the law. I found out later that had I been there longer than one week, I would have been shipped to Soledad, the scene a few weeks later of a riot and hostage situation staged by the Black Panthers. Several inmates were killed and some wounded and repercussions reverberated around that prison for months."

Above: Free. (l-r) Paul Rodgers, Andy Fraser, Paul Kossoff and Simon Kirke.
Photo: Harry Goodwin

Above and Below: Paul Kossoff in full flight with his Les Paul.
Photos: (top) GEMS, (bottom) Ian Dickson

Above: All smiles - Simon Kirke and Andy Fraser. *Photos: Harry Goodwin*
Below: Kossoff slumped on the floor was sadly to become a Free trademark.
Photo: Michael Ochs Archives

Above: Back Street Crawler. *Photo: Dick Barnatt*
Below: Kossoff jams with Bad Company (l-r) Paul Kossoff, Paul Rodgers and Mick Ralphs. *Photo: Michael Ochs Archives*

Above: Bad Company. (l-r) Boz Burrell, Paul Rodgers, Mick Ralphs and Simon Kirke.
Photo: GEMS
Below: (l-r) Boz Burrell, Paul Rodgers and Mick Ralphs onstage 1975.
Photo: Fin Costello

Above: Mick Ralphs and Simon Kirke backstage during Bad Company's happier days.
Photo: Fin Costello

Left: Paul Rodgers wields the mic stand.
Photo: GEMS

Right: Paul Kossoff and myself after an interview for *Guitar Player* magazine just weeks before the guitarist's sad demise in 1976.

Below: Simon Kirke
Photo: GEMS

Above: Paul Rodgers in defiant mood.
Photo: Fin Costello / Redferns

FREE LIVE, JIMI DEAD

Playing with Paul Rodgers helped me grow.

-Paul Kossoff

As if these inner-mounting flames weren't enough to burn their house down, Free, and particularly its guitarist, experienced another life-altering tragedy around this period. Jimi Hendrix died on 18 September 1970, and the instant Paul Kossoff heard the news he phoned his close friend Simon. Already on the verge of a breakdown, Paul couldn't contain his emotions. He and the drummer would often get together and jam on Hendrix's "Little Wing" and "Axis: Bold As Love". He had only met Jimi once, all those many years ago when he was a junior guitar salesman, but the impression his music had made on Paul would stay with him for life.

Hendrix's death came just five days after the band had recorded live at the Croydon Fairfield Hall. Island Records, sensing perhaps the disintegration, was determined to mine at least one final album and nothing is easier to assemble than a live recording – except perhaps a greatest hits package.

The death of Hendrix, the pulling apart of the band both musically and emotionally, and the almost uninterrupted pressure of years of touring and recording had torn down all defenses – Free was burning quickly. And Kossoff was the first one leaping into the inferno.

"I had a very morbid interest at one point in Hendrix. I used to listen to him and take all these drugs and I'd think, 'What point in my even playing? He's done it all.' And that was a bad way to be. I went through a big Hendrix thing, where I was infatuated by him, his music… and his death."

Simon had grown increasingly close to Koss and was probably his best friend. When James Marshall passed and he received the call from Paul, Simon knew that his longtime companion was dangerously near the edge.

"Koss was starting to ingest more drugs than was good for him. I think in retrospect, the non-success of *Highway* and the subsequent unrest within the band was starting to get to him. He was also in the throes of trying to find a 'sound'; not that he wasn't a superb guitarist already but he was very much influenced by Hendrix. He had become profoundly affected by Jimi's death and had started on a quest for that sound [which would manifest itself later with the Back Street Crawler albums and Kossoff's switch from Gibson Les Paul to Fender Stratocaster, the same type of guitar Hendrix shouldered]. It was a nebulous thing and was not something that Koss could articulate very well. He was starting to experiment with Leslies [the cabinets Hammond B-3 organs run through to create that swirling 'A Whiter Shade of Pale' quality; this was also the effect Hendrix used in producing his unique tone]. In the beginning he acquired only one cabinet but in later days would add another. They were enormous things and the bane of Graham Whyte's life.

"Paul's input of drugs started to spiral. He wasn't content with joints and beer. He started to take a lot of Mandrax, a loose equivalent to what Quaaludes were in the U.S. His speech started to slur and he would frequently nod out during takes. At first the difference was only slight but as the months progressed it got worse. This was absolutely frightening. His rhythm playing, not one of his strong points, got sloppy and his tremolo, once so piercing and strong, grew unconvincing."

The finish line was in sight.

STRANGE MAZE

Paul Rodgers cut me off at the knees.

-Andy Fraser

"The four members of Free, Paul Rodgers, Simon Kirke, Paul Kossoff and Andy Fraser, this week decided to disband to pursue solo careers. They felt they had achieved as much as they could within the group." Thus spoke David Sandison, Island Records publicist, in announcing the dissolution in May 1971. In another sick and twisted wrinkle, "My Brother Jake" had been crawling up the charts and reached number four in Britain. Here was the cleaving of a band, at each other's' throats, throwing the future aside with a hit single in their pockets. Unbelievable.

Trying to ride the unforeseen wave of "My Brother Jake", spin artists at the label leaked an announcement about the release, the following month, of a live album.

These fact-twisting doctors must have done their jobs because *Free Live!* catapulted to number four in England. In America, once again proving the dichotomy in the tastes of the two listening audiences, the record only climbed to number 89. These were brave and bold numbers played by musicians whose essence was distilled during live performance. Even with the technical muck-ups and instrument breakdowns, this has weathered time to become a milestone in live recordings and one of Free's most valued pieces.

The guitarist is a bit less generous in his appraisal.

"I thought it was OK for the time. It's taken me a long time to reach my style and the playing on the album was so exciting. It was energetic. But it wasn't what I became – I know what I'm playing now."

Given life in mid-1971, the album borrowed from the Sunderland shows, "All Right Now" and "The Hunter", with "I'm A Mover", "Be My Friend", "Fire and Water", "Ride On Pony" and "Mr Big" taken from the 13 September 1970 Croydon show. "Get Where I Belong" was a remainder studio track.

The band had split, in print and emotionally. Odd, that this group who had seemingly weathered so much had only managed to give birth to five albums before self-destructing. The live album went on to become a staple for fans and was a hearty sendoff. You could chalk the breakup to drugs and egos. Fair enough. But there was more at play here, more unseen challenges and ghosts.

Simon sums up this period.

"Our work load had taken its toll. Koss – dear, sweet, vulnerable Koss. A prodigy for Christ's sake! Cocky, confident, bordering on arrogant, great sense of humor, good driver. Think of the Artful Dodger in *Oliver Twist*. He took me under his wing during Black Cat Bones and I was with him for five years after that off an on. I ended up trying to protect him from himself and the parasites around him but ultimately addiction won.

"I only visited Koss' home a couple of times. It wasn't a particularly overt Jewish house. His mum wasn't Jewish although I think she converted along the way [she did]. His father was a well-known actor and seemed on the surface to be a nice enough guy. But there was something missing somehow. Koss had been in trouble with drugs at an unbelievably young age, fourteen or fifteen. Uppers they were, 'blues' and 'dexies'. Mild speed I had over the years. Nothing terrible. It made me smoke two ciggies at a time and you'd talk the hind legs off a donkey but the comedown was horrible and I never really took to them.

"I've seen it in other wealthy households; the kids don't get the attention they need and seem to spend their childhood playing catch-up to their father's success. And rebelling when it doesn't come quick enough for them. Money, gifts and privilege are the substitutes to quality time and a natural bonding process.

"Funny, I don't remember his parents coming to one show in London. Not even the 'posh' ones like the Albert Hall. You couldn't keep my parents away when we played Bristol.

"And Andy was a genius. Quite simply a musical prodigy. His bass playing was in another league. But his talents didn't stop there. He played great piano [witness 'My Brother Jake']. And drums. He had an unnerving habit of showing me a particular way of playing a song by jumping on the kit and bashing away. It drove me nuts – but he was usually right.

"He never played guitar though. I never saw him pick one up around us. And he never sang in Free except the occasional harmony but when I saw him years later in L.A., he played me some demos and his singing was sensational. Like Stevie Winwood. I was totally surprised. He was a flash dresser too although he was a little too poncy for my taste.

"Rodgers was the intense one. Yes, he was aggressive and moody but that was only some of the time. On a good day he was charming and had a great sense of humor. He was also very wise – an old head on young shoulders really. And as honest as a long day.

"And he was, quite simply, the best singer around. In all the years I worked with him I never knew him to have a sore or hoarse throat. And he hit notes that had dogs going in circles night after night. A complete and utter natural. Koss adored him. When we broke up this first time, Koss missed Rodgers' voice more than anything. The closest thing to him was Otis Redding – listen to Otis and you're listening to Paul Rodgers."

Andy Johns, the band's engineer on their debut, *Highway,* the live album and the swansong *Heartbreaker*, offers up his profiles.

"It was so easy working with those guys, they were so proficient. Andy had a great sense of arrangement. I showed them a few bits, here's a Mellotron, here's a harmonium, and he would just take it and go off. He was really very cool.

"And Simon would play little bits of acoustic guitar and sing backgrounds. I think he was a bricklayer or something and he had these huge biceps. They were all in on it.

"Kossoff would pretty much just sit and smoke big four-skin joints. But he was just the most wonderful guitar player. Never really made any mistakes, had this fantastic sound, and that man's vibrato! Still to this day, someone will play something and I'll go, 'Man, that's almost as good as Koss.'

"And Paul Rodgers? What can you say about the guy?"

Does Andy maintain that Paul Kossoff was the only member taking drugs?

"No, everybody smoked hash back then, some more than others. And he liked to smoke his joints and I suppose I did too. You'd get to a certain point where you thought everyone was looking at you – but it made the music sound really good. But you'd get rather paranoid which isn't good when you're trying to work."

PICKING UP THE PEACE(S)

The beauty of it could bring a grown man to tears.
-Richard Digby-Smith

It was almost perverse saying good-bye after the super energy released on the *Free Live!* album. How could they generate so much power and a mere 24 months later allow it all to dissipate into thin air? Most artists abandon ship after falling overboard into icy and unwelcome waters – the final resting place for commercially disastrous projects – but they had drawn on years of touring and playing before single-digit audiences to unveil a non-studio record that remains to this day a classic piece of work. So it's more than a little mind-tweaking to understand why the separation occurred.

Richard Digby-Smith reveals, to some extent, what was happening in the studio – the power plays, ego bashings and unfulfilled desires. The Englishman was there during the process, acting as engineer, tape operator and mixer. Working with this still tender and youthful troupe was no easy undertaking. Without warning, Rodgers would zoom into the studio, hurling often unintelligible instructions at Digby-Smith to start machines rolling and hit the 'record' button. A second's hesitation on his part and the singer would slam his headphones on the carpeted floor and unleash a stream of invectives. On one occasion the tape operator had innocently pumped in too much reverb into the singer's cans and Rodgers went ballistic.

But Smith, involved in the live mixes as well as "My Brother Jake", revered the band and in particular its singer. The verbal abuse – almost bordering on the physical at times – was part of the game and as a witness and participant he considered the rewards were worth the price. Richard felt as if he were part of larger picture, a religious moment, giving sight to the blind.

After the vocal was put on tape, Kossoff would then overdub guitars – a reversal of the usual process. But Paul loved to weave his six-string serenades around the singer's vocals and play off them as melodic ideas.

"Paul's singing affected me in the best way. Not being a singer, my best teacher was Paul as to how to enhance, blues-wise, a voice. I say that Paul is the best white blues singer you'll find."

This was never an issue. Everyone agreed. Paul Rodgers had the voice of a siren, capable of coaxing the listener to new and distant places. But he

—102—

was difficult to be with, had a mind of his own, and after just five albums with Free, left to form another band. Peace (a brand of Japanese cigarette) was where he landed, a trio that included bassist Stewart McDonald (from the English Outlaws and Quatermass) and drummer Mick Underwood (ex-Killing Floor). Though Island Records would have swallowed glass in order to keep Free together, they saw the writing on the wall. If you can't have Free you may as well have the pieces left behind, and consequently Blackwell supported Paul's new endeavor. And Glover would manage all three splinter groups.

The trio, with Paul on guitar and vocal, opened for Mott the Hoople's fourteen-city English tour during October and November of 1971, and it was here the singer first began a relationship with "All the Young Dudes" guitarist Mick Ralphs. Apparently he also befriended Hoople front man Ian Hunter, the singer making overtures to Rodgers about joining his band (although this is unconfirmed). Peace recorded six tracks when Glover booked time at Island studios, but an album was never completed. Titles included "Zero BC", "Like Water", "Seven Angels", "Heartbreaker", "Lady" and "Do Right By Your Woman". These first Peace offerings appeared on the *Songs Of Yesterday* boxed compilation, while the third and fourth songs ended up on the *Heartbreaker* album. But when Paul heard about the disintegration of Koss he shelved the trio, just six months after forming, and began to take steps to re-form Free. This, he felt, was the only way to save his close friend.

"We were all very shocked about Koss' condition. Whew! We all tried to do our little things but nothing seemed to help. It wasn't enough to call him up, it wasn't enough to invite him out to a jam, it wasn't enough to try and get him out of his house and that environment into somewhere else. Which Andy tried to do. Andy came to my sessions at one time and said, 'Look, Koss is in such a bad way, should we get the band back together?' And I said, 'Yeah.'

"Even though I had started recording with Peace, I stopped. It was a lot mellower (than Free) but I thought it was pretty good. My plan was just to tour without any stresses and strains – without any pressure. But that was probably a fairy tale idea. We did rehearse and got a set together and toured. But when I heard about Koss I put this aside."

At the same time Rodgers was rearranging his musical life, Andy Fraser struck out and assembled a trio of his own – bannered Toby. Comprised of guitarist Adrian Fisher and drummer Stan Speake, the three-piece made but a small splash. These sidemen, while adequate players, brought with them less than sterling credentials: Fisher had previously toiled as a tea boy in the Robert Stigwood Organization while Speake had been resigned to driving a dump truck. The latter player had been a Korner recommendation, however. Fraser kept searching for a singer, a difficult spot to fill after working with Rodgers, and after several failed auditions, stepped up to the microphone himself. Shows scheduled for December 1971 were cancelled. They hit the wall immediately and barely managed to assemble an uneven demo. Containing "I Ain't Done Yet", "Now I'm Waiting", "Travellin' Man", "John Lesley Sweet", "Loraine's Cable", "Jacob's Well", "Goodbye", "Yes Or No", "Over And Over", "Now I'm Waiting", "I Don't Know" and "209", these sessions have been rarely heard.

Kossoff, entombed in a daze of drugs and disillusionment, was somehow able to forge ahead on his own. In late 1971, he engaged in some perfunctory jams with acoustic picker John Martyn (a failed stab at resurrecting the troubadour's small-time classic "May You Never" later surfaced on Paul's *Back Street Crawler* solo outing as "Time Away"). This loosely knit jam employed Traffic's Jim Capaldi, Uriah Heep's Ken Hensley and American singer Michael Gately.

Other strange picking fests occurred with the group Uncle Dog ("We Got Time"), Uriah Heep keyboardist Ken Hensley and Traffic drummer Jim Capaldi. Koss strummed on Jim's tracks "Big Thirst", "Last Day Of Dawn", "How Much Can A Man Really Take" and the album's title opus, "Oh How We Danced".

Capaldi was a huge Kossoff supporter. Sessions for his album took place in Muscle Shoals, a studio Paul much revered. Still, he was dropping pills constantly and even when Chris Blackwell all but dragged him into a Miami rehab clinic, he escaped just a few days later.

Neither frightened nor concerned about his spiraling drug consumption, Kossoff constructed a new band with protector and friend Simon Kirke. Tetsu Yamauchi, befriended bassist, had been corresponding with Paul and after several letters discussing a mutual project, he flew to England arriving on 27 July 1971. As a trio they worked together for several months, writing and seeking an elusive sound that they couldn't quite find.

Working in the studio one day, they were visited by Island house percussionist Rebop Kwaku Baah, a Blackwell discovery who played on virtually every album of the Island stable. He mentioned Rabbit Bundrick as a possible addition since the keyboardist had recently arrived in England together with employer Johnny Nash.

Simon surmises that Paul needed someone to ease the rhythmic load he was required to shoulder, someone to cover the middle register. When Simon first met Rabbit he was intoxicated about the possibilities.

"I had never heard anyone play piano like that. He had an early Prophet IV synthesizer that revolutionized keyboards in the early seventies. We got in touch with him and asked would he like to form a group with me and Koss and Tetsu and lay some tracks down. And maybe do some touring."

John was ecstatic. "My Brother Jake" was still doing damage on the charts and the live album was flying high around this time. They built on these stepping-stones already laid before them.

The keyboardist (now playing with The Who) speaks about the undertaking and the manner in which he first came to hear about Paul and this other group.

"While I was working with Johnny Nash and Bob Marley in Stockholm, I knew a percussionist from Ghana, Rebop Kwaku Baah, who was with Traffic. Me and Reebop played all the time in my bedroom, recording our jams to tape, partying, getting stoned and having a great time. He made various trips between London and Sweden. He took some of our bedroom jams to Chris Blackwell and he ultimately played them for Simon and Paul. He suggested that they bring me in to work with them along with Tetsu.

"A meeting was set up with me, Simon and Paul in a little café in Notting Hill Gate so we could feel each other out. It went great. We went into the studio and to start some jamming and came up with the *KKTR* album."

Bundrick kept his day gig with Johnny Nash and stayed with him for several more months. He is heard on the singer's two subsequent British hits, "There Are More Questions Than Answers" (number nine) and "I Can See Clearly Now" (number five).

Long timer Richard Digby-Smith was hauled in to oversee the production of the KKTR project. But there was not much direction to be found and the self-titled outing disappeared in the record bins. The album barely registered in the hearts of Free fans left in withdrawal. Compositionally there was little to feed on – Paul's instrumental, "Just For the Box", the soulful dialect of "Sammy's Alright" and the Kirke-penned ballads "Anna" and "Hold On" held the hints of promise but in the end turned into musical lies. Paul was a pale shadow of what he once was; his playing had little heart and he approached soloing as an arbitrary chore. John runs down the scene.

"You can actually hear places where he's losing it. Although I can honestly say that Koss was in fine form on most of the sessions. Of course there were drugs and booze around. We were young but the project breathed new life into Simon and Paul. They had basically just split up from what was in reality a marriage to Free. So, a fresh start did them a power of good. There were no signs with Paul of what was to come later on. We stayed up sometimes three days in a row.

"We completed the album without any major problems, although there was one time in the studio when Koss was doing an overdub vocal on 'Colours'. We were all in the control room; he was in the studio ready to start his overdub. Just before Richard Digby-Smith started to roll the tape, Koss spoke: 'Hey, guys, turn out the lights in the studio, I want some atmosphere.' So, off the lights went, Diga rolled the tape, the song started and we waited for Koss to sing – and waited and waited. I switched the lights back on and, poor sod, there he was, sitting in a chair in the studio, sound asleep. We all worked and played so hard and the track 'Colours' was so relaxing and awesome, that it sent Paul to sleep in his chair. We just laughed, woke him up, and then he did a very sleepy rendition of lead vocal on the track."

Originally, the Kossoff Kirke Tetsu Rabbit project was going to call on Rodgers to provide vocals. Simon, constantly in touch with Paul and Andy, did call his old band mate to invite him down; Paul felt comfortable with the material but his commitments to Peace prevented him from joining.

Still, a day after beginning work with his newfound band, the guitarist appeared at a Peace gig at the London Polytechnic. On 15 October 1971, he came on stage and joined them for an encore. The doors, once closed tightly, were opening ever so slightly on what would be a full-blown reunion. And it started with this simple guest appearance and Simon's diligence.

Simon, ever the gentleman, the diplomat, was both peacekeeper and housekeeper on the project. If someone had a problem, they told it to Kirke and he helped them work it out. And when he wasn't busy with KKTR, he made attempts to seek out what the other half had been working on.

"I never saw Toby or heard them but I saw Peace. They were playing somewhere in the South of England and I drove down to see them with Tetsu who was living in my cottage at the time. They were pretty good; Paul seemed a lot more relaxed and his guitar playing was getting better and better. It was pretty emotional for me seeing someone else playing drums behind him."

KKTR, if nothing else, planted the seeds for the Free reunion that would come within just a few months. Whilst doing little to shake the musical world, the project did lay the groundwork for Rabbit's subsequent dealings with Free. He and Tetsu would later play on the auspiciously and appropriately named *Heartbreaker* album.

Only three months after this initial get together, they recorded for the final time. A loose jam called "Don't Make No Deal" was recorded on 14 January 1972. Nine days later Free would regroup and play an unannounced show at the Greyhound in Fulham.

Released in March 1972, the recording fell on deaf ears. Tetsu returned to Japan – but would come back for the *Heartbreaker* sessions and tour, while Rabbit remained in London to work on his own solo endeavors. Richard Digby-Smith produced the project and did a noble job. To this day Simon rates him as the best engineer he ever worked with, not to mention an affable and understanding personality.

However deftly Digby-Smith executed his technical obligations, the press didn't exactly grasp the project with loving arms. Simon counters the lack of exposure with a simple sentiment – he enjoyed the work. He found working with Rabbit a "revelation" and with Tetsu, the only other bassist he'd come together with in many years, a player both "steady and fun."

"The KKTR sessions were fun," reflects Kirke, dismissing the lack of sales as incidental. "It was a breath of fresh air after the stifling atmosphere that had permeated Free in the final months. But Koss was getting bad with drugs. Koss used to take these Mandrax; I took one once and it knocked me sideways. Went straight to sleep and when I woke up I couldn't talk properly for hours. Koss used to take them constantly. I helped him as best I could but in the end he was dragging me down with him so I just left and moved back into my own place. I lived with Koss for a while but I couldn't take all the guys coming around with the dope.

"Who knows what might have happened if Koss had straightened out? We might have gotten a singer and gone on the road. The album was pretty good but the vocals were weak. I had a go on 'Hold On' which I co-wrote with Koss. He actually played so well on the ride-out coda that I felt compelled to give him half of the song. Rabbit added a great air of professionalism; he was such a good player and Koss loved to play with keyboards. For a while, he was happy. But you only have to look at the photo on the cover to see what a mess he was in."

Though Paul seemed to have straightened out a bit following his return to England from the Japanese tour, within days of landing he was back in his drug den on Portobello Road scoring and swallowing.

The *KKTR* album, for all its problems and lack of focus, did bring to bear Kossoff's growing infatuation with the Leslie, the massive cabinet used to create the swirling effect on Hammond organs. He earlier talked about being enamored with the sound – it was a Hendrix mainstay – and this is his first experimentation with it. Borrowing Rabbit's cabinet, he crystallized the technique on the cut "Colours".

And this melodic document also chronicles Kirke's offering with "Anna," the song that would later appear on Bad Company's *Straight Shooter*. "Just For the Box" was another cut first auditioned here, later to turn up on the *The Free Story* anthology.

Free had divorced themselves from one another and these enterprises represented their first tentative footsteps outside the circle. There is little to praise here, save for the Kossoff work that highlighted the guitarist's and drummer's first in-depth songwriting chores, and the fact that the album was laying the foundation for the lineup of a future Free band.

Mention had been made about a possible KKTR tour but when no vocalist could be found for the tour, plans were shelved. Neither Rabbit nor Simon wanted to have a microphone stuck in their face.

As it turned out, the original members of Free were only apart from each other for a few months. There was a swift realization that the parts were not as muscular as the whole. Andy and Paul saw immediately that Koss would be dead were Free not to reform – and they did.

By late 1971, after having experienced terrible post partum depression, it was more than apparent to everyone involved – most specifically Blackwell, Glover, and the label – that three bands were not better than one. Calling Toby "dreadful" and Peace "not great", Blackwell instigated dialogue prompting the reformation of the original quartet. Johnny had established a close bond with Rodgers and approached him about the idea of a "farewell" tour – a final goodbye to fans. The ex-Peace officer neither shot down nor dismissed the idea. Money, once as easily earned as printing it yourself, had become a problem. Peace and Toby had sucked up funds like a mammoth vacuum cleaner. This was the obvious and external reason. Internally, Andy and Paul were grieving about their former guitar player and saw this as a chance to provide support.

Don't be misled – money was a very real and legitimate reason for re-forming. But it was not the only reason. While they might not have been cruising in the fast lane, they undoubtedly had made more than decent sums of income. The other whisper, and this may a bit closer to the truth, is that they felt naked without the comforting arms of Free. Egos may have been bruised and even blackened and blued when their individual works were trampled and tossed aside. They can't be faulted for missing the intoxicating allure and security of success. Nothing feels like it and nothing can replace it.

AT LAST – NOTHING IS FREE

It was very jagged, that album.

-Paul Rodgers

Peace, Toby and KKTR, the three solo projects formed after the band's unfriendly parting following the Asian tour, were, in the end, disappointments. Human nature dictates that what you do today will be measured by what you've already accomplished. And Free had certainly ascended to a high watermark giving future projects an almost impossible barrier to break. And they weren't the first. When Mick Jagger and Keith Richards set out to present themselves as solo artists (though the Stones were still intact), their work was scrutinized, analyzed and eventually held up to the bright reflecting mirror of the mother band. This same baggage dogged Jimmy Page and Robert Plant with their individual meanderings; was present when Pete Townshend recorded his one-offs; and tattooed almost every artist associated with a major band that attempted to break away from the mother ship to mold a life form of his own.

So, Paul, Paul, Simon and Andy were in good company. Around December 1971, word went round that the original players were preparing for a reunion. Under cover of secrecy, the reunited four began rehearsals. By early 1972, word was leaked to the press and once again David Sandison, Island's communications officer, was busting out information almost daily. During their previous tour of Japan, the jaunt to end all jaunts, a high-end promoter had promised them major dates if they ever wanted to re-visit the land of the Rising Sun. So, the press officer states: "This is really the farewell tour that Free never did. The group was talking about getting together for a tour of Japan because they loved it so much the last time they were out there. They also felt they hadn't done a proper 'thank you' to the fans in Britain ... so they thought it would be nice to do some British dates for the fans who have consistently written letters to them since the split."

To ensure the notion that this was indeed the farewell nod, David made mention that Rodgers would retire to Muscle Shoals to work on a solo project, while Andy would wing his way to Nigeria in order to study indigenous music. Of Kossoff, he spun a tale about working with Traffic drummer Jim Capaldi. Andy was similarly linked with this project. In the meanwhile, Tetsu and Simon would ostensibly team up with Graham

Bond. Bond and wife Diane had apparently formed Graham Bond and Heavy Friends with Kirke and Yamauchi.

When the weekly rags got hold of the news, headlines were emblazoned with major sentiment: "FREE ALL RIGHT NOW; FREE – STAY TOGETHER FOREVER."

Communications were reopened and on 23 January 1972, an impromptu show at the Fulham Greyhound was crammed full of hardcore Free worshippers. Island Records, delighted at the prospect of having Free back in the fold, didn't want to appear with egg on their faces. The band had completed a 'farewell' tour and in industry minds, this was the final plucking of strings and striking of drums. But the group, re-energized over the prospect of a new life, paid little heed to bean counter bravado. A 45-minute run-through encompassed standard material. Since the tour would probably contain new material, plans were set in motion about the possible recording of a second live album. No album was ever recorded but the results of the February dates were astonishing: all shows were sold out in advance and further performances booked.

Two-and-a-half weeks after opening the tour, the band was booked into the pinnacle of palaces, The Royal Albert Hall. Cream had made history here several years earlier when they performed a farewell show, recording and shooting the date for posterity. Cream had been historic – Free was causing hysterics.

In *New Musical Express*, a reviewer wrote: "The audience went mad from the moment Free were introduced at Albert Hall. Nearly every number was greeted with hoops and hollers, clappin' and stompin'."

Indeed, the atmosphere had been mesmerizing; the band was emotionally embraced. Still, the reception did little to bolster confidence. Kirke, in particular, was torn between exuberance and dismay.

"One of the highlights, and low, was our appearance at The Royal Albert Hall. It was a sold out show and across town the Faces with Rod Stewart were playing at the Rainbow. I remember *Melody Maker* doing a double-page review of the gigs. Anyway, Koss was gone and I mean he was shattered. Whether the status of the gig got to him or whether it was the fact that everyone who knew him was going to be in the place, I don't know. But he took something just before arriving. By the time we were due to go on, we had to ask Johnny Glover, our long suffering manager, to delay our entrance by fifteen minutes. Paul and I coached him through the opening bars of 'All Right Now' and 'Ride On Pony'. I was literally placing his left-hand fingers on the guitar neck where the chords would fall. Quite literally ... unbelievable!

"I felt that Paul and Andy and myself were subconsciously trying to compensate for Koss' state of health.

"And going back to the opening show, it still gives me chills. It was an out of body experience almost. We were flying. Although the tour was sold out and some of the scenes were unreal, it didn't go down without its own moments.

"We got through the gig seemingly OK. Koss had a couple of dodgy moments. He didn't actually fall but came close to it. The crowd helped us through for sure and the reviews, although slightly subdued, weren't nearly as scathing as I thought they would be. It seemed that we had survived another day."

This is the king of understatements. More than once fellow musicians would have to tutor Paul on what the exact chords were on songs he'd played a thousand times. And many was the time the band would have to excuse themselves from performances because of an "illness". And on the occasions when he was durable enough to stand upright and speak coherently, his playing was a pendulum, swaying from adequate to average. Rarely did he set worlds afire with his once inhuman sense of touch and technique.

Liverpool Stadium was the site where Led Zeppelin's box office record was broken. They were lords of London by selling out the classic Royal Albert Hall. But all was not diamonds and pearls. Kossoff's Les Paul was irritatingly out of tune and his normally feral stage presence would more properly be defined as retiring.

In truth, Kossoff was always ill, near exhaustion, and in fits of despair and bouts of depression he resented the efforts of his band mates. Desperately wanting to play in the manner he once had, and mentally determined to be the Paul everyone once knew, he arrived at the sickening and disheartening conclusion that that person had vanished, been buried and dissolved in a mound of pills and a vat of alcohol.

Following a warm-up set in Middlesbrough with UFO, they set sail on a British tour opening at Newcastle City Hall. No one, it seems, had forgotten about them. Full houses spilled over at every stopping point, but this was not momentum enough to stop the backflow. Returning to Newcastle on 21 and 22 February for makeup shows at the same hall, the group began running into the negative mojo Koss's illness had set in motion – and just general bad luck. During the first show, a coalminer's strike created fluctuations with the power and while playing on the second day the guitarist literally crashed to the floor. Another rainy daze date was set but this was cancelled. "Too ill to play" became a catchphrase.

Contracted for one final album, intermittent sessions took place during off days. As usual, Paul and Andy had a backlog of material; the former brought in "Soldier Boy", a nod towards Crosby, Stills, Nash &Young's *Déjà Vu* album, and the latter had written "Travellin' Man" and "Goodbye" (two tracks left over from the Toby debacle). Kossoff actually had a track called "Molten Gold" but this never made it to tape (A&M Records would later tap this as the title track of an anthology released in 1993).

They had dodged another bullet and lived to sing another day. But at what cost? Here, a band struggling for years, communally experiencing all the nasty things the world had in it, had finally scaled the mountain to the Mecca of live performance, the palace of queens. And yet Paul was so wrecked he could barely place finger upon fret. Had those musical hired scribes told the truth, maybe Paul and company would have been embarrassed or saddened or disheartened enough to forfeit the dream and drag this hollow man, kicking and screaming, for help. But probably not. The press is certainly not to blame – no one was.

There is an intriguing footnote here: while the tuneful tribe was scratching its way through a potentially pathetic performance, Rod Stewart was breaking down the walls in a show across town. Post-Free dialogue forever centers on the Rodgers/Stewart comparison – both singers emerging from accomplished bands, dredging up the blues and carving out solo careers. Rod, the man with elevator hair and limestone larynx, the Ray Charles-influenced troubadour who first found footing as Jeff Beck's vocal sidekick, would go on to pursue and attain phenomenal success with a boatload of monster singles and chart-topping albums. He'd end up, at one point, going disco and singing soft ballads and middle of the road slop – but he sold records. To this day, he remains a concert staple.

On the other hand, Paul has been unable to locate his solo Shangri-la, bouncing from project to project and band to band in pursuit of that elusive dream. Always a driver and never a passenger, this boy from the North country would often treat support players with an attitude less than respectful and in some cases borderline brutality. His early interaction with Digby-Smith was a harbinger of this attack dog mentality and is certainly a reason why he has not been able to settle into one project, with the same group of players, for any length of time.

If *Fire And Water* was their *Revolver*, then *Free At Last* represented this once-just-a-blues band's *Sgt. Pepper's Lonely Hearts Club Band*. The album dances and shimmers rhythmically and calls to bear on Motown and San Francisco pop and the essential blues qualities the band always possessed. "Little Bit Of Love" is a perfect pop specimen – 2:32 of chugging Kossoff guitar and edgy Rodgers vocal.

Maybe Koss was so high he could barely see. Maybe he could only function in an altered state. Whatever the situation, this record features some of the most original and moving guitar ever etched into vinyl. Trying to build on the guitar orchestration proffered during the KKTR sessions, he dabbled with different sounds and wandered into areas unknown. Andy was especially careful in not hooking him by the nose to show him specific parts.

"When you get to *Free At Last*, I think you have a real band called Free," invokes the guitarist. "To me, I think it was Free's most complete album. Free was a great band, especially this one. All the later albums were great.

"I liked my playing on that album. I started using a [Fender] Stratocaster. It was a white Strat with a maple neck but the neck was warped. It was beautiful to play – you couldn't play any big chords on it but it was really responsive. I don't know what year it was but it was an old one. I'm not into years and all that; if it sounds good and feels good, I'll use it. Also, there's no tremolo arm on that Strat. I've never used one because I've never been into it. Any tremolo I use is from the left hand. I just play with the amp full up and I control it from the guitar. I don't know, maybe I'm a little bit too limited with my sounds. I'm not sure. You don't play a billion notes, but you play a few goodies, hopefully like Freddie or BB do."

There must have been at least a smattering of "goodies" as the album topped out at number nine on the British charts. Across the sea, it only reached number sixty-nine. If the band was going into permanent hibernation, and if the legacy was now in the hands of the book writers and historians, they couldn't have asked for a more insightful and delightful listening experience.

Free At Last was the culmination of years of touring, writing, ego infighting and studio late-nighting. If, at the time, this represented the final document, it would resonate and echo throughout the years. Though Rodgers saw this as an uneven rendering, the remaining players sensed they had reunified to conceive a work setting a new benchmark not only in their own careers but also in the development of a genre melding blues with ambient strains and variations on pop/rock rhythmic figures. The band would assemble one last time to piece together *Heartbreaker*, a severely disjointed affair bringing in auxiliary players. Still, nothing could detract from the synchronous heartbeat of this, their reunion album.

"I think it's one of our best albums," declares Kirke. "There were some great songs on it: 'Little Bit of Love', 'Soldier Boy', 'Child' and 'Goodbye' – which turned out to be very prophetic. The music belied what we were all feeling. But you only have to look at the photos on the back to see the strain showing through. Koss looked particularly terrible. They were taken at A&M studios in L.A. I think we were touring at the time and it shows."

"Little Bit Of Love" should have been a crowning glory. It was the obvious single. With flip side "Sail On", this 45 was released on 5 May 1972. Disappointingly, this sublimely sensuous rocker only reached number thirteen. After the number four ranking of "My Brother Jake," this represented a blow to everyone.

Free At Last came out amidst a batch of records that are now essential milestones in the development of rock and pop: Alice Cooper's *School's Out*, Deep Purple's *Machine Head*, Jethro Tull's mini-opus *Thick As A Brick* and a mountain of releases by David Bowie, Mott the Hoople, Black Sabbath, The Rolling Stone's *Exile On Main Street* (the project Andy Johns oversaw after twisting knobs on *Highway*), ELP and Wishbone Ash.

America, too, embraced the album and even seemed to be in the clutches of an Anglophile mania. Anything English was good. Consequently, the band departed for distant western shores and were accompanied by the ever-present Glover and Graham Whyte and new recruits Jim McQuire and Pepe. Still, despite all the good cheer, positive thoughts and embracing energy, the tour was doomed from the outset, cursed like a zombie in a New Orleans graveyard.

Their first show, highlighted in the opening chapter of this book, was standard fare. Kossoff only grew worse. The *L.A. Free Press*, a weekly paper dedicated to leftist politics and contemporary music, covered that 20 April 1972 date: "Free would have quite easily stolen the show had they not run into personnel problems. It seems that lead guitarist, Paul Kossoff, was 'taken ill' prior to the concert, leaving the remainder of Free to fend for themselves. With typical British reserve, Free mounted the stage, explained the situation and promised to return and perform another date, and even went on to play two tunes before quietly leaving the stage."

What the underground periodical omitted was the mid-afternoon soundcheck and the "taken ill" reality (Paul was essentially unconscious) – not to mention the horde of screaming, irate attendees denied a performance.

Remaining dates in the south fell to similar deaths. They played support to Fleetwood Mac; Rod Stewart and The Faces; West, Bruce & Laing; and Joe Cocker. But the writing was on the wall and it didn't take much to read between the lines: Free was on its last gasp. Originally scheduled to perform sixty shows, many of these were cancelled with the increasing instability of the guitarist.

The final breath may have come with the death of roadie Jim McQuire. Jim had been hired to relieve some of the load Graham Whyte constantly endured. Indefatigable, James was a dynamo with a non-stop motor. Fatigued and absolutely exhausted, Jim was trying to catch up on some sleep in the back of an equipment truck. A cabinet toppled over and covered an air vent designed to allow the escape of poisonous carbon monoxide fumes. Destination reached, the back of the truck was opened to reveal the macabre vision of an asphyxiated McGuire.

This tragic accident was the coffin's last nail, the camel's back breaking straw, the final frontier – there was nowhere left to hide.

"Jim was a terrible blow to us," sighs Simon, "and one of the final straws for Andy. We also had to say good-bye to Graham because his work visa had expired and he had to go back to New Zealand. Andy decided to quit the band; I don't blame him, really. He had given it his best shot. He had served the band well and had given us some beautiful songs. He had established himself as a musical force, was considered one of the best players around and now wanted not only out of the band but out of the country as well. He planned to go and live in L.A. I wished him nothing but the best – he deserved it.

"I am unable to get into specifics here; my recollections are a bit hazy and quite frankly it is a very painful period for me. It's ironic because we recorded *Free At Last* around this time and it produced some beautiful songs: 'Soldier Boy' was one of Paul Rodgers' best, 'Travellin' Man' and 'Little Bit Of Love' and 'Child' were all great. But it was a bugger to make. Andy and Paul were writing their own songs now – very little collaboration between them. And Koss would veer from OK to awful. It was, to quote a Joe Cockerism, 'like pushing ten tons of gravel up a hill.'

"On that U.S. tour to promote the album, Koss got into such a state that we had to blow out a couple of shows. To our credit the rest of us went on stage and did a mini-set to try and compensate [referencing the Palladium fiasco]. We did the cover shots to *Free At Last* around this time in L.A. and you can see that the strain of everything was plainly written on our faces. It was also indescribably hot in the studio for some reason and we were all sweating. We still managed to produce the goods though. We received some great reviews and people who saw us still remember the shows with praise. God, what would we have been like with a healthy guitarist?"

But they'd never know. Paul fell deeper and deeper into the chasm. Andy's departure was in many ways a "sense of relief". Always the delicate dictator, he had been virtually unable to work with Rodgers in any creative capacity during those last months. And the antagonism between Andy and Kossoff was turning truly ugly.

Looking back, Simon realizes he and the band should have mandated that the guitarist enter rehab back in 1970. But that time passed. Even at that period those types of centers were not too prevalent. AA would not have been suitable since they catered mainly to older alcoholics, and the types of famous treatment centers now peppered about America (the Betty Ford Clinic and the Hazelden facility where Eric Clapton de-toxed) were virtually non-existent.

Still, knowing some decision had to be made, Kossoff and group flew to the Bahamas for a week in an attempt to dry him out. The hiatus provided nothing but lost revenues. Promoters were enraged over cancelled dates. Too little, way too late.

Misery, it is well known, loves miserable partners. Looming ahead was a monster misery of mammoth proportion – another scheduled Japanese tour.

THE LAST MASOCHISTIC MILE

His breakfast usually consisted of a bottle of vodka.

-Rabbit Bundrick

Amongst the seven albums this mini-organization compiled during an abbreviated four-year run, *Fire And Water* and *Free At Last* stand out as significant signposts. They invaded uncharted terrain and to this day remain landmark endeavors as salient as any Zeppelin or Cream recording. Even *Tons of Sobs* and *Highway*, while not heralding the promise and untapped potential of other contemporary debut and follow-up attempts (by the likes of Cream, Zeppelin or Traffic), revealed bright and shining moments. So why haven't they been bestowed with the kudos and across-the-board acceptance as their contemporaries? Record sales didn't tip any scales and, save for their breakout single, Free were resigned to relying on live performances in order to grow a fan base. If you toss in the ever-present personality clashes and drug-related episodes, a hazy picture is constructed.

Simon attempts to analyze the situation.

"Why weren't we as big as Cream or Zep? I think had we stuck it out we would have become as big as them. Remember, we were very young and had only been together just over two years before the initial breakup. Cream's members were in their mid-twenties and Zep's members were seasoned veterans – Jimmy and John Paul Jones had been on the session scene for some time before they formed the group. They weren't dogged by drug problems either – that would come later.

"We were bigger in England [than America] because we slogged around the country for two years laying a solid fan base foundation. I think we had played every major town in England at least twice. It's quite easy to do actually; England can fit quite comfortably into Lake Superior."

Did they accomplish what they initially set out to do?

"Well, yes and no. In terms of longevity we were only around for four years and people have this amazing affection for us 30 years later. Christ, they are even writing books about us! In musical terms, I wish we could have stuck it out for another few years. I think we were just getting started really. We re-formed for the wrong reason – i.e. getting Koss out of his druggy funk. You know, we had a shot at our own individual things and they hadn't worked out very well and that was an honorable thing to do.

But knowing what I know now about addiction, there wasn't a hope in hell of him straightening out in a group environment.

"Time has been kind to our legacy. It has preserved it and nurtured it. A lot of people grew up with our music. We had some great songs and pretty amazing musical abilities. Coupled with our cute looks and 'gang-like' demeanor, we were well on our way."

For all the good intentions, positive input and undying support directed at Paul Kossoff, Free had traveled way past innocence. A smile and a pat on the back wasn't going to get the job done and the reunion tour resonated with the same misplaced confidence of Custer's Little Big Horn massacre. Paul had fallen too far. Even Island Records was dubbing the reunion as a second-coming farewell tour and consequently the dates and future were already standing on an impermanent floor.

The final eighteen months of the group's reunification glued insanity to inspiration. It was as if, with nothing to lose, they opened the fortresses around their hearts and bled all the passion and paranoia onto stage floors and onto black vinyl records. None of the solo projects had generated any sort of feedback from fans or labels and when they ultimately made the choice to re-group, all the frustrations came flooding out like the angry surge of a burst artery.

These defeats, both personal and creative, manifested themselves in the uneven though sometimes surreal live performances. What the audience responded to was only the visual – what they didn't see were the internal battles being waged.

The Japanese tour, to be followed by an east-European visit to Hungary, was way too much for the diminutive Fraser to handle. On July 22 1972 he exited for the second and final time. With little time to audition replacements, Glover phoned Tetsu in Japan and as auxiliary backup contacted Rabbit, working as an Island support musician.

Rodgers, Rabbit and Kirke began rehearsing. There was no Kossoff in sight. The unthinkable was not digestible – Paul would not accompany the tour. The trio flew in advance to Japan and began working out the set. Tetsu swiftly joined them at Tokyo's King Records studio. With only two days to prepare, they went through motions only to encounter yet another disaster. One day before the opening night, Simon was taken ill.

"Somewhere in Hungary I contracted tonsillitis. It went unchecked for several days and by the time we made the trip to Tokyo I was in agony, We had to get there via Heathrow, the main London airport, and my plight was so bad that I went to the airport doctor. He said all I need to do was cough violently and the whole set of tonsils would probably come out by themselves. Seriously, he said I should go straight to hospital and have them removed. I told him I was in the middle of a tour and that was out of the question. He gave me the largest legal dose of penicillin and packed me off. The flight to Tokyo was alleviated by lots of booze and during my first night there I sweated through a fever of 103."

Kirke was rushed to the hospital and thankfully released the day of the show. Udo Artists Incorporated (Mr Udo has been the reigning king of concert promoting since western bands began coming to Japan) had booked the 35,000-seat Koraku-en Stadium in Tokyo for the opener and the smaller Koshi-en Baseball Stadium in Osaka. Opening for Emerson, Lake & Palmer, Free performed perfunctorily. The set highlighted new songs titled "Unseen Love", "Like Water", "Heartbreaker" and Peace's "Seven Angels".

During the Hungary dates, Rodgers and Rabbit had several verbal confrontations. Though outsiders may have claimed that Free was the musical offspring of Andy Fraser, insiders knew that the singer was the sire. You did not screw with him and when the keyboardist began embroidering the songs with different flourishes and harmonic elements, the wrath of Rodgers was incurred.

The dates were unexceptional. Rodgers played guitar adequately but nowhere near the tear-wringing fashion of the vacated Kossoff. Simon has scraped his brainpan about these dates as well.

"Paul Rodgers stepped in on guitar and we did a couple of creditable gigs in Japan and Hungary. His playing was a revelation, very sparse and soulful, and reminiscent of Albert King.

"In Budapest, we witnessed the brutality of the police. Some students had smuggled in a banner and during one of the songs hoisted it above the crowd. It was some anti-government slogan and the cops waded in. Their brutality was horrible. We stopped playing and the promoter was frantically waving us to play on but we said no way until the cops are out of the crowd. A message was relayed over the PA and the cops dutifully dispersed. Chalk one up for rock 'n' roll."

Meanwhile, Paul's health had leveled, if not improved, and by September 1972, everyone decamped to Island Studios to begin work on a track called "Wishing Well" – a single set for October release.

Rabbit was constantly butting heads with Rodgers. Paul appeared a bit jealous of the attention the pianist was generating and sliced him verbally on several occasions. Tetsu, handicapped linguistically, said little. John acted as interpreter and maintained Tetsu was a perfect replacement for Fraser – Chris Blackwell vociferously disagreed. He felt that Free was the original four-piece and that these makeshift mercenaries were bush league at best.

Glover, on the other hand, was fired up about the new development and sensed a feeling of positivism. But he also sensed an undercurrent of dissension, of tension, of players at odds with each other, and it was all attributed to Kossoff's ever-present pill-popping predicament.

A British tour was undertaken running through September and October 1972; and a week was set aside to appear in Italy and Romania. Yes, another visit behind the Iron Curtain. Hackensack opened on several dates and was later substituted with Smith, Perkins & Smith.

By now, the newcomers had found their niche and operated smoothly within the workings of the live set. But Kossoff was barely there, either emotionally or physically.

Eight shows into the tour on 15 September at Newcastle Mayfair, Kossoff touched the sweet wings of the oblivion angel. Falling to the floor, writhing in epileptic fashion, gasping for air and approaching physical rigidity, Paul was initially ignored. The performance was so grotesque that the band thought he was pretending. He was not. Fortuitously, one of the bouncers was also a nurse and was able to keep him breathing until a doctor arrived. At the hospital, the attending physician diagnosed an epileptic seizure; he concussed when striking the floor. The doctor ordered at least a ten-day stay at the hospital and shows were cancelled for the coming two weeks. At the Newcastle Royal Victoria Infirmary, promoter Geoff Docherty was stunned when visiting him to find none of his band mates in attendance.

Everyone had given serious thought to continuing without Koss. Rodgers had pulled off guitar duties in Japan and knew he could handle the double duty of singing and playing. But the little man who sits on the shoulder, that persistent whispering in the ear prevented this. They still felt the tour, and Paul's involvement, was all that kept him alive. Maybe so. But the former Selmer salesman was a heavy weight and kept pulling everyone around him deeper and deeper into the morass of marginal gigs, financial ruin and general career suicide. By September's end, still too debilitated to tour, the Italian dates were permanently cancelled. To compound the frustration, Rodgers was busted for possessing drugs, two motoring offences and fined £145.

There were other mishaps. After a set at the Redcar Coatham Bowl, a Free stronghold for years, the band were informed that they would never play there again. Kossoff had fallen headlong into the drum kit, midway through the set. Kirke, used to such shenanigans, looked on with amusement. Rabbit was irate and outraged, cursing Kossoff for his stupidity and lack of control. The outburst, borne of frustration and helplessness, was a knee-jerk reaction. The Texan visualized the inherent musical potential and was reduced to lashing out as a defense. He would never again attack Paul in such a manner and cursed himself for such a vulgar display of immaturity.

On 20 October 1972, Free, as a band, as a group once possessing the potential to be as historically successful as The Rolling Stones or Led Zeppelin, played their final United Kingdom show. But they did not travel silently into the night.

In gentle tribute to Rabbit, Kossoff smashed the neck of his very expensive Gibson Les Paul over the keyboardist's Hammond organ. The neck was broken – a not too subtle gesture signifying the end of his touring career. Paul worshipped his vintage instruments which makes the act seem all the more horrifying. Still, he cited this lineup, as unbelievable as it may seem, as his favorite.

"That last tour I did with Free was with Tetsu and Rabbit and it gave me a lot of freedom. We were a good live band to watch, really powerful.

"I like the feeling from the audience whatever it is; whether it's to get off, give us a kiss or stop pissing around. I can get off on that and still play even if there's a direct conflict."

Following the tour, everyone re-entered the studios to continue work. Rodgers was side-tripped when he did a final mix on a reggae song he'd earlier recorded in Jamaica with The Maytals. Titled "I Just Want To See You Smile", it featured Rabbit on keyboards and remained unavailable until the release on the *Songs Of Yesterday* box set.

On 23 October, just a few days after the final engagement, work began in earnest on what would evolve into the *Heartbreaker* album. This was a different band and a distinctly new inter-personal dynamic had developed. Paul Kossoff was now allowed more freedom as a player since he wasn't responsible for covering all the rhythm parts as well as all the soloing. Rabbit freed him up to adopt a looser style, covering the chordal parts he was previously required to lay down. And without Andy constantly in his face about what to play and how to play it, he settled into a more peaceful space – though still besotted chemically – and his work here reveals this newly found serenity.

These initial sessions produced "Common Mortal Man", "Seven Angels" (the Peace song here given new life), the title song, "Travellin' In Style" and "Come Together In the Morning".

"Wishing Well", the album opener, was an infectiously driven guitar line (reminiscent of Jimi's "Purple Haze") while "Easy On My Soul" and "Seven Angels" demonstrated the group's ability to switch seamlessly between rock 'n' roll and the rock 'n' stroll. Even Koss was aware of the artistry that went into this, Free's last stand.

"Wishing Well" saw light on 24 November 1972 and reached number seven on the charts. Though Kossoff had been a co-writer, he was too sickly to cut rhythm tracks and was barely able to overdub a solo. Still, the song is a soaring piece of work. On "Come Together In the Morning" Koss ran through a Leslie and though there is an audible pop on the track [created when he switched, either accidentally or deliberately, between Stratocaster pickups], his playing here expresses dimension and space.

NEW BLOOD AND HEART ATTACKS

Free are the monsters of creativity and soul.

-John Rabbit Bundrick

Kossoff, only able to play on a little over half of the songs, needed support. Contrary to common belief, his replacement was not brought in by the vocalist. Rather, Rabbit contacted long time Texas cohort Snuffy Walden, a versatile and accomplished guitarist working in London at the time.

"I used to get him into the studio every chance I could," explains Rabbit. "When Free were at a loss for guitar parts, I just mentioned I knew this guy called Snuffy. They were so desperate by then that they had to say 'Yes.' There was an album to be finished and when Koss wasn't around we had to do what we could. Snuffy came in and we got on with it. They were all happy with Snuffy's work. Sometimes you can't even tell if it's Snuffy or Koss. Snuffy is a good mimic when he needs to be. He fit in great. I think as far as having him in the band permanently was maybe too much Texas for their liking. They already had me and I was a handful."

Snuffy, born in Louisiana and raised in Texas, had been friends and musical buddies with Rabbit since the mid-sixties. Walden would often see Rabbit performing at The Cellar, a Houston dive, with a band called Buttermilk Bottom. In another strange twist of fate, future Back Street Crawler members Tony Braunagel and Terry Wilson were Bundrick's rhythm section.

Snuffy joined a band called Aphrodite in his home state and then moved to Colorado. Ending up as a trio after the original guitarist parted company, they were spied by one of Emerson, Lake & Palmer's road crew. Ultimately, this ELP employee left the trio to go and work with Snuffy and band. They relocated to England in search of a record deal but none came. Manticore Records (ELP's label) offered Walden a solo deal without the band and after divesting himself of these players found replacements and formed Stray Dog. This was the project he was working on at the time Free – and Rabbit in particular – gave him the call.

"Rabbit was doing his own solo records, Tetsu was doing records and I was doing session work for those guys. This was right around the time they were doing the *Heartbreaker* record and Kossoff was, at that time, sick. I came in and did some tracking with them and then, as I remember it, Kossoff came in for one day and did his overdubs on the whole record. I don't even know how many tracks I actually did; I don't even own a copy of it.

"I know I did 'Wishing Well' but the lines were all pretty blurred in those days. Besides the drinking and the drugging, there was so much different stuff going on."

There were moments when Koss and Snuffy were in the studio simultaneously and the feeling in the air, claims Walden, was "vibey". During one session while the Texan was working, Paul entered the Island facility and was visibly upset. Apparently he did not know why this other guitarist was there though he certainly knew who he was.

"He didn't like me much but it was an awkward situation. At that point Kossoff's drug thing meant they needed somebody else to track the songs. Kossoff at that point just wasn't in any shape to be recording. So I was called in to do some work and I wasn't credited. They thanked me but didn't credit me because it was a band thing. I was a hired gun."

Pointedly, when the album was finally finished, Paul Kossoff was listed as a session man – and not a band member.

At the end of the day all that remained for Snuffy were the flaws. He was not particularly happy with his work but does admit to being impressed with Paul Rodgers' direction and forceful ideas.

"He was intense, but talented."

Vague overtures were made regarding future work, deciphered in Snuffy's mind as live dates. Again, the scenario was bloated with politics and shadowy movements since no one wanted to replace Koss but at some point the reality had to be faced. In any event, he turned down the suggested offers to continue work with Stray Dog. Instead Wendell Richardson, a picker from Trinidad formerly of the group Osibisa, was given the nod to tour with the band for a US tour supporting Traffic. A strange choice indeed.

"I was a Free fan," declared Walden. "I thought Paul was a great singer and Free was a great band. That whole process of coming into a band like that is just filled with problems. That's like trying to replace Todd Rundgren in The Nazz. It wouldn't work."

Snuffy's decision didn't exactly please the singer. Someone demonstrating a world of patience one moment but capable of coming to a full boil in seconds is the type of person you want to approach with extreme caution. There was never an exchange between the two on the subject so Snuffy bases this solely on his own feelings.

While Koss was variously incensed and de-sensitized about the entire situation, when he did sober up, pleasure was expressed.

"There were very good songs on *Heartbreaker*. In fact I used to have mixes of 'Seven Angels' and a lot of the other tracks that I rough mixed when I was there. And they turned out better than the guy who was mixing it (a comment remix engineer Andy Johns probably wouldn't be too happy hearing). He [Andy] picked out all the stuff I didn't want to hear. 'Seven Angels' was a Rodgers tune and it was really special. And on the album the wrong track of guitar has been mixed in."

Still, Kossoff had tried to endure and ended up picking on five of the eight tracks. The other members made every effort to accommodate his unpredictable moods. Rabbit slid in sweetly and brought dimension and dynamics through his keyboards.

"Those sessions were great, but things started going downhill for Koss then. Sometimes he was so sick he couldn't even make it to the studio, so we had to make do. It all worked out in the end though. It's a great album. We were sad for Koss though, that he couldn't do all the guitars himself. But it was impossible.

"It wasn't hard fitting in with Free at all. As a keyboardist, there were loads of holes and spaces to fill out, feel out and get stuck in. I had total freedom to play whatever I felt was appropriate and being a 'pro muso' and them being such a great band, it was quite an easy job. My best job to this very day, in fact. I never had it so good as when I was in Free. They knew I could write songs as well so that told them I knew how to add to arrangements with good ideas. No problems there.

"A typical session would be a few joints, a trip down to the pub for some beers and back to the studio for some jamming to construct the song we were going to record that day. We'd mull it over, talk about it, jam it a while, then go for it, and usually get it right in the first take or two. Brilliant band."

Rabbit certainly left his hand prints all over the *Heartbreaker* album. He was immediately embraced by the surviving members and played a pivotal role in the development and eventual sound of the record. His inspired use of the Hammond organ, the sound that defined Procol Harum, Traffic, Joe Cocker's Grease Band and Deep Purple, became one of the album's inspired motifs.

"I played on every single track on *Heartbreaker* and wrote two of its songs, 'Muddy Water' and 'Common Mortal Man'. I co-wrote 'Wishing Well' and 'Travellin' In Style' with the rest of the band.

During the interim between the *KKTR* and *Heartbreaker* records, Rabbit worked on his own solo projects in off hours from his main role as an Island session player. Chris Blackwell encouraged this midnight mania and later signed the keyboardist to Island Records, releasing *Broken Arrows* and later, *Dark Saloon*.

Simon Kirke also recalls the making of Free's final album.

"*Heartbreaker* was a tortuous album to make. Although it had many great songs on it like 'Wishing Well', 'Come Together In the Morning' and

Seven Angels', it charted the ultimate demise of Koss as a player. Snuffy
played on several songs – hell, even I played guitar on 'Common Mortal
Man' – and the whole affair was underscored by this tragic air."

In December 1972, just prior to album completion, Kossoff abandoned
ship, once and for all. He accompanied Chris Blackwell on a vacation to
Jamaica, where the guitarist raided local pharmacies for his daily stash.
This same month, engineer Digby-Smith handed in the mixed tapes to the
Island king. He was less than thrilled.

With all of this madness about, Chris Blackwell was forced into one of
his rare displays of authority. Listening to the mixes left him speechless with
embarrassment, calling them thin sounding and useless. So he brought in
mix whiz Andy Johns. Johns, booked to work with The Rolling Stones in
Jamaica, was only available for a brief duration and consequently ordered
the entire band from the studio and set about trying to ressurect the tapes.
He did. *Heartbreaker*, while not on a level with *Free At Last* or *Fire And
Water*, nonetheless was a strong indicator of where the band might move
musically – blending keys and more structured arrangements with a bigger
sound. But at the same time they knew this was the end and not a new
beginning.

"I was at Island doing something, I forget what it was, Average White
band or something," recalls Andy. "I went upstairs at night and there was
Blackwell and he said, 'Look, they've just handed in this album and it's not
right. Can you do anything with it?' I said, 'I bet I can but I've got to go
to Jamaica in three days to do the Stones.' And he said, 'Oh, well that'll
be enough time.' And I went downstairs and this fellow, Diga, who had
recorded it, was a nice enough bloke, he's a nice fellow and everything, but
sometimes it's good to have outside ears. I then mixed the thing basically
in two or three days.

"And then, there I am in this hotel in Kingston, Jamaica, with the Stones,
having breakfast one morning and who do I see coming across the patio
but Paul and Simon. 'Oh, hello Andy, can you introduce us [to the Stones]
blah, blah, blah?' And I introduced them to Keith and everybody. I asked
them what they were doing there and they go, 'Well, man, that album you
just fixed up sounds fucking awful.' I said, 'No, wait, wait, wait, no, that's
a mistake, I bet I know what it is.' And what had happened was when
it went to mastering... they hadn't realigned the machine so it was all distorted. Chris Blackwell was in Kingston when I was there and I called him
up. I wasn't rude but I said, 'C'mon, man, what the fuck is up? This isn't
cool – you're making me look bad here. Just have them master it again.'
And of course Simon and Paul proceeded to smash to pieces the room
they had, which was next to mine. I said, 'Oh, guys, why you doing that?
I'm going to be here for another two or three months, you're going home

tomorrow, and these people won't like this at all.' And that was that. But that was a great record, too. There were some wonderful bits and pieces on it."

Andy reflects further on his relationship with the band.

"I used to hang out with them a bit; they used to come over for dinner and all that. And we'd sort of sit there and wonder what to talk about as my wife handed out food through the hatch in the kitchen. We'd finally say, 'This isn't working, let's go back to the studio.' I worked with Andy later with Sharks; I started off and then I sort of disappeared because it was dreadful. It wasn't happening. And then I worked with him a few years later in L.A. in the late seventies, some dreadful demos he was doing, and he decided he was a singer now and sang like Stevie Wonder. He'd taught himself to do that but I don't know what was going on.

"Paul was fine, I never had any problems with him in the studio and then I started hearing things about how he'd gotten, I don't know, a bit impressed with himself. I saw him at a Bad Company gig at the Forum [in Inglewood, California] in about '77. I saw Paul and he was sitting at this table with some chick and I went over and said, 'Hey, man, how you doing?' And he completely blanked me out. And I thought, 'What the fuck is all that? How ridiculous.' It was just stupidity, I don't know. And I really shouldn't talk out of school; maybe he was having a hard day. And I heard stuff later on but I shouldn't say anything because I wasn't there to experience it. But the guy can sing, pal. I would like to work with him again because he was just a dream."

Andy looks back on all his work with Free and smiles, an emotion not instantly forthcoming when questioned about other artists (to remain anonymous). In the same fashion that Kirke loved making the *KKTR* record because it was fun, Johns enjoyed these sessions for the simple sake of the music's obvious leanings towards greatness.

"In those days it didn't take so long to make records. I don't know if we were better at it or what, but you didn't do these marathon sessions. Free would show up about one, leave about ten, and you'd only spend about two or three weeks on the music. Those guys would probably knock out a song a day and then you'd mix it at night."

By the close of the *Heartbreaker* sessions, daggers hung in air and the atmosphere surrounding everyone was so thick those same dangling long blades could have cut the tension. When Kossoff was ranked as a session player on this album, he all but fell to the floor, and in an attempt to save some shred of dignity, made the announcement he was quitting – before they could fire him.

LIFE AFTER FRASER

Maybe we retired into ourselves.

-Andy Fraser

Free, seemingly, had been scraped raw, their insides hollowed out and all the lust and passion they'd once exhibited now tossed aside. *Heartbreaker* was released on 19 January 1973 and Blackwell, ever the master of publicity, arranged for the group to perform for an American television special titled *Rock And Roll Superstars*. The reasoning behind the performance was to air the program on stateside shows in advance of an impending US excursion. Somehow, no one is certain if the variety spot was ever even shot. To prepare for the tour, dates were arranged at various college sites.

The tour was an Island family affair, teaming Free with John Martyn and Stevie Winwood's Traffic. This seventh album was denting the American market and local shows were cancelled in order to extend the overseas visit. Thirty coast-to-coast shows were earmarked. By the thirteenth hour, there were still glimmering hopes that Kossoff might be able to attend the festivities. This fell through and the English pen-pushers resignedly wrote that Paul would pursue his own project and "concentrate on writing and arranging for a solo album."

With Paul a definite no-show for the tour, and Snuffy Walden turning down Rodgers' overtures, Rabbit came up with Wendell Richardson to handle the guitar chores – an odd, nay, terrible choice. His sound was very high-end and though he drooled over the prospect of cranking it up through a stack of Marshalls (his own gear was pitiful by comparison), he was not a crunch player, not a soloist with deep-rooted blues influences. Nicknamed 'Del' his inclusion was a miserable decision. Good player, but would have been more at home in Santana or even Bob Marley's band.

From the outset, the tour was a low rent affair, doomed like a one-legged long-distance runner. America was the death knell, the kicking of the dead horse, the not-so-grand finale. Kossoff replacement Richardson had been playing Afro-based music and couldn't even begin to understand how to solo over blues changes or thump out hypnotic barre chords. It still remains a mystery as to why Rodgers and Kirke agreed with Rabbit's choice.

"That final Free tour did stretch the bounds of credibility," underscores a by-then totally burned out drummer. "We had Wendell on guitar who was actually very nice but his style was nothing like Paul Kossoff's. I think by adding Rabbit and Tetsu we had opened the door to all sorts of influences and quite honestly we were dying to play with other musicians.

"Quite amazingly, the tour went off without any major incidents (save for the Rodgers/Bundrick clashes), but that was definitely it for me and Paul. With all our commitments honored, we said to each other, 'No more.'"

Glover, running the personality-clashing marathon, tried to balance obligations to Free with the ever-growing popularity of Amazing Blondel. Even Chris Blackwell, once a sort of fifth wheel in the machinery, was devoting more time to Traffic.

All this culminated in a brouhaha of bruised egos, dissatisfied musicians and, more times than not, inebriated principals. Rodgers was seriously ruminating over his decision to accept Richardson and was usually in an intemperate mood, drinking and lashing out at Rabbit – perhaps in retaliation for the keyboardist's choice of guitar player. Paul could have said no, easily, but he didn't. Taking it out on Bundrick, who had proven to be an invaluable asset both as a writer and live performer, was childish – just another example of the singer's growing inability to control his destiny. Simon retreated into himself while Tetsu, with his limited English, could often be found comforting Richardson. As a newcomer, he well understood how difficult that gauntlet was to steer through.

But Rodgers was unstoppable on stage and always gave a gallon's worth. Two weeks into touring, he sprained an ankle, but ever the soldier, missed only a couple of shows, spurred on by sheer determination and force of will. The battle was won but the war was being lost.

Bad luck struck again when Wendell lost his prized guitar in New York – a 1961 Fender Stratocaster with maple neck purchased in a Chicago pawnshop during an Osibisa tour. He had become so disillusioned that he gave serious thought to leaving the tour.

Drugs became the norm – marijuana, alcohol and a growing dependence on cocaine – and this fueled the ever-mounting distrust growing between singer and keyboardist. Peripherally, the album was doing well back home and an English tour was being arranged on their return. Rabbit, confronting Rodgers daily, was nearing the end of his tether.

Anyway, the US tour was a debacle. Rabbit incurred pretty serious gashes and bruises during regular knockdown fights with Rodgers. He also had a mirror-smashing tantrum after the band's final performance at the Hollywood Sportatorium in Florida on 17 February 1973.

"I was pissed off that the band I loved when Koss was around had turned into a traveling shambles. Here I was, with the best band in the world, touring with Traffic and John Martyn in America, with a Trinidadian guitarist replacement for Koss who was ill back in England. This wasn't the band I wanted to be in. This was shit. So I got drunk after the last show, went into my dressing room, which was full of mirrors – like a chorus girl's dressing room. Mirror after mirror. I went through each one and smashed them, venting my sadness at Koss's illness and his inability to fulfill his obligation to me as 'my guitarist'. Chris Blackwell understood and allowed me to wreak havoc and after I'd done the job, he calmly walked into the dressing room and quietly stated, 'Do you feel better now, Rabbit? You know you're going to have to pay for all this don't you?' I wanted to cry with laughter.

"Paul Kossoff's guitar playing was like the evolving world around me. Evolution was taking place there and then. There was nothing like it before. The guitar as a voice to the world was making new ground. Koss was so brilliant, innovative and expressive. He was as powerful as Paul Rodgers' voice. The two were equal in every respect."

With this out of his system, he conceptualized a clearer vision of why Kossoff fell so far so fast.

"I can say that what tilted him over the edge was definitely the breakup of Free. That was his life, and he never understood why the other guys couldn't get along and enjoy it like he did. Obviously it wasn't their fault, and no blame can be assigned to any one but Koss. You make your own bed in this world. It's up to you whether you sleep in it or not. I know the rest of Free had to just watch him fall apart, and that was hard for them. But it was beyond their power as mere mortals to fix the problem. Koss was sort of supernatural, not of this world.

"He belonged in Free or failing that in another world. So when things fell apart, he naturally started drifting off to that other world. We all helped as much as we could but we're not supernatural Gods. We're musicians and that's it. It's hard to see a family member reach the beyond help stage but it's like trying to figure out how the universe began. Who the fuck knows? If there was a simple way to switch the lights back on, don't you think we would have flipped the switch? We were all in the dark with Koss and no one could find the light."

SOMEBODY WROTE ME A LETTER

There was a lot of his dad in Paul.

-Terry Wilson

Once back on English soil, the band was treated to a minor surprise when "Travellin' In Style" came out and re-kindled the interest of former fans insulted by this Free Mark II band. Still, about four weeks after the March 1973 release, the band members isolated themselves and barely spoke.

Rabbit, as prolific as ever, worked on solo material with Jim Capaldi, Tetsu, Kirke, buddy Snuffy, percussionist Rebop Kwaku Baah, Conrad Isadore and Johnny Nash's Dundee Horns. Kirke, the adventurer, hid himself in Brazil and the jungles of South America. Richardson entered the studio to try and jump-start his own solo career. Tetsu had generated interest from Rod Stewart who had actually included "The Stealer" in his own set. Shortly after Ronnie Lane's departure, Tetsu was first in line as replacement. Believe it or not, Andy Fraser was also given consideration but prior commitments barred entry.

Rumors were spun about the vocalist joining Deep Purple to replace Ian Gillan. Ian and guitarist Ritchie Blackmore were known for their classic displays of temper and egos inflated to the size of zeppelins. The highway star even documented in his biography, *Child In Time: The Life Story Of the Singer From Deep Purple*, "I know I wasn't the only one thinking of going, as Ritchie was thought to be cooking something up with Ian Paice and Phil Lynott of Thin Lizzy fame. Paul Rodgers, associated with Free, was also in the frame somewhere."

"Purple called me because they were in the middle of this American tour and the singer wanted to leave," explains Rodgers. "I wasn't sure what I was doing at the time and I thought about it and decided against it. I didn't really have anything against their music but I didn't think I would fit in there too well. The newspapers got hold of it and all of a sudden it was fact, and it was only a matter of one phone call. So it was just all blown out of proportion."

Ritchie Blackmore had often mentioned in print how mesmerizing he found Paul Rodgers. Kossoff, antithetically speaking, could not imagine "his" singer teaming up with Blackmore and had less than shining comments to make about him.

"I don't want to talk about Ritchie Blackmore. He upsets me. I don't understand his appeal. Well I suppose I do understand his appeal but his tremolo arm stuff? It's a thing and I ain't into that thing. If he's doing well, good luck to him."

Another almost-was incident involved Paul's teaming with Beck, Bogert & Appice. Like the Deep Purple fairy tale, this amounted to no more than a proffered proposal.

The band had tried to do everything in its power to help Kossoff. Saving Paul was now not even an option; all they wanted to do was try and keep him alive for another day, keep him happy and away from the drugs he'd come to rely on and require daily. Where was Paul's dad in all of this? David Kossoff can't be blamed for Paul's illness. He did not put the drugs into his son's hands, and he obviously didn't encourage the addiction. The elder Kossoff, years after Paul's passing, put on a benefit titled *The Late Great Paul* in honor of his son. The former actor wrote and presented a series of shows designed to illuminate his archived works in the form of a live stage performance. *Melody Maker* writer Brian Harrigan covered these events.

"Actor David Kossoff has written a one-man show as a tribute to his late guitarist son Paul. The show is called the *Late Great Paul* and is basically a theatrical biography of the former Free and Back Street Crawler guitarist interspersed with examples of his work, a number of which are unreleased."

"I'm attempting to tell people something about my son Paul," said David Kossoff, "his rise and his fall and his problems with drugs. It is perhaps a campaign, with possibly no great effect, but even a small effect is worthwhile."

In an attempt to present a complete overview of Paul, this author contacted Mr Kossoff. Questions were posed to him regarding the partnership they shared, what he felt about his son's music, what were the happy and sad moments that passed between them.

Here is his reply.

Dear Mr Rosen

Thank you for your letter which I found of some interest. It was not the first such questionnaire about Paul that has come to me over the years, though not often with the request for exactitude as in your own.

You seem already to know a lot from various sources about Paul, who indeed has been much written about over the years.

As to your many questions I must tell you I am not drawn to it. I am now over 80 and do not like to give time to such picking over. Soon Paul will have been dead longer that he was alive. Free has emerged as one of the great sev-

enties groups and their music sells still world-wide. A memorial, and in this
family, a reminder of tragedy & waste.
   Every good wish to you.
   David Kossoff"
Dec 3/00

This author found it hard to understand this somewhat dismissive response and tried once again to elicit a response from Mr Kossoff – but with no success.

Unfortunately but predicatably, after leaving his beloved Free, Paul didn't stop his evil ways. Somehow he would hang on and linger for about another three years before moving on. But those last three years found him living in a haze, a distorted reality where the band, the greatest love in his life, could no longer hold sway over him.

R.I.P.

Andy finally threw in the towel.

-Paul Rodgers

After all the huzzahs and mayhem of Free, Andy Fraser was trying to sort out his professional life. After quitting, he formed Sharks with guitarist Chris Spedding, drummer Marty Simon (from recently departed Holy Smoke) and singer Snips (ex-Hull). Their debut surfaced in 1973 and though *First Water* found a home with diehard Free supporters, the record did little to resuscitate his career.

Chris Spedding, growing up in Sheffield, England, had been recording and playing guitar for some time before being tapped by Fraser. He had worked the A-list, doing sessions for almost everyone: Bryan Ferry, John Cale, Jack Bruce, Dusty Springfield, Gilbert O'Sullivan The Sex Pistols, Donovan and Robert Gordon. He was even in line for the coveted spot of becoming Mick Taylor's replacement in the Stones.

In 1972, right before Andy hailed him, the former member of the Battered Ornaments band (featuring then fledgling vocalist/lyricist Pete Brown) was playing in the jazz fusion outfit Nucleus. He quit and joined the ex-Freeman.

Spedding stayed with the band, releasing a follow-up album titled *Jab It In Yore Eye* in 1974, then the bassist left to pursue work with vocalist Frankie Miller and a group that included Mike Kellie on drums (ex-Spooky Tooth and later The Only Ones), Henry McCullough on guitar (who would later play with McCartney's Wings and would also follow Koss to the grave) and keyboardist Nick Judd. The Scottish vocalist was intrigued just a bit too much with drink and Andy was soon forced to vacate this position to form his own self-named band. *The Andy Fraser Band* album and the subsequent *In Your Eyes* revealed little of the boy genius who, just a few years earlier, had helped write and play on some of the most rough and tumble rock ever crushed into vinyl. This latter offering was recorded in Muscle Shoals and was an attempt to capture the white soul he so loved.

With punk music about to safety pin itself to the hide of the world, Andy was swallowed up and spat out. About a decade following his stint with Sharks, Fraser released another solo album; *Fine Fine Line*, oddly enough, featuring drum tracks by Back Street Crawler's Tony Braunagel.

He moved to the California desert and now lives off his Free royalties and earnings from writing material for the likes of Chaka Khan, Robert Palmer, Joe Cocker, Joan Jett and Paul Young.

Several attempts were made to contact Andy for this book. Paul Rodgers and his management both made gestures and were turned down. Simon also encouraged Andy's participation but to no avail.

"Andy was in L.A. and we never kept in touch," sighs Simon. "Free was our common ground and once that had been transgressed I found we never had that much in common. He made a couple of solo albums and did some songwriting. I saw him last year, in 2000, when I toured with Ringo and the All Starrs. He looked pretty much the same; he was the little bopper, full of pep and bouncing around. He played me some of his songs. They were pretty good, kind of soulful with a jazzy feel. He has this amazing voice, a bit like Stevie Wonder. I never witnessed it in Free."

Paul Rodgers, following the breakup, seemingly went into hibernation. He vanished during the spring of 1973, though he did chat with various press people and mentioned work on a solo album as well as helping Kossoff with a project of his own.

In the summer of 1973, rumors started circulating about a liaison between Rodgers and ex-Mott the Hoople guitarist Mick Ralphs. No one would or could confirm this and with but a brief exhalation, Free was over.

FREEWAYS

I learned a lot from my Free experiences.

-Paul Rodgers

While Andy Fraser was drowning in Sharks, Paul Rodgers had been in communication with Mick Ralphs. The former Ian Hunter band mate had grown weary with the direction his band had taken, forsaking the blues and elemental riffs to venture off into the coiffed glam/spandex stylings of David Bowie and Gary Glitter. In August 1973, Ralphs finally left the group, and as one of its main writers had pocketed almost an album's worth of material including "Ready For Love" (from the *All The Young Dudes* album), "Can't Get Enough", a song Hunter had sneered at, and "Movin' On", a composition cut by Island label partners Hackensack.

Ian Hunter, seemingly, had read the writing on the wall as well. He was acutely aware of Mick's growing disinterest in the band's direction and their growing cinematic stage persona.

"The *Mott* album was good because it was me, Pete (Overend Watts, bass) and 'Buff' (Dale Griffin, drums) who did that, because Mick Ralphs was already leaving. Mick would just come in a couple hours late and put his parts down. He didn't like the songs; he didn't like 'Whizz Kid' – he didn't like none of 'em. He didn't like '…Memphis'; he didn't like any of it. He said, 'You're playing all these chords, why don't you do it simple?' I said, 'I can't do it simple because if we do it simple nobody in the band can sing simple.' We always had to structure it either in a diminished (minimalist) way or in that cut-and-dried way of '…Memphis'. Otherwise we didn't have a singer who could sing the songs. Mick would go, 'Yeah, but we can do it.' But I mean we couldn't do it – that was the point.

"So off he went and found himself a singer. He couldn't have really picked a better one, could he?"

Did Ian have a taste for Mick's replacement vocalist?

"I went and saw Bad Company and the first two-thirds of the set I was bored like I used to be with Free. I always used to walk out on Free and walk back in a half-hour later – and they'd still be at it. But I used to think they were great. That's a funny thing when you can walk out on a band and walk in a half-hour later and still think they're great. I didn't think they were going to happen and then the last 30 minutes it became a top line band.

"What they needed was a couple of years. They came up so quick I almost felt sorry for them because it was frightening. Because how do you follow number ones all over the place? There's always a kickback, always a backlash. And they were just waiting for that. But they seemed real solid together. I hung out with them a lot in New York and we messed around a lot. They seemed to like each other a lot; there was a lot of sympathy between them."

Simon Kirke returned from his four-month pilgrimage to Brazil and immediately contacted Paul. They spoke and the singer invited him out to the house. Also in attendance was Jess Roden and there was talk, more murmured than articulated, of plans to compose a monster band. A coliseum band. The king of all comeback bands. Bad Company was then but a twinkle in the eye – but a twinkle nonetheless.

In the meantime, Paul Kossoff was still in constant turmoil. After his ultimate decision to leave Free in December 1972, the now-solo artist drifted in and out of Island Studios, tying together the loose ends of ideas intended as his first breakaway album. Blackwell facilitated these patchwork sessions by allowing him free studio time to assemble his thoughts. Digby-Smith, too, was put on the case and together they collected a pile of material.

The material ran the gamut from garbage to gold; there was the unused "Molten Gold" track, a leftover from Free days (that would bring together the four originals for the final time); Basing Street Band jams including "I'm Ready", "Tuesday Morning", and "Back Street Crawler"; and the "Time Away" collaboration with John Martyn.

This hodge-podge assemblage took a more defined shape when outside players were enlisted: Alan Spenner, Alan White (Yes), Trevor Burton, Jean Roussel (Cat Stevens, Jess Roden), Clive Chapman (Jeff Beck Group), John Martyn, Tetsu and Conrad Isidore (Crosby, Stills & Nash).

Koss dubbed the conglomerate Back Street Crawler, the moniker attached to his debut solo record. This self-described affair was released in November 1973 and the press, normally gentle with Free and its offshoots, diced him like a carrot. No tour dates were scheduled since he was barely able to stand much less travel about the country to promote the album. This was a bleak period, the worst of times. He had been arrested while driving under the influence of a controlled substance and his Mews home was a revolving door for every drug dealer and hustler in the area. Everyone knew Kossoff had money and shadowy characters would persuade this fragile figure to sign checks they would later cash at the Island facility. Through all this, Sandhe Chard, supporter, friend and confidante, tried to keep the madness to a minimum. She failed, but not for lack of trying.

"We went through a lot and in those days it was tough. There was this bet as to who would die first – Chris Wood from Traffic or Paul [in the event, it was Paul who died first]. Those were the days when I don't know how I was so strong. They were hellish times. Chris would come over and four days later couldn't remember where his car was. It was the seventies; it was the world. I did everything I could. He had so much to live up to, he had so much he wanted to do."

Earlier, when the band had re-formed and recorded the *Free At Last* album, even that was not enough to save him from the clutches of cocaine and the promise of a feel good hour or two. Though the reunion resulted in what was arguably the band's most explosively hypnotic music, he was already past the point of no return.

"The thing was by then Paul wanted to express himself and felt he couldn't do it with Rodgers and Fraser," expresses a still heartbroken Sandhe. "He loved them to death, they were his brothers and his life, but there was something inside him that wanted to do his own thing. That started with the first *Back Street Crawler* record; we got all our friends to come in and it was a blast. It was the first time I saw him in the studio happy. I used to carry the guitars, I was the roadie."

Perhaps now is an appropriate time to mention that Sandhe has revealed here, for the first time, many of her deepest feelings and memories. Her greatest concern was not to anger the elder David Kossoff because, she says, "There would be a war."

For Paul, the light grew dimmer and dimmer. In 1974, after attempting to enter several rehab clinics, he essentially tossed in the towel. Ingesting pills of all descriptions – uppers, downers, screamers, howlers – and most sadly, turning to the needle. Late in 1974, managing to focus himself, he played some wonderful guitar on Amazing Blondel's "Hole In the Head," a track from their debut DJM album, *Mulgrave Street*.

In this same year, he worked intermittently with Van Der Graaf Generator's bassist Nic Potter, Fleetwood Mac's Peter Green and even Graham Bond.

Graham Whyte, the exiled Free roadie, was granted green card status and upon returning to Britain promptly contacted his old friend. Graham made desperate attempts to organize the player's chaotic and shattered life, sitting with him at home and listening to bits and pieces of songs in an attempt to find material for another album.

Geoff Docherty, longstanding promoter, had also been keeping tabs on Kossoff while working with a local outfit called Beckett (they had opened for Free's 20 October 1972 show in Newcastle; Paul broke the neck off his Les Paul and Beckett guitarist Arthur Ramm lent him his Gibson). Struck by some whimsy, Geoff introduced Paul to Beckett vocalist Terry Slesser.

After many ups and downs – essentially Kossoff standing and then falling to the floor – the duo started bonding.

Terry Wilson and Tony Braunagel, the bass/drums rhythm section backing Rabbit during his Texas days, had recently arrived in London to play on the keyboardist's *Dark Saloon*, his second Island solo album. They remained in Big Ben's backyard and, like Rabbit, became hired session rats for Chris Blackwell's stable of artists.

"Koss was trying to find his feet – alas, he never did," recalls a heartbroken Bundrick. "It was a different band from Free all the way around. I introduced my two mates from Texas and they made it different than Free. Just due to the fact that they were Texans with a different 'root' than the English guys. We had Terry Slesser, a Geordie from Tyne-and-Wear, who was brilliant. It was a bit like trying to recreate KKTR but with a different lineup. It was fresh, new songs, new creativity but without the backing and support of the fans and the record companies. In other words, we didn't have a single like 'All Right Now' to guide us along the way. It was tough but we were good. Maybe too good.

"Koss was the only star in the band and he sometimes could barely pull his weight. Most of the time he really was off the rails. The amount of times we had to throw guys out of his hotel rooms who were giving him drugs was amazing. His dinner usually consisted of three or four bottles of Mateus rose and no food, just topped of with drugs. He was in a bad way. But we stuck with him, and by him, 'til the end."

For several weeks the quartet – Kossoff, Bundrick, Wilson and Braunagel – rehearsed and composed. Rabbit, however, was knee-deep in session work and, unable to meet commitments with Back Street Crawler, left on his own accord. His replacement was Omaha, Nebraska-born Mike Montgomery, a friend of Terry and Tony. Mike had also replaced Rabbit in Blackwell (the band) when John left them. Montgomery's lineage included a band called Bloontz that cut the original versions of "Long Way Down" and "Jason Blue", two songs that would end up on Back Street Crawler's *The Band Plays On* album.

Bassist Terry Wilson had known both Rabbit and Tony since high school days in Texas. The rhythm section had toured all over the state, backing Johnny Nash, Jimmy Reed, Lightnin' Hopkins, Rocky Hill, and playing together in Bloontz. They would often jam with Stevie Ray Vaughan and Jimmy Don Smith. When the keyboardist gave Terry and Tony the call to come to London, they were on the first jet out.

Wilson first met Kossoff though Glover and Blackwell. Tentatively, the bassist agreed to have a play with Koss to "check it out" but wasn't making any commitments. Well aware of the perils of playing with Paul, he and

Braunagel met the guitarist in an empty store basement below their Chelsea flat.

"I wasn't sure if this was for us. He wasn't very together at the time. A roadie showed up with a stack of Marshalls. Koss showed up later with his man Johann, a good guy who looked after Paul and was tour manager for the whole Back Street Crawler ordeal.

"Paul and I had a good relationship, I think. We were pretty upfront and honest about things. Paul confided in me once that we, Tony and I, were more sophisticated musically than he was and sometimes that bothered him. But he knew his limitations as a player and he was very clear about what he wanted to do in his approach. He was a soul player; he loved the simplicity of good, heartfelt stuff. He loved Otis Redding's phrasing and how he simply sang the melody without overdoing it or using vocal 'melismas'" (clusters of sung notes).

Tony Braunagel, like Wilson, came from a Texas background steeped in R&B and blues. The son of a country and western guitar player, he left that environment for the chrome and steel façade of New York during the early seventies. This is the period the drummer toured with Johnny Nash, in the backing band that included Rabbit. Though Terry and Tony had played with the keyboardist during those long hot summer Texas nights, this was the first time all three ever had a chance to really feel each other out.

Terry and Tony, while in New York, recorded the *Bloontz* album with Mike Montgomery. Chris Blackwell heard this, spoke to Rabbit about it, and offered them the opportunity to become in-house music soldiers for the Island machine. For six months, they made up the rhythm section that backed virtually every Island project and when Rabbit left to pursue tour work in the States with Eric Burdon, the pair decided to remain in London. It was then they first met up with Koss.

"We met him in the studio and he wanted to put a band together," informs Braunagel. "He saw that we were these two strong Texas, R&B rock'n' roll musicians that had a lot of roots and experience."

By mid-April 1975, band intact and rehearsals in motion, a nine-date tour was announced for May and June. Kossoff managed to endure and even caught the ears of Atlantic Records president Ahmet Ertegun and A&R heavy Phil Carson (who'd later work with The Firm). Offered a huge advance from Atlantic records, this hybrid amalgam entered Sawmills Studios in Cornwall and later Olympic studios in London to lay down tracks.

Another tour was set up for August 1975 to coincide with the release of *The Band Plays On*, but Kossoff took ill, resulting in cancelled dates, and even was pronounced dead when he suffered a cardiac arrest. He was in the ether worlds for 35 minutes. His 25th birthday was spent recuperating.

A replacement tour was scheduled and just a month after almost closing his eyes forever Kossoff was once again abusing. Shows in Liverpool and Glasgow would have been comical had they not been so horrible. Kossoff fell about the stage, collapsed and played miserable guitar. An appearance on *The Old Grey Whistle Test* featured a sickly and wan looking creature.

Mike Montgomery was dismissed when Rabbit returned and the band winged its way to America. Despite trying to will him to improve his health and playing, the band and crew gave in to the inevitable. Dates were cancelled and rearranged. Touring, now an impossibility, was replaced with recording dates. Hopping from rooms in Houston to Electric Ladyland in New York to Crystal Sound in Los Angeles, the band finally anchored in a small Burbank, California studio called The Producer's Workshop.

Johnny Glover attempted to ride herd over an increasingly reckless guitarist. During one day of recording, Paul was so high he couldn't function. Glover lost his temper after Paul tried to concuss him with a whiskey bottle and ended up breaking two of the player's left-hand fingers.

Stranded in the ocean without a boat, never mind a paddle, they tried keeping heads above water – a typical routine with the Paul Kossoff syndrome.

1976 would be a short – and desperate – year.

COMPANY MEN

This was another level.
We wanted the equipment, we wanted the lights,
we wanted the management, we wanted the record
company behind it – and that's what Bad Company was.

-Paul Rodgers.

Rodgers, having given his life to the band he helped create, to a band that was perched on the edge of acclaim and commercial success, had nonetheless fallen into the abyss. Egos, drugs and the de-sensitizing of human needs had trashed Free. With "All Right Now" they were poised and positioned to make a great stab at the heart of the music beast. Unable to achieve what Led Zeppelin had accomplished, leveraging the press and creating hysteria before the band had even formed, Free were left to fend for themselves. But Paul, a wiser and more hardened player, would not make the same mistake twice.

From the outset he knew that to build his vision, the parts must first be in place. There was real energy expended in finding the right players, the proper management and "to make the kind of music that I wanted to make." In actuality, Peace was initially configured as the group to administer to those musical needs, but Peace ended in war so Rodgers, in a new partnership to be called Bad Company, continued with the Free tradition. Many people believe that the singer wanted to divorce himself from what had come before – but this is not the truth. The rapport Rodgers and Fraser had initially enjoyed as co-writers and co-creators was what the vocalist now wanted to build on. Though that communication had all but eroded during the interminably elongated conclusion of Free, there was hope of reinventing a new parlance with new musicians.

Rodgers teamed up with Simon Kirke and Mick Ralphs – the former an almost obvious choice (though not an immediate one) and the latter a musician befriended during the Peace period when Paul's trio opened for Mott the Hoople. Sharing the same dressing room, both bands made use of a single tune-up amp resulting in mini-jams and discussions about songwriting. At one of these water cooler warm-ups, Mick played "Can't Get Enough", the bombastically driven chord tune Mott the Hoople had passed on. On first listening, Paul knew it was a potential breakthrough single.

Still, these early interactions weren't all diamonds and gold. They were essentially sorting out the never-ending conundrum experienced in their former bands and at its essence this affinity boiled down to "mutual frustration with the business and musical directions."

Paul Rodgers had strong and defined ideas about direction. And herein lies the rub. Free, as history has chronicled, began as a blues unit covering standards. Personal frustration set in when Paul suggested the writing of original blues-based material; tension set in when these proffered suggestions ran contrary to Andy's visions. The ex-Mayall employee wanted to break out of this format and embrace more pop, more verse/chorus/hook-grounded anthems. Added to this was Kossoff's ever-diminishing role as a writer and instrumentalist.

Mick Ralphs found himself in an almost identical position within Mott the Hoople. Born 31 March 1944 in Hereford, England, his career began in earnest when he founded Silence, which quickly transformed into Mott the Hoople upon signing with Blackwell. Having recorded a catalogue's worth of albums with the Dickensian-named band (*Mott the Hoople*, 1969; *Mad Shadows*, 1970; *Wild Life*, 1971; *Brain Capers*, 1971; the breakthrough *All The Young Dudes*, 1972; and *Mott*, 1973 [his final work]; he began to feel ill-at-ease with the increasingly glam direction they were taking. While touring with the Peace trio, he found an ally in Paul Rodgers and plans were drawn up to combine energies.

"I wasn't feeling too happy with the way the [Mott] material was heading. We were about to embark on a new album and I got to talking with Paul and he felt a bit like me. I had met Paul several times on various occasions on the road. We used to be with the same record company and we'd tour a lot when Paul had Free. After the initial Free breakup, Paul had a group called Peace and they did a tour with Mott the Hoople. On the tour I used to go out and watch Paul on stage and we used to get together and talk and jam in dressing rooms and stuff like that. We found we had a lot in common musically. We were both in situations where we weren't entirely at liberty to do what we wanted to do. We were kind of restricted by the format we had gotten ourselves into. We began writing songs together, just putting things down on the tape recorder for the hell of it. And suddenly we found all this material coming up. And then we thought, 'wouldn't it be nice if we could put a band together and do this stuff on the road?'

"I could see myself going in different directions to the way the band was going as a whole. I didn't want to jeopardize Mott's thing, so I thought it was best I left and got into something I was more into.

"To me, they went the way Jethro Tull went – very visual and theatrical. What we wanted to do was much more basic and earthy. For me, I have a lot more scope as a guitarist to be myself rather than have to play a certain role. The basis of the band is guitar, bass, drums and vocals [the initial intent was to create a quartet structure, much in the same way as Free], but because Paul plays guitar and piano on a couple of numbers and Boz and I sing, it varies the sound. So it's not like, after you've heard the first number, that's it. It's constantly changing."

The wish was answered. Mick and Paul decided to work together. Simon had just come back from four months in the Brazilian jungle. Upon returning, he heard that Paul was stirring up the musical mélange, and jumped into the brew headfirst.

"I went to Paul's cottage in Surrey where he and Mick were playing away. The vibe was great. Mott had been such a zany band. I mean – they were the Monty Pythons of rock. And Mick had this lovely full sound and he wrote great simple rock 'n' roll songs.

"I think I ended up staying the night at Paul's. We all helped convert a barn into a studio at the back of the cottage. We played songs the next day and the rapport was so good that they asked me if I would like to join the band they were thinking of putting together. I said, 'Yes please.' There has always been a decent working relationship between me and Paul and we have retained a fairly respectful atmosphere between us."

Though Kirke seemed the workingman's choice, the position of drummer was not a slam-dunk decision. Many stick-beaters were summoned; Alan Spenner from Cocker's Grease Band was one. "He was great but he'd show up three days late for every rehearsal," recalls Paul. Auditions were held to pinpoint the perfect player capable of interpreting the collaborative efforts Paul and Mick were composing daily.

Finding a bass player was also a complex task. A wish list was made up of names like Tetsu, and even Roger Hodgson, later to form Supertramp. At the bottom of the roster was Boz Burrell, recently booted from Robert Fripps' ever evolving King Crimson.

"I was still uncertain by the time we got to Boz," admits Rodgers, still a bit gun shy after his ongoing tug-of-war with Fraser. "But I thought we can't go on forever, we'll go nuts."

Simon, too, was a bit hesitant. He reasoned, "He had a couple of strikes against him because he was with King Crimson, who we didn't like, and he had only been playing bass a couple of years. But he came to our rehearsal in the New Kings Road and looked great. He seemed very confident and when we started the first song, 'Little Miss Fortune' – how do I remember this? – Mick would shout out the chords and Boz would work the rest out as he went along. Very impressive. At the end of the afternoon we had a little huddle and it was agreed that Boz was in. We were a foursome. Before Boz, we had a Welsh bass player with us whose name escapes me. You have to feel sorry for him really; he came that close to being in one of the biggest groups of the time."

The reason the band ran through a bassist gauntlet was because the instrument was an integral part of the sound Rodgers had in mind. Beginning his career as a four-string plucker, he realized any band is only as strong as its weakest point. Bass playing is often overlooked within the scope of rock music and the old proverb reads, "If you can't play an instrument, play bass."

Boz Burrell cut across several styles; he managed to break into idioms ranging from prog-rock to art-rock and hard rock. Born Raymond Burrell on 1 August 1946, this multi-faceted character began singing in 1963 in a quaint conglomerate called The Tea Time Four. Their only significant credit resided with the inclusion of future Small Faces keyboardist Ian McLagan. They dissolved into The Boz People then Burrell evacuated this appellate to become part of The Sidewinders, a quartet sporting Mark Charig, future cornet player on Crimson's *Lizard, Islands* and *Red* albums, and Soft Machine alumnus John Marshall. Boz, as he was then simply known, jumped ship once again and landed in Feel For Soul, a featureless outfit that finally bade farewell in 1968. In this same year, he recorded a version of Bob Dylan's "Down In the Flood" for EMI's Columbia label (credit read: *Boz)*. Though the cover was less than sterling, it did feature a remarkable band consisting of Deep Purple's Ritchie Blackmore, Ian Paice and Jon Lord. They were moonlighting while working with ex-Outlaw Chas Hodges.

"I'd been in the business for about ten years, earning a regular wage of about £4 a week and I decided I've got to get myself a gig and earn some money – or I'm gonna swallow it. I've always been a bit of jazz freak and they played some nice, up-tempo 6/8 things. It was good experience for me.

"They couldn't find a bass player because at that stage Bob Fripp wrote songs and he heard them in his head and didn't give any other members in the band any leeway for their own expression. He wanted to hear them exactly as he head them in his head. So I really learned the bass parrot-fashion if you know what I mean."

"They" of course was King Crimson, and in late 1970, Burrell broke boundaries when asked to enlist in the Fripp-controlled corporation. Robert, lead guitarist and visionary of the ever-evolving unit, had made a living by locating singing bass players to front the band. Boz, part of the lineage that included Pete Giles, Greg Lake, Gordon Haskell and John Wetton, stayed with this always-morphing musical museum for about a year-and-a-half. For his efforts, he was able to tour the world and record on the *Islands* and *Earthbound* albums.

Fripp, arrogant, overbearing and singularly sighted, drove the bassist from the fold. He then teamed with other ex-Crimsons, (drummer) Ian Wallace and (saxophonist) Mel Collins, the horn player later appearing on various Bad Company tracks, and formed Snape, along with an ever-visible Alexis Korner and Peter Thorup. They recorded one album, *Accidentally Born In New Orleans*.

"They made a publicity thing of the fact that it was some sort of super-group – members of Free, members of Mott the Hoople, members of King Crimson," recalls Rodgers. "Although I don't think Boz was really a King Crimsonite; he joined the band at a later date. I'm not putting them down in any way but he was more of a jazz/blues/soul player rather than whatever King Crimson was. They were more psychedelic, weren't they? He was even more far out in terms of listening to blues, he was more obscure. And away we went and it was just a question of management."

Band lineup intact, Bad Company as they were now named (a moniker, depending with whom you speak, derived from either an old Jeff Bridges film of the same name or a cartoon lifted from an old English text called *Victorian Morals*), sought out representation. In this new ensemble's earliest stages, brief thought was given to the idea of carrying on under the banner of Free. But Free had suffered too many traumas and Paul sensed that an audience now saw that quartet as not very well organized. They toyed with the idea but decided on a new name and new identity.

"We could have called the band Free and been readily accepted but that doesn't give you an incentive or a challenge," Ralphs relates. "We had thought about the Zoom Club but we eventually decided on Bad Company. We did think about The Lounge Trousers and Four Millionaire Bubbles and Spitfire and The Black Bombers. We thought about The Piddlers; we sat up all night thinking about names. Concrete Parachute. But we always came back to Bad Company. We had a bit of a difficulty persuading the record company and management. I think they'd had a word with Simon and they said for him to come 'round my house because they wanted him to talk to me about not using the name. I turned him back around and sent him off and said, 'This is what we're gonna call ourselves, it's too good to miss.'"

Moniker intact, Rodgers was immediately aware that an experienced administrating body was essential; Free had tried to self-govern and it had ended in disaster. Paul had a mutual friend who knew Peter Grant and upon contacting him discovered that the former bouncer and Led Zeppelin manager was assembling his own label, Swan Song, and was searching for artists. When Grant arrived at a rehearsal, the band was still without a bass player. They did, however, have material ready including "Rock Steady", 'Bad Company" and "Can't Get Enough". Grant was hooked.

Zeppelin's five-year contract with Atlantic Records had expired in December 1972, and both Jimmy Page and Grant believed that by running and controlling the business they'd reap greater creative and financial rewards. Bad Company had come to their attention and Peter readily agreed to represent them. Within weeks the fledgling label would also sign The Pretty Things and Maggie Bell.

Percussionist Kirke sketches out the Grant persona, a feat requiring boxes of charcoal.

"Once the lineup was completed, we were straining at the leash to be under way. Remember, we had years of frustration tugging at us. We had a super manager in Peter Grant. He was an imposing man, around 300 pounds. He had held many jobs in his life; two of the most interesting were as a wrestler and as road manager for Gene Vincent. As Zeppelin's manager, he was one of the most powerful men in the business. It was alleged that he had ties to the underworld and in truth, he appeared to surround himself with some pretty dodgy characters: Johnny Bindon and 'One Punch' Ray were amongst the most colorful.

"I asked him in all innocence if these rumors were true and he just smiled and put his hand on his heart and said, 'Absolutely not.' I think his fantasy scene in *The Song Remains The Same* would be nearer the truth (in it, the gargantuan one portrays a slick criminal type).

"But he loved his bands. He was more of a mate really and wasn't scared of any man alive (during a Zeppelin tour, he allegedly had his henchman beat a security guard senseless when the hired muscle denied Robert Plant's son access to a backstage area). He spoke his piece and when in a temper could be very intimidating. His business acumen was legendary and I think he saw in us a chance to put it to the test again. Zeppelin were the biggest band in the world and kind of ran themselves; he liked us and wanted to groom us for the big time, the really big time. He succeeded, too."

Chomping at the bit to begin recording, this newly assembled troupe underwent serious pre-production at Headley Grange, Hampshire in the fall of 1973. Working in a bucolic setting, they hammered out the material already amassed and fine-tuned the edges. Zeppelin had stationed a mobile studio at the home, a recording bus similar to the Pye-wagon employed years earlier when Free were cutting tracks for the *Free Live!* album. Grant informed the boys that Page and crew would arrive in about two weeks time, but if they could compile and complete an album during that time, they were welcome to make use of it.

Rodgers, who recorded six albums with this band before departing on a solo career, theorizes on the recording of the simply titled first album.

"It was interesting because it was very unformed; we didn't go in with any preconceived ideas at all. We had a load of songs, we were just gonna record them, and pick the best ones and put them on an album. And that's why there's such a mix on there, all the way from 'Seagull' to all these other things. And it was kind of nice in a way. And I think we were probably the first band to have a song written around their name. So it presented an instant image that we didn't even realize."

Bad Company was completed in the allotted time and became a milestone, an absolute landmark in the chronology of rock music. At the heart of it were majestic pop/rock tunes orchestrated with elementary guitar/bass/vocal arrangements. And yet the arrangements and harmonic content lent an aura of musicality never before touched upon by electrically driven bands.

Ron Nevison put this all down on tape. No newcomer to the business, he had previously worked with Zeppelin and even had pushed faders with Peace, Toby and the re-formed Free.

He had earned his patches working the sound for various artists, including Joe Cocker's Mad Dogs and Englishmen, Derek & The Dominoes and Traffic. After being on the road from 1967 to 1969, Nevison had been harboring an increasing desire to enter the studio proper. Like so many others, this American with wanderlust in his veins and a head full of dreams was given passage to the Magic Kingdom – London – when Chris Blackwell offered the young man an entry level engineering position at the Island complex.

Groups such as Curved Air (featuring the awe-inspiring Sonja Kristina) and Spooky Tooth entered the studio, and in-between working these and other artists, Ron had become acquainted with The Who's Pete Townshend. The whirling windmill had created TrackPlant, a company that designed studios for musicians and, through Pete, Nevison was introduced to Ronnie Lane from The Faces. The bassist/vocalist had sketched out an idea to create a mobile studio and implant it in an Airstream Caravan. Much like the Pye piece of yesteryear but on a much grander and more quality-controlled level.

While the engineer was constructing this rolling recorder, The Who was building a studio proper in Battersea. They had begun sessions for *Quadrophenia* but the control room had not yet been completed. Pete, Roger, Keith and John hired Nevison and his moveable multi-track and were so pleased with the results that they hired him on as engineer.

After the *Quadrophenia* sessions, the engineer's stock tripled in value. Led Zeppelin gave him the call to come work on *Physical Graffiti*, recorded, like *Houses Of the Holy*, at Headley Grange. Here, a relationship was forged with manager Peter Grant.

Nevison, who would go on to work with Heart, The Babys, Chicago and other headliners, had to forgo working with Zeppelin when The Who tracked him down to oversee the *Tommy* film soundtrack.

By this time, late 1973, Grant had taken over management for The Paul Rodgers Band, a moniker hung on Rodgers, Kirke, and Ralphs before finding a bass player and finally re-naming themselves. Nevison takes over the narrative.

"To me, Mick and Paul both had tunes they couldn't use with their groups – the conflict between Paul and Andy, and Mick's conflicts with Ian Hunter. That's what made Bad Company so good; they had a lot of stored up material they'd been saving. Paul's ballads and Mick's rockers – you don't get any better. That's why the first album was such a gem."

He was hired as engineer because the band was seeking that "live" sound Zeppelin had created at the Headley Grange house. Downtime was required when Nevison had to return to the *Tommy* project, but still, in all, the entire *Bad Company* album only ate up about fourteen days of recording time. An additional two days were devoted to horn and background vocal overdubs away from Headley Grange. Mixing, undertaken at Olympic Studios, was accomplished at the rate of two or three tracks per day. An astonishing feat, much like the speedy timetables established by Andy Johns in his work with Free.

The band had come well prepared – they had spent months composing the material and the sessions went extraordinarily smoothly. After a basic track was captured – guitar, bass, and drums – Mick would then return to overdub a solo or double a rhythm track. Paul would then go in and lay down vocals and the odd embellishment – piano on the title track, for example.

Nevison was well aware of the group's previous work, particularly Paul's career with Free. In fact, while working at Island studios, he'd often come across a Free session. So he was concious of the tempestuous and fragile moments that had arisen. He was, in fact, hired solely as engineer, and told in no uncertain terms that they were not seeking another producer – an animal they'd had to battle in previous bands.

There was a bit of friction when Bob Pridden, the Who's sound overseer, expressed an interest in producing and/or engineering Bad Company. But Nevison was green-lighted and for a salary of about £75 a week, assembled the pieces.

So did he not benefit from back end sales from the album?

"Fuck no," he vehemently insists. "Even after they had success, they treated me like shit, to tell you the truth [he was also the tech on *Straight Shooter* and *Run With the Pack*]."

Simon, infatuated with this new conglomerate, has his own story to tell.

"I think that first album was recorded in about ten days at Headley Grange. Zep had booked Ronnie Lane's mobile studio but midway through recording John Paul Jones had taken ill, so in what was to be the first of many of Peter Grant's astute moves, he said to us to go ahead and put some tracks down. The complications of our former contracts were preventing us from touring so all we were doing was rehearsing day in, day out. We were building to such a peak that Peter saw this and instead of letting us stew, gave us a golden opportunity. I think the next couple of years were some of the best of my professional life."

Those legal battles with Island made touring an impossibility and Johnny Glover, once their champion, delayed the release of the album for almost three months. This premier effort was completed by Christmas 1973, but red tape stalled its appearance. Island Records actually released *Bad Company*, followed by the next three albums, while in America Swan Song licensed and distributed the band's output via Atlantic.

Danny Goldberg, a young turk publicist, was coaxed away from Solters & Roskin, to head up the label, announcing, "Our entire team is going to be fully concentrated on Bad Company." A media blitz assaulted print and radio outlets, overseen by merchandising and promotional honcho Pete Senoff of Atlantic Records. Amongst these advertising gimmicks were 10,000 colored posters, mobiles and billboards with the strap line: *Does Your Mama Know You've Been Keeping Bad Company?*

A brief English mini-tour accompanied the album's release and in a déjà vu scenario, the British press embraced the quartet as conquering heroes. Returning to Newcastle City Hall in March 1974, they jumpstarted the tour at this bastion of former Free worshippers. Select dates also took place in Frankfurt, Germany, followed by a six-week tour of America beginning in mid-July. Though everyone had visited the US on numerous occasions, this was, according to Mick, "Just like your first group, everything you do excites you."

Simon agrees. "Newcastle was one of Free's most popular (strongholds) and sold out in no time. It was quite a night. Both Peter Grant and Chris Blackwell were there – one relinquishing control and the other taking it on. The gig was fantastic. The crowd took us to their hearts. We came off glowing; no one to carry off, no one to worry about, no guilt at having played a sub-standard set. Just four guys, supremely confident in knowing that they were destined for great things."

An understatement by anyone's definition. The debut soared to number one in the American charts and the world bowed in supplication.

Simon underscores this growing sentiment in relaying, "We were on fire; the shows in England were an instant sell-out. There was such a buzz created by the personnel from three of the most loved bands of the day that interest was instant. The joy of this was that we could back it up. We were seasoned pros who had put their past behind them and had found a common goal – to be a fuckin' huge band, play good music and at last … have some fun."

Rodgers, too, was gnawing at the bit, to perform live once again.

"It was really great to get back on stage because it had been a while since I'd been in an organized unit playing music. What was nice for me was I was playing a bit of acoustic guitar and piano."

Most importantly, though, was the band's own feeling about the image they'd created. Paul was especially pleased with the outcome and felt his new four-piece had demonstrated greater potential at this early stage than Free had done at the same juncture.

"We did capture a moment in time and I think that's what an album does. And it was very laid back in a lot of ways. We had this old big mansion with a mobile studio which was unusual in those days because everybody went to a studio which involved driving down freeways, parking a car and all the stress of that. It was kind of hippie-ish in a way; someone would light the fire, someone would cook breakfast and we'd have our wives and girlfriends around and it was real communal and vibey. And we just did what felt right that particular day. Yeah, it did capture a great period of time and it had a lot of promise to it.

"Each of the players was really good at what they did and they really understood each other. I actually wrote 'Rock Steady' in the studio; the button was on red, and I was explaining the song. I was working things out right there under the gun and I loved it."

Early on in the process, this proto-super band knew intuitively they were on the right track. The album lodged itself in the stratosphere and even reached Top Ten status in England. Within months this first musical step had sold five million copies and "Can't Get Enough" turned up as a number five chart single. Where it had taken Free years to break into the American consciousness, Bad Company had established themselves within months of forming.

During that first American road trip, this author conducted one of the first major interviews with the band for *Rolling Stone* magazine. The San Francisco-based periodical followed a strict code of rules and paramount amongst these was that no band was ever interviewed or given page coverage before the release of the album. This writer knew, even before receiving advanced test pressings of *Bad Company*, that this new amalgam would be embraced internationally upon release of the debut. And convincing the editorial barons of *Rolling Stone*, undertook to interview the four disparate personalities. The interview appeared in the 15 August 1974 issue under the banner *Paul Rodgers' Bad Company*.

To convey a sense of how bonded these individuals were, it seems appropriate to present an excerpt from that interview. Save for the minimal quotes in the story proper, these responses have never before been published. The day following our interview, this scribe accompanied the Company on that fabled bus excursion outlined in this book's opening chapter.

THE GOOD, THE BAND AND THE UGLY

Bad Company ... had a much broader vision than Free.

-Simon Kirke

The Continental Hyatt House was the location for this summit meeting. Hollywood was basking in typical sunshine but up in the room air-conditioning was functioning at full throttle and everyone was comfortable and content. Though Paul, Boz, Simon, and Mick knew this interview would be their first major spread – *Rolling Stone* was the bible for musicians back then, and still is to this day – they pulled no punches and were more than forthcoming in responding. The interplay amongst the four reveals a great deal about this embryonic period. The world was theirs for the taking – and they knew it. This is but a portion of the entire proceeding, a talk that lasted for well over an hour. These responses, in hindsight, now seem a bit like old news but it must be remembered that this Q&A conference was the first time all four musicians had spoken about the band – all in the same room, at the same time.

Do you find that you've had to approach the writing in a different fashion than you did with Free?

Paul Rodgers: "Yeah, yeah, wow. It would be hard to say exactly how but unconsciously you adapt to each other's playing and the songwriting does that too. We've really yet got to see exactly how because a lot of the numbers were written before we were actually a four-piece. So it's hard to know exactly what will come out. But the great thing is there's an amazing amount of potential and we have a lot to draw from each other and learn from each other. And that's bound to reflect in the songs and what we're saying.

"With Free, that situation didn't exist. There was personality clashes, as simple as that. We weren't leaving each other enough room to develop in our own way."

Mick Ralphs: "Yeah, with this band, we've already started laying down stuff for a second album. We always have new ideas coming up, me and Paul write a lot of stuff, and even Simon has some new ideas. We were putting stuff together even before we had a bass player."

Boz Burrell: "I had been doing sessions for about a year – Alexis Korner, Eddie Harris, and people like that – to improve my actual playing. I planned to do sessions for about a year and then hoped I'd find a really good unit to get into. This is more my music than Crimson was. I found Crimson a little uncomfortable – the singing mainly. I had to sing in different voices, that tweedy sort of English voice. But it was great because I had a chance to really start learning the instrument. Now I just play bass and leave the singing to the man over there [nods at Rodgers]. He does it a lot better than me. I do some harmonies because it broadens the scope of the music."

Simon Kirke: "Yeah, while Boz was doing sessions, I just wanted to lay back for a bit when Free finally split. I didn't have any musical plans at all; I just wanted to get my head clear. It wasn't really a case of approaching me, we just sort of naturally got back together."

Paul Rodgers: "He just charged into the session and said, 'I'm the fuckin' drummer!'"

Mick Ralphs: "He'd just returned from holiday and just showed up at Paul's house and we had all these songs going."

Paul Rodgers: "The whole beauty of the formation of the band was from beginning to end everything seems to have been a natural thing. There was no planning. Obviously we wanted to form a good, solid band but we didn't want to make any compromises. The people in the band had to have the right sort of personal chemistry which is why it took quite a long time for the thing to get together."

Mick Ralphs: "If the people are right as people then the music follows suit. You can get ace musicians together but they don't make good music because something doesn't gel. With us, we get on so well as people, and dig each other musically, that it works."

Boz Burrell: "I think we get on well musically because we're all at the same stage. We're all very enthusiastic and not jaded. Paul is getting into learning guitar and Mick finds it a new experience, and me too."

Mick Ralphs: "We'd tried out bass players who were technically brilliant but they didn't get off on what they were doing. They just did it. We did try different people; we didn't go specifically to Boz. We had the singer and guitarist and drummer and we didn't really know that many bass players."

Paul Rodgers: "During the time the three of us were planning material, we'd formed a certain way of …"

Mick Ralphs: " … doing things. And we wanted somebody to complete that. With Boz, he just turned up, played a couple of notes, and it seemed to work. That's how the whole situation has been. With the songs, Paul and I had written just about everything before we went into the studio. A lot of bands, the ones I was with before, you'd suddenly be on tour and there'd be a panic and Ian would lock himself away for a week and bash like hell on this piano. He'd suddenly appear with ten skeleton tunes and he'd say, 'Right, we've got to do it like this.' And it was the wrong way to make music to me. The way we're doing it is more natural and the material just flows. Talking about songs, it's funny because we do "Ready For Love" (previously covered by Mott the Hoople) but Paul heard the song and liked it. We had all this new material and didn't want to do anything that had gone down before. We tried it and it sounded so much better with a good voice singing it. It's how I heard the song when I wrote it."

Simon Kirke: "And we do a couple of Free songs, 'Stealer' and 'Easy On My Soul.'"

Mick Ralphs: "I'd never heard 'Easy On My Soul' before."

Simon Kirke: "The way Mick said the way we do 'Ready For Love' was how he would have liked to have heard it, conversely, it's the same with 'Stealer' and 'Easy On My Soul.' It's how we would have liked to have heard them."

Paul Rodgers: "I switched the radio on and this song came on and I said, 'Hang on, I know that song,' and it was one of our songs. Bob Seger had done 'Stealer" (on his *Back In '72* album from March 1973) and they did it great so we stole their arrangement."

The album appears to have been an easygoing affair. You recorded it in just a few days so you must have been well prepared.

Mick Ralphs: "Yeah, we did it in a house in the country on a mobile studio that belonged to Ronnie Lane. It was a sixteen-track you park outside; normally you're in the studio and you think, 'Bloody hell, this is costing 30 quid an hour,' but here, if you want to record you switch the machine on, and if you don't you just switch it off."

Boz Burrell: "It's great, you can pop on down to the pub for a game of darts. It's much more relaxed."

Mick Ralphs: "I can see bands who don't have it together could waste a lot of time in the country. But we had it together and went down there to work – but it wasn't like work. It was easy. We produced it ourselves because we felt we knew what we wanted the band to sound like. It was just a case of transmitting that via the engineer." [Ron Nevison].

Paul Rodgers: "The album is very raw, very basic, very under-produced."

Mick Ralphs: "We could have gone mad because all the songs lend themselves to lavish arrangements but we did it very basically using the instruments we could play between us. As a result the songs stand up much stronger to me."

Have you found that coming from three pretty visible bands – Free, Mott the Hoople and King Crimson – that those previous successes have followed you into Bad Company? Either in a positive or negative way?

Paul Rodgers: "No, they don't expect to hear another Free but we do have the followings of those three bands. The material is original enough to wipe out all the past."

Mick Ralphs: "They come out of curiosity like on the British tour [which took place prior to this interview], people coming to see Paul and Simon and see what I was into and the same with Boz. They came out of interest and not really expecting a version of the bands we'd been into; they came to see what this band was like."

Paul Rodgers: "The critics did come to see another version of Free but we'd spent so much time getting our original material together, that the people who left the hall went away thinking of Bad Company. Not ex-Mott or Free or King Crimson."

Boz Burrell: "There was very little heckling because when I joined Crimson Mark 10 or whatever it was, you used to get people shouting out tunes from other albums. But we got none of that from the audience, they dug what we were playing. And the only people who went away not impressed were the critics."

These veterans, these battle-wearied soldiers, had withstood the grueling artillery of ego wars and personality clashes and internal conflicts. In Bad Company they'd been able to set aside the agonies and sidestep the landmines that beleaguered earlier sound squadrons. For the moment, they flew with gossamer wings, on the backs of sweet butterflies of success. But life is not always forgiving and within a few years similar problems that had plagued Free, Hoople and Crimson would once again emerge.

WHEN THEY WERE KINGS

Those albums were the cornerstones of my career.

-Ron Nevison

FM radio was ready for Bad Company and the band was ready for radio. Not only did "Can't Get Enough" insert itself into regular rotation but "Movin' On," and the title song also became on-air perennial favorites. In order of mention, these tracks rated number five and number nineteen while "Ready For Love" and the title piece also placed highly on the US boards. Peter Grant, in collaboration with the massive publicity campaigns designed by Atlantic Records in America, managed to break them virtually worldwide.

In order to capitalize on this once-in-a-lifetime universal visibility, the group re-hired Ronnie Lane's mobile wagon and this time stationed themselves at Clearwell Castle in Gloucestershire, England. But foremost in the singer's mind, despite all the wild success swirling about him was the absence of Paul Kossoff. Not a day went by without Rodgers' musing on what this band would have grown into musically had his friend been able to beat back the ghosts.

"We always had a good relationship, Koss and I, and I loved him dearly. I wished and hoped that he would pull himself together to play. I miss him even now, he was a great player, and we had almost an esoteric understanding of each other's space. Sometimes if I was going to overdub a vocal and there would be an ad lib space at the end where Koss and I would exchange lines, he would put his parts in and leave gaps knowing where I would be. We could read each other that well. Had Koss still been around he would have been the guitarist in this band."

Paul Kossoff had his own opinions about his replacement.

"I saw my style in Mick Ralphs. He tried to rip me off that way. I just wish he'd do it a little better. I'm sorry, Mick. But he does some things that I don't do. His strings always sound so loose, like he's using rubber bands – it just sounds that way to me."

But Rodgers had to forge ahead and in Mick Ralphs he'd found someone simpatico, a like-minded collaborator. Time was ticking and there was no time available to dwell on what might have been.

"The thing is I formed Bad Company, I had this music, I had to do it and I couldn't deal with wasting too much time. I really wanted to be organized and get out there and do it but there was always a great deal of respect and love for Koss and his ability."

Kossoff shared the same sentiment for his longstanding vocalist partner. He even attended one of the first British dates to see Rodgers and Kirke perform with their new associates. Sandhe Chard regales us with this very touching, and oh-so-terribly sad saga.

"Paul Rodgers and Simon were, to him, his brothers. So he went and saw them at the Lyceum, I think, and stood in the aisles. He wouldn't even go to his seat. They started playing and he started crying and goes, 'My brothers, my brothers.' And we had to leave – he couldn't handle it. He loved them so much but it was the Fraser/Rodgers thing; he could not write, he could not create because of the Fraser/Rodgers thing."

Simon negates this tale. "I don't know that Koss had ever seen the band in concert; if he had I'm sure we would heave heard about it," is his rebuttal.

Clearwell Castle became ground zero and with the Ronnie Lane portable parked outside and Ron Nevison once again performing technical duties, work ensued. The port-o-track, located in front of the house was fitted with a closed circuit camera. Whenever a microphone adjustment had to be made, Nevison had to bolt from his seat in the van, run inside, make the correction and trot back to the truck. *Straight Shooter*, the always devilishly difficult second album, was recorded following the group's heavy touring schedule. Well aware of the numbers racked up on the first venture, they attempted to re-create that magic. They came close. This one would perch itself at number three on both American and British listings and would reveal a slightly different personality. Having played together on the road there was more of an ensemble feel but gone was the spontaneity of the debut.

Paul saw this album as a "snapshot" of where they were at the time.

"It reflects the fact that we'd been on the road and were blooded in a way and we'd done a lot of shows. And here we were having to follow up the first album that was so... easy... because we didn't really know what we were doing. There was more pressure and I think it reflects that but I think there are some good things on there."

No argument. "Good Lovin' Gone Bad", the first single, rose to number 36 in the US to be followed by the riff-laden "Feel Like Makin' Love" (original working title: "Think About Love"), a now accepted standard of FM roll calls clamoring its way to number ten. Simon provides perspective.

"*Straight Shooter* had some classic stuff on it: the two singles, 'Shooting Star' and 'Weep No More', a personal favorite of mine for obvious reasons [he wrote it]. 'Feel Like Makin' Love' got us a Grammy for Best New

Group if memory serves me well. We were away on tour so Keith Moon accepted the award on our behalf. 'Shooting Star' was written by Paul and is one of his finest songs. He played some of it at the airport prior to a States tour and damn me if he hadn't finished it by the time we arrived. It was to prove prophetic, sadly, a year later when Koss died. 'Feel Like Makin' Love' was an amalgamation of two songs cleverly intertwined by Rodgers and Ralphs. It was arguably the most popular and definitely the sexiest song the band ever produced. I loved 'Weep No More'. Paul sang it better than I could have hoped for; Mick played a lovely solo and also added some touching piano and the string section gave me chills. One of the best songs I ever wrote.

"We recorded it at a castle in Wales using Ronnie Lane's mobile studio once more. We loved that vibe of being able to just plug in and play whenever we felt like it. They used to have these dinner parties for paying guests at the castle – you know, sort of a baronial meal, all-u-can eat for twenty quid. Boz and me gate-crashed one of their soirees and I dimly remember dancing on the long table, groping the ladies, insulting the men and generally having a high old time. The guests were thoroughly amused and thought it was part of the night's entertainment – although we were asked not to provide a repeat performance."

Nevison and company were flying high during the work schedule for *Straight Shooter.* So high, in fact, they shot off rockets and mixed the sounds in on "Shooting Star". "'Don't you know you are a shooting star, whooooossshhhh.' We shot off these bottle rockets and recorded it. And of course we got in trouble for that because the locals said their cows weren't giving milk and shit like that. We ran into some problems there and we went to Air Studios where we did some overdubs and mixed. It was in Oxford Circus in this big office complex where I mixed the *Tommy* film and UFO. I never did use Island much, I didn't like it."

Ron Nevison was only too happy to engineer this second project, his salary being raised from £75 per week to an astronomical £200. It should be understood that he was never hired to participate in backend royalties (nowadays, many top-tiered producers are given 'points' on the albums they oversee, a percentage of retail resulting, in the case of a hit record, fees surpassing their regular salary). Ron views his work with Bad Company as a major jumping-off place for future endeavors.

"I was never hired as a producer, it was me and the band. I would have thought after this second, or at least the third album, I would at least have gotten some bigger credit or a small slice but I went into it knowing that wasn't happening. I think my manager at the time, after the second album, approached them with something like that and they said, 'Fuck off.'"

If asked his opinion, he'd offer it up, but musically, the bus was band-driven. Like the first outing, he tried to keep the production simple and uncluttered. On hindsight, listening to those albums years later, he hears "tracks that would not now make it as keepers, but there was a basic 'charm' element and honesty, a thrill just to be involved."

"I think in their mind I was just the engineer and anybody could have done it; I truly believe that. I don't know if you talk to them about me but I don't think they give me much credit. I've talked to them through their different managers about doing another album but they weren't interested. So, I can't figure it out."

Simon, still the ambassador of goodwill and the even-tempered one, provides a possible insight.

"Ron was brought in by Peter to engineer the first album. Initially he did a good job, so good in fact that he worked on the first three albums. But then elements of grandeur crept in and he wanted a producer's credit. We felt that the band was really producing itself and that we, in essence, were the producers. So his demands were unjustified. We parted ways soon after the third album and he went on to fulfill his wish and today is one of the top producers in the country."

Nonetheless, Nevison compiled a bold and driven record. Singles buzzed the airwaves like jets in the sky and on the strength of these rock delights, the band undertook yet another mammoth assault on America.

PACK RATS

Paul was the talented one out there in the limelight.

-Sandhe Chard

Returning from yet another monstrous cross-country American circus, Bad Company began work on the album that would become *Run with the Pack*. Material came easily these days and the recording of their first three albums took place in a period of less than three years. And yet accompanying all this external validation – full houses, high-flying singles and spiraling bank accounts – was the pressure to perform. That monkey on the back, crack in the façade feeling that what you're doing now had better be stronger and more commercially appealing than what you'd done before. This is a subtle process, a gradual change in personality and temperament. Hindsight shuffles in on quiet claws and a re-thinking occurs, a second looking at material in trying to determine if the songs possess the permanence of earlier works.

The mistress of Fame and Fortune is a bitch. She is never satisfied and is always ravenous. This same beast was visited upon Free when they sat on the throne with "All Right Now". This silent but deadly little night stalker infected the band, turning one upon the other, inflating egos and crushing creative desire. Now, she was back and feeding on the pack. Her venom is not always deadly and some survive. But Bad Company did not and with the poison flowing through their veins, a slow-acting chemical, they would begin to show signs of the disease in the not too distant future.

As the first artists signed to Grant's Swan Song label, there was an unspoken pressure on them. They had become the company's major breadwinners – Maggie Bell and The Pretty Things barely registered as blips on public radar – and for this, their third release, it was critical to keep the banner raised. *Run With the Pack* had flags flying full mast. There was cohesion, a precision here, a more stylized sound emanating from the tracks. The band, having played together for three years now, performed seamlessly. Clocking in at number four on British charts and number five in America, the album borrowed an old Coasters' classic, "Youngblood" as its first single. They kept a remarkable progression intact by creating yet another Top Ten 45.

Retiring to Pontoise, France, in September 1975, they began work on record number three. As tax exiles they were only allowed to spend 63 days each year in England so the south of France became a logical choice. But Ronnie Lane did not want his money-making mobile shipped to the continent, so he turned the project down. Nevison, already returned to Los Angeles, was phoned and flew back to England to accompany these rock nomads to France. The villa, near the French Riviera, was the type of opulent accommodation normally rented out to visiting dignitaries. This area of European geography, certainly one of the more beautiful places in the world, is also a region known for its tiny back roads and winding cobbled streets. Cute, yes, if you're in a tiny Citroen or Renault. Not so cute when you're towing the Rolling Stones recording truck.

"It's tiny and narrow and when the truck got there, it couldn't make it up to the house," recalls Nevison. "It couldn't make it around these bends. And then something else happened – I think Simon Kirke fell off a motorcycle and messed up his arm. So we had to rent another house for the recording. This was out in the country in Grasse, France, which is famous for its perfume.

"Even then neighbors came with guns because we were making so much noise. We had to start earlier and stop when the police came. Even though it was a farmhouse, it thundered through the valley."

Despite these problems, the group did not succumb. In fact the album caressed the ears with more complex arrangements, acoustic flourishes, and on the title song, orchestrated string parts. "Run with the Pack" was in many ways a follow up to the "Bad Company" track, showing that same ideology of "us against the world". The image of the pack as rock band has a beastly beauty. And in lush counterpoint, the lyrics are swept away by sweet violins.

"That shows a different aspect of us," admits Rodgers. "The song and the album were much more polished, much more produced. And it's very good for that. Like with the strings on this song, I wanted them and I could hear what they would do. Jimmy Horowitz [arranger] came down and wrote out the scores; while the song was playing I was telling him where the strings would be – and he did a great job of interpreting that. It was a more polished approach, more clinical in a way. But I hope that we still captured the feel."

Indeed, that feel was there. Kirke continues the tale.

"Yeah, I remember that. *Run With the Pack* was the third in a triumvirate of albums which, I modestly think, were among the finest in rock 'n' roll. They were the bedrock of Bad Company's repertoire and sealed our impact on the musical world. However, I think the standard of the material of subsequent albums wavered a bit after this. Veering from brilliant to dubious.

"Those were great songs. Great camaraderie – the best of times really. 'Honey Child' was conceived at a sound check on an American tour; it just burst out one day. We all looked at each other and said, 'Fuck me, what's this?' I never forgot the goose bumps. We did it in one take in France. The title track was a blast, check out the strings on that one. 'Do Right By Your Woman' was recorded around a campfire – listen closely and you can just about hear the flames crackling. 'Live For the Music' was another of Mick's rockers. I was outside the mobile during a playback and the whole vehicle was rocking back and forth as all the guys' feet beat out a tattoo on the floor."

With recording completed, Nevison brought the master reels back to Los Angeles for mixing. These Gods of guitar returned to California to pursue some promotional junkets in support of the album. Ron turned up at the Record Plant one day to continue work on the mixdown – and found the tapes and the band had vanished.

"They apparently didn't like my mixing of that album. I had mixed maybe half the album and they were gone, they didn't say anything to me. They got Eddie Kramer to mix it and that's the last I ever saw of them. People ask me where the snare drum is on that third album and I ask you Eddie, 'Where's the snare drum?' I loved Paul Rodgers' voice, as we all do, and I tried to keep it as clean as possible. A lot of singers are prone to doubling their voices (laying down two tracks of the same performance), putting it through a harmonizer, phasing and flanging it. When people hear their own voice they don't like it too much. Their albums got more processed but I tried to keep it clean, a little reverb, and put his voice right out there where it should be. And that's probably why I got fired, I was too vocal about keeping it clean. But after all, it's their production and they should be able to keep it the way they want it. Just because it's my taste doesn't mean it's necessarily their taste."

Peter Grant actually brought in the American because of his work with Zeppelin. And while the Page band bears no sonic similarities to Paul's troupe, there is an overall treatment running through both projects.

"First of all, the Zeppelin drum sounds from Headley Grange were created by setting up John Bonham in an entryway made of marble and wood," says Nevison, recalling the recording of the *Bad Company* album. "It had a really high ceiling. But it didn't work with Simon because he's more of a finesse drummer; he wasn't this power drummer. You couldn't have had two more different drummers than Simon and John Bonham. Simon had a couple of tom toms and more of a groove thing, a hypnotic style and Bonham was the power drummer.

The ultimate goal was to produce a steady rhythm track; most of the original takes resulted in keepers, save for the odd double. An auxiliary song called "Superstar Woman" was laid down but never used. Upon completion, the album was organized and at the end of each track a space was cut out to eliminate the count-off for what followed. Nevison overlooked the splicing of the intro to "Can't Get Enough" and that resulted in the verbal countdown into the song. Everyone became attached to the intro and it became the opening for the album.

Even with the marvelous first step Nevison had taken with the band, the second and third albums didn't come easily. *Run With the Pack* was hands down the most difficult endeavor, owing to Simon's untimely accident and a myriad of distractions.

After mixing the first two records and beginning the third, Ron was given his marching orders. He maintains that the group was not happy with what he'd assembled but those in the know adopt a different slant. They declare that he allowed out-takes to be distributed to friends and were incensed on discovering this.

The engineer would be the first to fall prey to the invisible animal. Oddly, he would work once again with Paul years later on a symphonic project – a classical orchestra interpreting various rock standards. "He still treated me like an engineer, 'You just push the buttons.'"

Paul Rodgers was nominated as the ideal candidate for a medley of "Imagine", "Penny Lane", "Blackbird" and "Come Together" – an eleven-minute piece completed in one day. Anne Wilson from Heart and Paul knocked off a duet of "Norwegian Wood". Paul's mood was less than jubilant upon seeing Nevison once again. "You could tell there was something there; it wasn't like the feeling I got from other artists I'd previously worked with."

Engineer Eddie Kramer, he of Jimi Hendrix and Led Zeppelin fame, was the replacement soldier who stepped in to complete the *Run With The Pack* project. Kramer cut some tracks, did overdubs and mixed the entire proceeding. By the time Eddie entered the picture, the affair was extremely "organized". He had previously worked with the band on an edit for an earlier single (Kramer seems to recall "Feel Like Makin' Love" as a likely title but this is not confirmed) and was already acquainted with their work.

"It was probably because I had a knowledge of the band, was British, had worked with Zep, and had edited the single that made them very happy. The office called me up and said they were coming to California and would I help them? Of course I said, 'Yeah.'"

Sessions took place at Kendun Recorders in Burbank, California. In an elevated mood since ousting Nevison, they plowed through the material. Kramer recalls this as a "fun time."

"It was a good mix of talent, the band sounded wonderful. I was very concerned about getting the mixes as good as I possibly could. I remember going back to the house and sitting with Mick and making sure that the record actually sounded the way they wanted it to. They were very devoted to getting the record sounding right. I think we achieved that."

KOSS KEEPS CRAWLING

*Inspiring, tragic at times, emotionally
up and down ... always Kossoff.*

-Rabbit Bundrick

While Bad Company was firing engineers, finishing albums and undergoing major promotional and marketing strategies, Paul Kossoff was simply trying to make it through another day. Unable to complete the album begun in Los Angeles, he opened the door, for the second time, to guitarist Snuffy Walden. The Texan underscored all the six-string parts and Kossoff, when he was able, would come in for a quick round of soloing and embellishment parts. With a finger splint adorning his left-hand, this was a rather cumbersome ordeal.

Koss had bonded with Zeppelin's John Bonham, a notorious drinker and mean drunk. No good came from this association and on many instances Paul could be found with his new friend in the studio bathroom, inhaling and downing everything in sight.

Tony Braunagel and Terry Wilson, the drums/bass rhythm section out of Texas, took on double-duty when Kossoff became increasingly difficult to manage. With no real producer on staff, they helped coordinate sessions, scheduled overdub periods and generally kept momentum going.

"I don't know if anybody would appreciate me saying this but those two records we did with Crawler (*The Band Plays On; 2nd Street*) didn't really have a producer; we were the ones who really saw it through," recalls Braunagel. "We made sure shit actually happened and got onto tape and got overdubbed and somebody actually mixed it. It was our spearheading that pushed it all through. And I'm not saying that to take credit away from anybody but oftentimes Paul was not together enough to be in the game.

"We tried to do everything live, even vocals. Paul, if he got a good rhythm track was cool, but he really liked to get out there and overdub. Paul liked to get out there and crank up two 200-watt Marshalls and it was so incredibly loud. It was so loud that other studios in the complex would say, 'Hey, guys, what's going on? A spaceship landed?' It was raw and I just got big, fat wide-open drum sounds and played. We just went for it; we got high and had a ball. Everything was there – drugs, girls, the whole thing."

While Back Street Crawler was in L.A. and attempting to pull together the pieces of the record, Bad Company was also in town to play two sold-out nights at the 17,000-plus Inglewood Forum. Kossoff's finger splint had been removed and the band was booked into the Starwood, a sweaty 400-seat rock bar. Communication was re-opened amongst the principals, Johnny Glover and Peter Grant, and Koss and blood brother Kirke. A call was made to Andy Fraser to see if he might want to join his former crew on stage. To no one's shock, he turned the offer down. The ex-Mayall minion would never see his friend again and would not even attend his funeral.

This crossroads, this nexus, is alternately scintillating and morbidly sad. Here, on the one hand are Paul and Simon, re-defining arena rock and selling records as quickly as they could be pressed. Headlining two nights at the famed Forum, the grand palace that had played host to everyone from The Rolling Stones to Jimi Hendrix to Led Zeppelin, they had returned as conquerors. This was the same venue Free had played years earlier when opening for Blind Faith. On the other hand, Paul Kossoff, openly accepted as one of the most innovative and soulful players to ever strap on a guitar, was holding court at a small, though highly regarded rock den in front of a few hundred passionate observers. History weaves a mighty web and entangles us in inescapable predicaments. It just seems so strange, so acutely bizarre, that the three former band boys would not be on stage together. Well, they would in a patchwork fashion.

"Kossoff had broken his fingers and they asked me to come in and do a record with them," maintains Walden. "And I did and Kossoff came in and played across that record once I'd done the tracks. And again I don't even know if I got credit on the record.

"I was only out [on tour] for a short while and I'd go out and play and Kossoff would come on and play. He'd broken his fingers and come on and do one or two solos using one or two fingers. It wasn't an extended tour; I maybe did a week or two. I always thought they were really talented and was honored to go do what I did."

Paul and Simon ended up jamming with Back Street Crawler on their closing numbers, having had to race across town after their Forum appearance. This was the last time Rodgers and Kirke would see Paul alive. Even Boz and Mick joined Koss on stage, somehow sensing the curtain was being lowered.

"We jammed together." Rodgers' words are simple, and yet the impact on his former guitar player was immediate and immense. Kossoff was absolutely glowing and maybe he had been waiting for this fated moment to finally allow himself to slip into that long and restful sleep.

But those feelings of ecstasy were quickly erased. *The Band Plays On* had been a perpetual disaster and *2ⁿᵈ Street* was no different. Recorded variously in New York and Los Angeles, the sessions ran along the same chaotic lines as its predecessor. Snuffy Walden was brought in for another appearance and Kossoff, when functional, would record the odd overdub. Rabbit replaced Mike Montgomery and the feel on this follow up album has a stronger southern Texas R&B groove than the first.

Richard Digby-Smith was again pulled in to keep Koss as sober as possible and enlisted Johnny Glover as watchdog. In fact, according to Tony Braunagel, Glover could sense the guitarist's speedy flameout and suggested they finish the *2nd Street* album as quickly as possible. The record company didn't seem to mind Paul's decline and hastened the recording process. Glyn Johns, Andy's older brother, was recruited to mix the album.

For the rock glitterati, limits are always pushed and boundaries continuously expanded. Barely able to hold a guitar or speak in an intelligible fashion, Kossoff was given the green light to undergo a twenty-date British tour commencing on 25 April 1976. We expect so much from those faces adorning album covers, from those names we hear *ad infinitum* on the radio and television. In some respects, they are held to a higher magnification – they're expected to live forever and in so doing provide us with the soundtrack to our lives. We can't accept their mortality and upon playing their last notes, we're almost angry with them for leaving us alone, abandoning us to our silent rooms and spaces with no melody.

But Kossoff was still in the City of Lost Angels and his descent back into addiction was swift and perilous. Having seen his former Free friends, he was bolstered for the moment. But this gave way to the never-ending high.

"There were times when Paul had so many friends around who just wanted to comfort him," eulogizes Wilson. "I remember one time at the Sunset Marquee during the *2nd Street* record, I was close to quitting the band because of the turmoil. He had broken two different fingers different times by falling down from overdosing. I walked into his room and he had a couple of his friends there that brought some barbiturates and some other stuff. I walked in and was so pissed at the girl who was there. Her name was Leslie I think, but went by the name of Dale. She said we, the band, didn't understand him and his needs; I proceeded to tell her that there was a girl or guy in every town who said the same thing, who would go score him something just to get closer to Koss and hang with him. She didn't know he had overdosed a couple of months earlier and had doctors' warnings to stop all drug use. These very doctors had revived him from an earlier death. She was not happy with me and went for me – knocked my glasses off of my face. A roadie ended up pulling me off of her. I wanted to scare her so bad that she would not come around again. A day later we were on the plane going to New York to play Atlantic Records the new album when Koss died – from the very drugs Dale or Leslie or whatever her name was scored for him. It turned out he had gotten heroin, valium and seconals from her."

The label wanted to talk about upcoming tours and hear the mixed masters of the *2nd Street* album, so a stopover had been planned on the way home to England. Terry Slesser decided to stay over in Los Angeles and didn't join the band for the four-hour flight to New York. Paul Kossoff sat next to Tony Braunagel on that flight. When the plane began its descent, a stewardess inquiring as to the whereabouts of his friend awakened the drummer. Koss was not in his seat. Braunagel takes up the narrative.

"I was sitting next to him on the plane when we took off and I woke up in New York and he wasn't sitting next to me. I could feel the plane coming down and I was asleep because it was a redeye over-night. I had a couple of cocktails and I don't know if I took anything, a valium, and I just passed out. Paul was on his way out. He'd died earlier; his heart had stopped, about a year earlier in England when we were back there after the first record.

"Paul was in the hospital and they brought him back and told him if he ever did drugs again he wouldn't live. He was clean for a minute but not much more and when we did the *2nd Street* record he continued to stay incapacitated. That's why we had Snuffy come out and play some of the gigs and do some rhythm tracks.

"I can't tell a romantic story, I won't lie. We had a meeting the night before and there was some unrest. When you're that young, you really don't pay close attention to every conversation that goes on. We were staying at the Hyatt House and it was absolutely nuts rock 'n' roll going on, chicks room to room, everybody high, drugs all over the place – it was great.

"So we had a meeting with Paul and I remember him saying something like, 'I don't think I'm going to be playing with you guys when we get back to London.' And I'm thinking, 'That's strange, that's really strange.' I knew that he was really loaded and that next night we left to get on the plane, I knew that he was packing drugs. He even offered me some of them. An array. I just said, 'No thanks.' He and I liked each other and we got along well and he liked my spunky spirit. And I'm a small guy, not as small as he was, but smaller than most of the guys around me, and yet I always have a tough persona. So we got along real well in that respect and we talked. He offered me drugs and I said no, I had my own.

"We got on the plane and he was sitting next to me in the middle seat. I woke up and looked in the seat next to me and he's not there. I looked at the road manager a few rows up and said, 'Hey, Johnny, where's Paul?' and he says, 'I dunno.' That's when the plane started coming down in New York City and I see people running up and down in the aisles. The next thing I know, the plane lands, they get everybody off the plane, and they get all the guys in the band over to the side. We find out then that they had to break into the bathroom. And he died."

On 19 March 1976, one of the world's finest and most emotional guitar players had closed his eyes for the last time. Shockingly, Paul Kossoff was only 25 years old.

Braunagel, in a lighter mood, mentions that he had drugs on his own person and here they were, the entire band talking at close quarters with the New York Police. Not sure if the group would be searched, Tony asked a policeman, "Hey, can I go to the bathroom?" The cop replied in the affirmative and the drummer went into the facility and consumed the drugs he had on him.

"I was high as a fuckin' kite and that's how I started the day. Paul being dead. Pretty decadent really."

With this catastrophic turn of events, the machinery ground to a halt. Atlantic Records, and label president Ahmet Ertegun, saw in Kossoff's Back Street Crawler a band with a huge future. Kossoff was being groomed as the next Eric Clapton or Peter Frampton.

"If Paul had been at even half health, we could have been a big rock 'n' roll band. Who knows? But it all failed right there with his death and that was pretty much it."

The New York label, home to Led Zeppelin and others, tried to keep the wheels turning but the game was up. Tony blames much of this on manager Johnny Glover.

"I never dug management, the guy has ripped us off. He's taken outtakes and re-released and re-licensed stuff. I've never seen a publishing statement. He says Terry and I signed a paper that gave our publishing to him. We'll never see any money from the Crawler stuff because of this guy and he's still out there doing it."

Geoff Whitehorn came in to replace Kossoff but by this time Atlantic Records had cooled on the band.

"The thing with replacing Kossoff was like this," Whitehorn recalls. "Back Street Crawler, or more to the point their record company, wanted a name guitarist to join the band to replace Koss and had asked Mick Taylor (Rolling Stones) if he fancied doing it. Mick, having already done the 'dead man's shoes' routine with Brian Jones, was understandably reluctant to do it again. I was working with a friend of Mick's, Colin Allen, who happened to mention this to me at the time. I expressed interest, and my name was put forward as a possible candidate.

Just before I was offered the Crawler gig (1976), I did an audition for Andy Fraser, got the gig, and spent the next few weekends going down to his house in Woking. At the audition he played (very fine) bass, and there was a drummer there too (Tony Hicks, ex- Back Door) who I never saw again, and Andy never picked up a bass again, either. All he wanted to do was play the piano. I made my excuses, and Andy moved to California very shortly after that.

"They never really told me that I'd got the Crawler job, but we sort of drifted into a rehearsal situation, and then, all of a sudden, we found ourselves onstage at the Marquee club doing a couple of gigs for a drug charity (with Koss's father, David, in the audience), followed by a short British tour (with AC/DC as our opening act!). I was extremely apprehensive about how the audiences might react to this new guy playing guitar that most of them had never heard of, but I needn't have worried. They were all very supportive and we just took it from there, really, making a couple of albums and touring incessantly.

"Eventually, we had to do our third album. The band kind of relocated to Houston, Texas, which is where Braunagel, Rabbit and Wilson were from originally, and we rehearsed, wrote and did demos and all the usual stuff. Meanwhile, Rabbit had had an offer to join The Who, and he was agonizing about this, because he didn't want to let us down. So, we fired him! Just to let him off the hook, really, and of course, he's still working with The Who to this day. Without Rabbit, we did some demos for this third album and the record company decided to dispense with our services forthwith (this was early 1979). Punk music was the thing, and Crawler was a luxury they could do without!

Playing with Rabbit was (almost!) always a pleasure because he's such a creative guy who just lives for his music. I consider myself reasonably dedicated, but Rabbit is in a different league. If you were to take his music away from him he would literally die, I'm sure of it! We still work together on various projects, mostly by post (God bless modern technology). The last time we actually toured together was on a Roger Daltrey tour in 1994, and Rabbit got fired from that for drinking too much (again!). He's now given up drinking altogether, and is a much happier man on the strength of it.

In 1990/91, I played with Bad Company on the Holy Water tour, and, of course, Simon was the only original member of the band. He was naturally very fond of Koss, but I don't recall the subject coming up very often. I also worked with Rodgers from 1995-8. He, too, was pretty reticent about Paul K, but I do remember him once saying that, had Koss still been alive, they would still be working together in some capacity."

Around the same time, Glover was replaced with Abe Hoch, formerly working with Peter Grant and Swan Song. Crawler was trying escape from Atlantic's clutches and from Glover. Hoch released the band from both contractual obligations while Tony and crew went to Glover's house to retrieve master recordings the manager had been hoarding.

Tony does have memories of Paul when he came back down to earth. The band had caravanned between Los Angeles and New York in order to lay down tracks but on Braunagel's suggestion, the group headed south to Texas, his stomping ground. He and Terry thought re-locating to the land of oil wells and cowboy boots would prove to be a positive shift. A small rehearsal room was found and Koss actually improved his physical and mental outlook. The trio visited a local bar where blues guitarist Rocky Hill, brother of ZZ Top's Dusty Hill, was performing. Dusty was a pure-bred Texas player with an illustrious pedigree and "knew every blues song in the world."

"Paul got up and sat in and man, he was clear and lucid, and I heard the kid. This is the kid who started playing guitar and then formed a band called Free. This is the kid who played on 'All Right Now'. I was amazed and it was wonderful I was getting the opportunity to hear this. He had that crying single vibrato thing that was so totally Paul and there are so many guitar players who knew he was famous for that. A lot of people copied that style later on and that's why Ahmet Ertegun saw 'Jeff Beck, Eric Clapton, Paul Kossoff.'"

Braunagel, a sensitive soul locked to a crazy rock temperament, knew the time in Texas had paid dividends. Paul pulled himself together – at least for a moment – and during this period the pair would talk about music and personal issues. As many Kossoff comrades would suggest, a not-so-positive relationship with his father may have triggered a large part of the guitarist's cravings.

"There was father/son friction which is to be expected if you're growing up in a Catholic or Jewish family where they expect you to be a doctor or lawyer or in my case, a priest. I think there were some clashes there and I heard people saying his dad was rough on him for that. I don't know if his dad was nicer to his brother or just what the dynamics were – if you could call it dysfunctional. But I do know when his dad came around there was friction. Some people try and tell me things his dad didn't do right during that time but I don't really fault anybody. I'd like to say his dad did work hard in supporting the whole thing at the end."

While Braunagel still retains less-than-loving feelings about management, he has kept in contact with the other players. Communication has even escalated to the level of conjuring up a New Millennium version of Back Street Crawler. Terry Wilson, Rabbit, Terry Slesser and Geoff White-horn have been in e-mail contact regarding a reunion. Tapes would be mailed via the post with each member adding his part to existing tracks. So far, Bundrick has written seven tracks, sent them to Terry and Tony to add bass and drums, and then these tapes were mailed to Geoff Whitehorn for guitar overdubs. Rabbit has coaxed Slesser into recording vocals. When the tracks are completed Terry and Tony will mix the twelve to fourteen tracks, send the completed record to various labels and hope to secure a small advance.

Terry Wilson, who will present several of his own songs to this future Crawler project, has his own edited memory of that fateful flight.

"We got to La Guardia and I'm waiting at the baggage carousel for my bags and the rest of the guys. I had met a girl on the plane and was talking to her when Johann (Paul's bodyguard) came up to me and said Paul was in the plane's bathroom and they couldn't wake him up, couldn't revive him. He didn't say he was dead and finally someone came down and told us he was gone.

"All I could remember was the last conversation I had with Paul. He came up and sat down on the arm of my aisle chair halfway through the flight and was asking if I was going to quit the band? What was I going to do? I remember telling him that I was just tired of the whole Back Street Crawler rock 'n' roll thing and the drugs getting in the way of the music and I didn't know what I was going to do. That we would go back to England and mix the album and see what was going to happen.

"Then at the airport we get the news and we go immediately to Atlantic Records to make phone calls to his dad to tell David of Paul's death. There was a couple of hours of waiting before we got a hold of David; he was somewhere in Scotland on one of his talking tours. When David returned the call I had to tell him of Paul's death. It was pretty weird – I think David knew Paul was not long for this world.

"A couple of years ago (circa 1999) on a tour with Stephen Bruton in England, I had lunch with David Kossoff at his house. I asked him about that very phone call and his clarity, the questions he asked about Paul. He said he had time to think about Paul's life and about Paul maybe dying soon and had wondered about what Paul was going through – was he happy at the end? What was he playing like? What were his spirits like?"

Tony, like Terry, was close to Paul if not exactly soul mates. The bassist admits he was not ready for the skyrocket he'd been attached to. But his greatest wish was that Paul would have healed sufficiently for the band to continue touring and recording.

"I think that if Paul had gotten through the drug thing he would have been a much better player. It would be great if we could have met up later."

Bad Company, in New Orleans, received the news via Peter Grant who had been contacted by Glover.

"It was soon after we jammed with Paul that he died. That was the last time I saw him." Paul Rodgers, one of Kossoff's closest friends, was brokenhearted. He and Simon sent a wreath to Paul's home.

Close companion and bearer of the Kossoff torch, Sandhe Chard probably knew him as well as anyone. A part of her died with the gentle Koss on that doomed flight.

"There were some nights I thought Paul was dying and I'd call an ambulance. I needed help and I'd call his parents even though I knew he'd be mad at me. Financially they helped. He didn't have a good relationship with his dad. It was just a bad situation. It was a struggle and we did the best we could.

"I met Slesser for the first time since the funeral at an old pub in England and he went into a tirade how he loved Paul. I think I'm the only person in the world who loved Paul. To me it was just a struggle to keep the man alive. I had Paul and that's all I could want out of life.

"He would blow so much money on drugs; we lived about two blocks from Island Records. My neighbors actually went out on Portobello Road to sell fruit and vegetables and they'd feed us. I'd go and help the neighbors with the stalls and they'd leave their kids with Paul; he might not wake until noon but he'd take care of those kids. They trusted their children with Paul.

"He always had about nine guitars set up and was always playing. He tried to sing but he couldn't. He always had the reel-to-reel going and he'd let me do the tambourine. But he loved his friends to the end and they loved him. We'd all sit and listen to Muddy Waters albums, the *Highway* album which was one of Paul's favorites, and the Champion Jack Dupree album he did with Simon [with Black Cat Bones]. Hendrix was banned from the house because he'd get stoned and listen to him. And of course Cream. My cat was called ECPC, Eric Clapton pussy cat. And Paul got the guitar Eric gave him and I had a new bridge put on; I bought all his new strings and carried his equipment – I didn't know at the time I was his old lady, I thought I was a roadie. He had a great [Gibson] Melody Maker but one of the cats knocked it over and broke the neck. And then he had that white Stratocaster he used with Back Street Crawler that he got from Jimmy McCulloch, my boyfriend before him.

"That's all I can tell you about him. He was an intellect, a great reader. His face when he played was … God. He went there. He went to places we don't know. What I find interesting is the man has been dead for what, twenty-four years, and there's still so much interest. Hendrix was his idol but he loved Clapton. We named our cats Layla, Derek, Ginger, and Jack – I stopped naming them Jack because they ran away.

"I was in L.A. while they were recording [*2ⁿᵈ Street*], stayed with him, went back to Detroit to fly home, and that's when they called me and told me he died on the plane. Nobody ever called me, Johnny Glover was supposed to – and I got a call from Jennie. I said, 'He's alive,' and she said, 'No, he isn't.' That's when I lost it.

"The bad times that stayed with me for about fifteen years are gone, and all I can remember are the happy times. I didn't know this many people wanted to know about this man."

A touching and heartfelt tribute to this master musician.

WHEN THE MUSIC'S OVER

I contributed my whole life and soul to Crawler and Free.
                                                -Rabbit Bundrick

With Paul gone and Back Street Crawler paroled from the shackles of
Johnny Glover's management company and Atlantic Records, steps were
taken to re-kindle, if possible, the band's diminished profile. Abe Hoch
organized a deal with CBS/Epic Records and this new lineup was once
again perceived as the "happening guys". Their first plunge was *Crawler*
and contained "Stone Cold Sober", a radio-friendly track that attracted
broadcast exposure. With heavy label support, Crawler, their new abbreviated appellation, was poised to break big. But the cigar-smoking heavies in
New York, those kings of caprice, lost interest. They simply linked these
gritty survivors to bands such as Foreigner, Boston and Kansas, the groups
du jour. Crawler was a far more R&B tinged outfit, splattered with soul
drippings, and consequently the debut and its follower, *Snake, Rattle &
Roll* (released in 1977 and 1978 respectively) slithered swiftly into obscurity.

"The second album was produced by Gary Lyons but we were kind of
co-producing our own stuff," offers Braunagel. "We came up with our persona and music and when we went to make a third record, we went back
to Texas. We had about twenty songs but Gary didn't hear any hits that
would compete with Boston's latest huge hit or Styx or any of those other
fuckin' bands. He misrepresented us and went to the record company and
said, 'I don't hear any songs' and they dropped us."

Lyons was not the sole destroyer. Rabbit, who had taken to drinking
heavily, was offered the prime position of backing The Who. Tossed around
were the ideas of either carrying on as a trio or locating a replacement keyboardist or guitar player. Braunagel was faced with the option of moving
back to England or remaining on home turf; he opted for the latter and
six months later re-located to the West coast and has resided in California
since late November 1979. Within a month of the move, he was already
backing Eric Burdon on three movies, touring and engaging in film work.
Rickie Lee Jones summoned him and had the drummer accompany her on
several tours. Bette Midler, similarly, used Braunagel as her touring percussionist. Through Jones, he was hired on by Bonnie Raitt and stayed with

her for over eight years, touring and appearing on a couple of tracks from her landmark *Nick Of Time* album and the successor *Luck Of the Draw*.

Suffering from the road dog blues, he then opted out of touring engagements to remain in town and pursue studio work. Jack Mack and The Heart Attack became a regular client until Taj Mahal's management contacted him. Taj has become an integral part of his musical pursuits and he has appeared on Mahal's *Phantom Blues* (1996) and *Senior Blues* (1997).

On the lighter side, Tony has become a member of Jim Belushi's backing band and occasionally does a Blues Brothers combo when Dan Aykroyd joins the late John Belushi's brother on stage.

"I'm still great friends with everybody in the Crawler band. And if Paul was still alive and healthy, we'd still be doing it. I hate to make it sound like Paul made it all fall apart but it was all about Paul. When he wasn't healthy, it all fell apart. At the end of the day, I loved Paul – I look back on him and I smile. That's why it's so hard for me to be honest with you and tell you one thing and knowing in my heart I liked Paul. Paul was a loveable guy, had a great smile, you had to love the guy. He was very sweet and not an obnoxious kind of asshole. Especially when you compare it to being around Paul Rodgers; Paul is difficult to be around – edgy and full of himself. Simon and I were friends."

In yet another twisted coincidence, Tony played on Andy Fraser's *Fine Fine Line* album.

"I got a call to come play with him. I went to play with him at his house in the hills. We'd rehearse and it was coming together, we had a cool band. We went in to make a record and we were backed by Kim Turner, assistant manager for The Police and Sting. And Andy was another weirdo. We rehearsed all these songs at his house and then when we went in to do the record, he started taking LSD during the sessions. Showing up and standing in the corner with his arms folded over his chest with sunglasses on and wanting to change everything we'd rehearsed. I asked him what the problem was and he said, 'It's just not happening.' Non-communicative. In the end I didn't even get fired; I called up there one day and they had another drummer. That all fell apart and Andy moved out to the desert and continued doing drugs. I don't think he's doing well right now. But he had a great voice and didn't play bass in this project. He had a good voice and wrote really good upbeat songs.

"I hope he's doing OK and I didn't hold this against him. I tried to contact him after all this went down and got no response. That album was really fuckin' good but it just never happened – punk, New Wave and all that was happening so maybe it was the wrong time."

After the final burning down of Back Street Crawler, the other members found their own way in the world. Terry Wilson and Terry Slesser have remained out there battling the beast. The former bassist has toured and recorded with Stephen Bruton and features on *What It Is* (1993) and *Right On Time* (1995). Wilson has enlisted wife Teresa James and performs on her solo debut, *The Whole Enchilada* (as of this writing, still unreleased). The vocalist was the singer on Charlie (1983), a project involving Terry Thomas, the producer who'd later work with the revamped Bad Company on *Holy Water* and others. Much in demand, Slesser has blasted his tonsils with Geordie and Iron Maiden. He turned down an offer from Wishbone Ash.

Keyboardist Mike Montgomery surfaced in The Score, a band with Charlie Tumahai from BeBop Deluxe. He formed Rough House after moving back to New York but was presented with the horrific diagnosis of lung cancer and succumbed in 1991.

Snuffy Walden tried to revive Stray Dog after the crumbling of Back Street Crawler and managed to assemble *Stray Dog* and *While You're Down There*, in the years 1973 and 1974. The Texan went on to work with Laura Branigan, Rita Coolidge, Eric Burdon, Donna Summer and Stevie Wonder. He finally quit the road in 1984 after accompanying Chaka Khan on her world tour supporting *I Feel For You*.

Like everyone else around him, he battled a cocaine addiction – as did Rabbit and Kirke – and in 1996 began an association with the New Age label, Windham Hill. His contributions appear on *Winter Solstice, Summer Solstice* and *Wood & Steel*, compilation records featuring various label artists.

But his greatest notoriety has evolved from his work on television theme music. He now works on more than seven shows concurrently and in September 2000 garnered his first Emmy for *Outstanding Achievement In A Main Title* for his renderings on *The West Wing*.

John Bundrick, after Kossoff's passing, remained a Crawler and was part of the two Epic records, *Crawler* and *Snake, Rattle & Roll*. In December 1978 he was invited to join The Who and has remained with them ever since. *Face Dances* (1981) and the Townshend/Ronnie Lane collaboration *Rough Mix* (1977) sport Rabbit's key thumpings. He would have appeared on *Who Are You* had he not broken his wrist during an evening of Keith Moon madness.

Like Walden, his session career is mind-bending: John Martyn, Jess Roden, Amazing Blondel, Bob Marley & The Wailers, Speedy Keen, Donovan, Jethro Tull, Snowy White, Sandy Denny, Eric Burdon, Jim Capaldi, Mick Jagger, Roger Waters and Joan Armatrading are a few of his entries.

His two Island solo albums have been discontinued but never one to allow hands to remain idle, John recorded *Dream Jungle* in 1988. Many

Bundrick bundles followed including *Same Old Story, Run For Cover*, and *Tour Guide*, the latter reuniting Whitehorn, Slesser, and outsiders Snowy White and Janne Schaffe.

Always intrigued by America's indigenous peoples, he created *Moccasin Warrior, Quanah Parker: Moccasin Warrior II* (with Whitehorn on guitar and Dobro aficionado B.J. Cole), and a third as yet unreleased finale titled *Taiowa*.

Tetsu Yamauchi, after breaking ties with Free in 1973, became one of the Faces and his first recording with them was *Overture/Coast To Coast* a year later. He attempted to create a solo persona in his native Japan but was greeted with mixed reactions. In 1972 an eponymously labeled record was released and four years later *Tetsu & The Good Times Roll Band Live* was issued. His fledgling work with Samurai can be found on the *Samurai* and *Kappa* albums (1970 and 1971). The bassist now resides and rocks in Japan.

Wendell Richardson returned to his original home of Antigua. There he performs with his own creation, The Digital Interface Band, and recently released *Odello Super Groove* in 1999.

CLOUDY WEATHER

Despite all science ...
we will never understand the sadness
of certain notes.

-Ethan Canin

While everyone was trying to forget the unforgettable and Paul and Simon had buried their grief along with their best friend, a world still awaited Bad Company. The marketplace had embraced the band with open arms. Their first three albums had found the mark in the commercial world and swept away not only Free acolytes but new converts as well. *Bad Company*, *Straight Shooter* and *Run With the Pack* were essential listening and the expectations created by this triumvirate had raised the bar to lofty heights.

Weary from the road and still hurting from Kossoff's recent death, the quartet may not have been completely prepared to begin work on the fourth album. But just as night follows day and time inexorably marches forward, so do the wheels of industry never cease turning. According to Simon Kirke "striking while the iron was hot" became an unspoken credo and at the outset of 1977 everyone ventured back to Pontoise, France, to set the wheels in motion.

Burnin' Sky became the first Bad Company project not to break into the Top Ten, stalling at number fifteen (a still remarkable achievement by anyone's measuring) while the title single limped its way to number 78. The British press, sensing a slight trickle of blood, questioned, "Is there a crack in the sky?" Like vultures they circled over the developing sessions and, cunning animals as they are, their instincts were not far off.

"That album was a little bit tired," confessed Kirke. "It suffered from a touch of burn out. We'd been touring constantly and we had been on the album/tour carousel for nearly three years and quite frankly we needed a rest. We were all a bit knackered. But there were a couple of good songs there."

David Bowie and Iggy Pop were stationed at the same studio and were running behind schedule by three or four days. This odd couple were in France working on the ex-Stooges first solo album, *The Idiot*. But the delay was taken in stride and the whole crew spent the time French romping.

Says Simon, "We hung out together. Bowie was a fascinating guy and we struck up quite a rapport with him. I never realized what a great sax player he was. Witty and charming, we quite forgave him the fact that he was delaying the start of our next album."

When recording began in earnest, these perpetual tax exiles were confronted with a sobering thought – material was not exactly in abundance. But they made it through and *Burnin' Sky* revealed itself as a quirky assemblage, strident at times, but balanced with the anthemic pulse as demonstrated by the title track.

"The title track was like a movie theme," gushes Kirke. "Great imagery. Boz spiced it up a bit by suggesting that jerky beat. It was a bugger to begin with but I eventually nailed it. I like 'Heartbeat' and 'Leaving You'. Perhaps the strangest part of the album was the 'Knapsack' song, an old tyrolean song which was a mild hit in England in the early fifties. God knows why we did it but it just seemed like a good idea at the time.

"The other song which raised a few eyebrows was the ultra-stoned 'Master Of Ceremony'. It was late at night, we were all pretty gone. Mick sat at the Hammond organ, Paul sat in a corner with a hand-held mike and we just jammed. It was a funky groove but in retrospect was an unlikely candidate for inclusion on the album."

Rodgers acknowledges the difficulties with this fourth step. Touring, the black hole created by Kossoff's passing and a general malaise all combined to create a mildly toxic brew.

"That was quite a tough album to make and I didn't think we were ready to go into the studio. I wrote a couple of songs in a hotel in Paris the night before we went to Pontoise. One of them was 'Burnin' Sky' and the other was 'Heartbeat'. Actually 'Burnin' Sky' would have never been written except for that pressure so in a way it's a good thing, I guess. I had that chorus floating around in my head for a long time and I thought, 'Wow, we need some songs for tomorrow; we've got to make an album – my God!' I sort of remembered that song, 'when the sky … is burnin'. So I got to the studio and what I did was work out some chords for the verses but I had no lyrics. And I got the band to play it and they thought it was cool and asked, 'How does the rest of it go?' And I go, 'I don't know, I haven't got any lyrics yet.' So we played it and I actually made the lyrics up in one take."

On recent solo tours, Paul has included the song in his set. He's also been told that fighter pilots, going into battle, would use this as a musical focus.

Even with Paul's immaculately conceived title piece, the album was not without its darker moments.

"We had a few glitches," chides the drummer in that wonderfully under-stated mode. "The classic one was after two or three days, I noticed that the stereo wasn't spread like it should be. I went from speaker to speaker and realized that there was no fucking stereo at all. A hasty conversation ensued with the engineer, whose English was not too good, and we found that one of the stereo drive speakers had blown. We had to re-record three songs.

"Paul had acquired a small caliber hand gun and used to practice on a little shooting range at the back of the house. Peter Grant came one day and during dinner we heard these shots. BANG. Peter says, 'Well there goes the engineer.' BANG. 'And the lead guitarist.' BANG, 'the bass player.' I was 'safe' inside at the table when I heard BANG BANG. They weren't even going to leave anyone alive to do a solo album.

"But the days were pretty good; thank God the weather was fine. But looking back we should have waited a bit before we went into record it (less than twelve months separated this album from *Run With The Pack*). The reviews were not very favorable though, and during the States tour to promote it, we definitely were not up to par.

"The main reason for this was our drink and drug intake; we all indulged although Paul gave up drugs during the recording of the album and never went back. But me, Mick and Boz all indulged to excess. Well, we were at that bulletproof part of our lives, our records were selling like crazy, we were pampered 24 hours a day – we must have been doing something right. So we indulged. Ah… the late seventies, nostrils and livers getting hammered left, right and center."

Another mushrooming concern was the growing hostility between Paul and Boz. Burrell, emerging from a jazz and blues fusion background, was bringing in different rhythmic textures. He'd created that tug-and-pull feel on "Burnin' Sky" and had matured into an inventive and stylistically char-ismatic bassist. In fact, when he'd talk about "chops" with Mick, Ralphs would kid him by retorting, "What the hell do you mean? Pork chops?"

Rodgers, whose rages would bedevil him throughout his solo career, felt "threatened" to use Kirke's terminology, by Boz.

"Boz added a different slant sometimes with his jazz background. He was very much a feel player in those days, relying on intuition rather than technique. He was playing an Ampeg Scroll neck fretless bass which was a monster to play in tune. A plunge in the deep end if ever there was one but he handled it pretty well. Paul, who is a mean bass player himself (this might account for some of the antagonism), picked it up once and put it down a few minutes later shaking his head.

"Boz was always trying different approaches to songs (in the same fash-ion Andy had). It was his jazzy leanings I suppose. God knows where

Paul got the idea from but he certainly had this particular burr under his saddle about Boz. We were all doing too many chemicals at this time and although Paul had stopped, he still drank. The hours were crazy – night had become day and vice versa. Paul was going through stuff at home but he never told us about it; he was a very private man."

EVERYBODY FALLS DOWN

It's the beat generation...
it's the beat to keep,
it's the beat of the heart,
it's being beat and down in the world ...

-from Jack Kerouac's *Desolation Angels*

Though *Burnin' Sky* did not do as well as the earlier albums, the group had set in motion an artistic and commercial tidal wave that carried them on yet another US tour. That safari, fueled by drugs and alcohol, pulled up to sold-out arenas and saw records still flying off the shelves.

In March 1979, Ridge Farm Studios in Dorking, Surrey, was the location where work began on *Desolation Angels*, a record trumpeting the addition of synthesizers to what had been an essentially organic sound of guitar, bass and drums. The hybrid worked. Ostensibly titled after a Jack Kerouac book, this fifth checker on the board became a number ten slot holder in Britain and ascended to number three in America. Serious pre-production focused on the sculpting and scratching out of material. The timeless "Rock 'n' Roll Fantasy", which reached number thirteen, spearheaded the affair.

"Paul had written that and it was a belter," enthuses Kirke. "The album sold very well and the tour was virtually sold out coast to coast. It was probably the best States tour of those years. But it was all coming to a crashing end."

Prophetic words indeed. The tidal wave was washing in on itself, creating undercurrents of frustration and animosity. Emotional heads were barely above water, the same precarious place they'd been so many times before. Out of a darkening sky, career-consuming predators were circling, seeking the weak and the unsure. You could hear the squawks and shrill warbling echoing around the night sky, these devil creatures zeroing in on any vulnerable bobbing head. Bodies were sinking under the weight of the very things that had once buoyed them – success, camaraderie and an unquenchable thirst for respect in an industry that did not even know how to spell the word.

Paul had grown increasingly disenchanted with Bad Company. Feeling shackled and stymied, this Middlesbrough man had been lashing out at fellow musicians – and not just Boz.

"I didn't feel Mick was pulling his weight about this time. I thought that we needed some more songwriting from his area. 'Rock 'n' Roll Fantasy' was a good single and that's what we needed. In those days particularly you needed a couple of singles anyway from a record to make it really kick in. And that was one. And I would include that in my [solo] set as well.."

Paul played all guitars on that track which was built around a Roland guitar synthesizer, one of the first midi-driven instruments of its type.

"This one was incredibly unreliable; it was all right if you didn't touch it or move it. It would cut out so it was terrible to take on tour. It was a bit of a problem. But it got a great sound in the studio and when I played the chords it sounded to me like a rock 'n' roll fantasy. And I thought, 'Hmmm, that's a good idea for a song.'"

The song registered at number thirteen and was followed by "Gone, Gone, Gone," a 45 release that barely edged its way into the Top 60. But more importantly, it was the song, as the title so accurately divined, proclaiming the band's final ride.

GOOD TIMES, BAD TIMES

I think it got a little crazy
for me at the end of the day.

-Paul Rodgers

Personal frustrations, ego battles, drugs and keeping secrets from one another – a witch's brew and a potion guaranteed to sicken the body within which these nasty venoms course. If this list of toxins sounds familiar, they are. This is what eventually destroyed Free, even prior to Kossoff's own self-victimization. Simon, however, maintains this was not the same predicament his first band had suffered. He felt Bad Company might have been saved, if only temporarily, had they been allowed to indulge in simple down time. Maybe they were simply confronted by a massive workload. But more importantly, the group required a steadier hand from manager Peter Grant, a man undergoing his own hellish torment.

1980 was a terrible year for the Zeppelin overlord and any specter haunting him, haunted his bands. On 25 September 1980, about a year-and-a-half after the completion of *Desolation Angels*, John 'Bonzo' Bonham was found dead at the home of Jimmy Page. He had choked in his sleep, a gentle term for suffocating on your own vomit, after a night of serious binge drinking. Less than three months later, on 8 December, John Winston Lennon was assassinated in front of his New York apartment. Mark Chapman, a psychopathic killer and avid Beatles fan, fired five bullets into Lennon's body. These two events, these two senseless and unimaginable moments, would forever change the destiny of four musicians who had come together as Bad Company.

Rodgers was and remains a devoted Beatles fan – a zealot – and the termination of his idol affected him deeply and personally. Paul's performance at Liverpool's famed subterranean rock den years later was a mere surface scratch in representing his devotion. He devoured books about the Beatles and was entranced by the songwriting partnership between Lennon and McCartney. Similarly, over the years, Simon had forged a bond with Bonham and when he passed, anger and helplessness ripped a hole in his soul. With an already rocky road laid out before them, musical differences now resulted in personal confrontations. It came as no surprise to anyone when Paul cut the cord.

"I think it got a little too crazy for me at the end of the day. I felt myself losing touch with reality. I think a number of things came into play, one of which was the death of John Bonham. I thought, 'Wow, man, what is the point? What are we doing? Where are we going with all of this?' And I just wanted to step back from the whole thing and understand what was going on. Again, it became this roller coaster that you were on and you had less and less control of. I just hate spinning out of control too much. I don't mind a little bit of it because that's unavoidable but when your whole life is spinning out of control and if music is your whole life and that's where that is, then you don't have any control. I just wanted to step back and stop being dizzy for a while."

Simon well understood his singer's sense of emotional vertigo. Touring, recording, promotional activities and just general synapse collapse had similarly affected the drummer.

"Paul was coming to the end of his rope with the endless workload and I think his domestic life was suffering too. When Lennon was shot, paranoia hit a lot of people – suddenly stars and celebrities were not safe anymore. No one had ever shot a rock 'n' roller before and the fact that this man was so revered by everyone just magnified the shock.

"Not surprisingly it was around this time that Paul said he wanted some time off to record – the dreaded words no group wants to hear – his own solo album. I think we all breathed a sigh of relief. We needed a break and Paul had been wanting to do this for some time. And so began a strange period for the rest of us. This break became extended more and more; weeks turned into months and before any of us realized it, a year had gone by.

"Bonzo's death signaled the end of Led Zeppelin and the subsequent demise of Peter Grant. It is common knowledge that he did a lot of drugs and about a year before had taken to his room and become a virtual recluse. This had frustrated us and Zep immeasurably and relations between us and him had deteriorated. Zep were pretty much running themselves and Peter was just not available to anyone. So during that time several members of the band had invoked a clause in their contracts allowing them to depart. It was a sad time all round. When Bonzo died it was like a house of cards crashing down."

Simon's kinship with Bonzo was a strange one. Where the former was quiet, intellectual and a gentleman while drinking, the latter tended towards the larger than life, turning up the volume both vocally and physically when partying. He is known to have spilled drinks on more than one journalist for asking indelicate questions. But they were both drummers, a fraternity unto themselves, shared the same label and management and, in each other, found kindred spirits.

"Bonzo deserves a whole chapter to himself. Me and him were mates. He was the greatest hard rock drummer ever. Hands down. He did stuff with his single bass drum that people couldn't do with two – witness 'Good Times Bad Times'. He was a very down to earth guy, mad on hot-rods, motorbikes, everyday guy stuff.

"We had a mutual appreciation of each other. There was a time when Bad Company was playing in Birmingham in the Midlands. We had just signed to Swan Song and on the first tour. When we arrived in their home-town, Bonzo and Robert Plant were there along with Jimmy Page. Now they hadn't played together for some time so we invited them on stage during one song. Bonzo was playing a couple of congas and at first when I went to hand over the kit to him he politely declined. But I wasn't having any of it. Percy [Robert Plant] was already up there and Jimmy was about to plug in. I insisted politely, 'Come on, you wanker,' and I kept the beat going with one hand while he played with the other while we swapped places on the drum stool. The crowd went nuts. I don't think Zep had played in England for years and here was three-quarters of them on stage.

"One time he dragged me out of bed when we were both staying at the Riot House (Continental Hyatt House) and he had this funny car in the garage. Well we shot out of the garage and down Sunset topping, I don't know 80-85. Sure enough we were pulled over by a cop. And Bonzo was all smiles when the furious cop comes up. After the usual questions Bonzo announces himself to be Zep's drummer whereby the cop's attitude does a 180. John pulls out some tickets for that night's show and the cop departs smiling, giving us a warning to just 'turn this thing around and go back to the hotel and we'll pretend this whole thing never happened.'

"I played drums alongside him on Zep's last ever tour of Europe. I went to his hotel suite and we practiced 'Whole Lotta Love', all 30 minutes of it, with hands on knees, me sitting opposite him on the bed. The show was incredible, we really locked in. I have a tape of it somewhere.

"I think of him most days …"

FOUR GONE CONCLUSIONS

If I don't really feel satisfied with the way the music is going …
I have a tendency not to put up with it for too long.

-Paul Rodgers

Everyone realized that the problems swirling about Bad Company had created almost insurmountable obstacles. Still, taking an eighteen-month hiatus to re-group and re-examine priorities, they came back together at Ridge Farm Studios in 1981 to record their sixth and final album with the original lineup. *Rough Diamonds*, as the appellation suggested, was meant as a return to their roots, a junking of synthesizers and overblown production values, in order to re-capture the crystalline earthiness that defined their earliest and most savagely intriguing works. But somewhere in the mix signals were crossed and good intentions went wrong. This final act, save for brief moments, recalled few of the primal tracks that danced barefoot on those records from 1973 and 1974.

"That was a strange one and we came in for a certain amount of criticism because… it wasn't rough," admits Rodgers. "People expected it to be almost a return to the roots of Bad Company and to be rough and I guess it wasn't. It was a little polished.

"I wanted the band to remember its roots. I got a gig together in a local village hall down where I lived out in the country. I didn't want to advertise it as Bad Company because it only held 200 people or something. So I advertised it as a band called Rough Diamonds. I sort of spread a rumor that it might actually be Bad Company so we had a whole cross-section of people there. We had Hell's Angels, Teddy boys, the local gentry; it was so funny because we had all these layers of society. There were near riots outside but it was a great gig."

Rough Diamonds still became a Top 30 insert on the US charts but "Electricland", the single, barely broke the Top 100. Disillusioned and still haunted and hurting from the deaths of Lennon and Bonham, the artful Rodgers had actually exited Bad Company following the release of *Desolation Angels*, but returned having spent time writing and in self-examination. In many ways the situation was reminiscent of Paul Kossoff's dilemma many years earlier. Koss had felt the need to spread his wings but knew he could not take flight within the aviary constructed by Paul and Andy. Though he was grounded on many occasions because of his chemical habits, the player ultimately broke free of constraints. And the singer felt compelled to do the same.

Simon sensed Paul's unease, having been there many times before. Recognizing the symptoms, he was waiting for the final cue.

"It all came to a head when Paul had disappeared for a couple of days. That was unusual; he was normally on hand for most things. But he came in one night where we were sitting in the house and launched a violent attack on Boz. Mick joined in and that kiss of death ensued – a fistfight. So that really was it. Paul's frustrations had spilled over and the band was teetering towards disintegration.

"We still recorded *Rough Diamonds* though and in spite of everything, I thought it was a decent album. 'Electricland' had great imagery from Paul; 'Gone, Gone, Gone' from Boz and 'Old Mexico' from Mick. 'Downhill Ryder' was good. But tensions were running high between us."

As high as the tidal wave upon which they'd been riding for six albums: national tours, high-spiraling singles and coverage in every music publication from Oklahoma to Okinawa. But the flow was ebbing and the waters turning icy.

During the hiatus between *Desolation Angels* and *Rough Diamonds*, Paul had been composing material for his own album, a project he'd mentioned more and more frequently during these waning weeks. Angry at the way the music was developing and physically confronting the people around him, Paul recorded his first solo album. Titled *Cut Loose* – he was never one for ambiguity – the 1983 Atlantic project was a pretty standard undertaking. He played all the instruments: drums, bass, guitar, keyboards and obviously vocals, at a studio newly-built at his home.

"It's not a vast departure from the stuff I've been doing with Free and Bad Company. But I think it's more of a self-expression. This album is a one-off thing really and something I had to get off my chest."

Rodgers may have seen this album as a temporary side trip but he had no foreseeable intention of returning to Bad Company.

"Bad Company came to a natural end. I am happy with the newfound freedom; it's nice to be back there again. I think Bad Company could have gone on for ten more years, but personally I didn't like the idea of becoming a national institution, although I wouldn't knock anyone for wanting to do that. [Actually Paul was quite incensed when Simon and company continued touring/recording without Rodgers]. But personally I wanted to find something that had a bit more of a challenge. We had a thing there and we could just slide into this routine. This new album is the ultimate challenge, I guess."

A typical session revolved around recording the main instrument on which the song was written – usually guitar or keyboards – along with a drum box rhythm track. The electronic drum kit was replaced with a real set and then vocals and guitars and miscellaneous overdubs were overlaid. Vocal keeper tracks were usually captured in one or two run-throughs in order to maintain spontaneity. This process was as foreign to Bad Company as a Martian would be in Manhattan.

"What we got into doing was to rehearse a song like mad in order to thrash out any arrangement faults. When you play a song for a long time, things that didn't appear obvious at first become apparent. We used to hammer things into shape that way.

"Everything [on the solo album] is new except a couple of the tracks are ideas I had kicking around for a while. Being an integral part of that band, I think I'm going to take away certain influences with me. I'd like to get some more material together to draw from so I'll probably record another album, something different again, and probably tour on the strength of the two albums."

While this first band deserter has been working on his own material, little attention was paid to the his former co-workers; he was only marginally aware of Simon's participation in Wildlife and Mick's solo album development. Still, there was no official announcement heralding the parting of ways, leaving the avenue open for reunification. Again, this bears an uncanny resemblance to the politics surrounding Free's first divorce – members went their separate ways but the door was always left slightly ajar pending reconciliation.

"We never actually made an announcement to the effect the band had split," states Rodgers. "Because after the first year we were apart, there was a chance we'd get back together. We all knew we needed to do other things and then maybe come back together refreshed. But it's been three years now and the chances are very slender indeed that we'll get back together.

"When I look back, the high point for me was the last tour we did in 1980. But it did leave us very burned out. The first album was special because we were an unknown band and we were instantly successful. There is a lot of pressure but it's not impossible to handle. It wasn't as if Bad Company had to split up, it's because we wanted to – to go into new things. The Stones went on, The Who went on, and on, and on. But I don't think that's necessarily what they wanted to do. We're different people and we look at it in a different way. I didn't want to get too much into a mechanical thing. I wanted to stretch out a little bit; it's risky but at the same time it's exciting."

The last records they completed, particularly the *Rough Diamond* finale, were a "little low key." Paul was "not too happy" with it, seeking a more explosive energy.

Cut Loose saw the light of day on 31 October 1983. Prior to this, Simon Kirke had supplied rhythm tracks on John Wetton's (another King Crimson renegade) 1980 endeavor, *Caught In the Crossfire*. He began working with Wildlife, a quintet guided by Steve and Chris Overland, and recorded one record named after the band in 1982. Mick Ralphs produced the album and from the ex-Bad Company connections, the group landed a deal with Swan Song. The drummer would re-pay the favor by playing on Mick's first solo step, *Take This!*, released in 1984. Simon had heard a Wildlife demo and when told that they were seeking a drummer and bassist, expressed an interest in joining up. Within the first five minutes of playing together, everyone sensed a bond and work began in earnest in building the first album. His decision was an easy one since Bad Company, now on a sabbatical running into its third year, left few fallback options. After Kirke's one-time workout with Wildlife, the group sought a new identity with a name change to FM.

"It wasn't working and we're not together at the moment and there is nothing planned for a long time," said Kirke at the time. "Paul and Mick have solo albums just completed and Boz is touring with Roger Chapman (ex-Family and Streetwalkers) in Europe. Everyone is happy doing what they're doing."

Wildlife, in which Simon replaced Pete Jupp, allowed the drummer more freedom. He readily admits, "I wasn't playing too good towards the end of Bad Company." Having grown bored and frustrated playing the same numbers, he saw in this new combination an opportunity to simply make "lovely noise".

Stewart Epps, Jimmy Page's house engineer, recorded *Wildlife*, and according to the stickman, was "the loudest engineer I'd ever worked with." The album, much like *Cut Loose*, had a distinctively live feel, a technique employed by both Free and Bad Company.

"I guess I've been involved in bands that are good live and if they are good live, the sound will come naturally in the studio."

Guitarist Steve Overland agrees with Simon's vision. He admits that with the inclusion of Kirke in the band it was "the break we were looking for." In addition, Wildlife managed to sign Peter Grant on as the lead management figure.

Wildlife, rounded out by Bob Skeat on bass and Mark Booty on synths, opened for Michael Schenker and despite regionally respected live performances, was devoured by the media monster and succumbed in mid-1984.

Since no corporate statement was made regarding the dissolution of Bad Company, there was always the hope – particularly in the mind of Simon Kirke – that reconciliation might be reached. But as weeks dissolved into months and months flowed into years, the concept lingered in the dead zone. Paul, in fact, was so absorbed in his new solo status, he barely kept in contact with the other members.

"For a couple of years, Mick, Boz and myself were involved in other projects. I took a band under my wing called Wildlife; played drums with them and made a pretty decent album. Mick got his solo band together and made an album and did about three gigs; but Peter Grant never really had his heart in the project and neither of our projects really got off the ground. Paul made the solo album he had long wished for but then came other projects, and the ARMS tour.

"We never had officially broken up and I think the three of us hoped that one day with the solo thing out of his system Paul would come back to the fold and off we would go again. But he joined the ARMS tour, which had the lineup of all time on it, and it was during that time he collaborated with Jimmy Page and sowed the seeds for The Firm.

"This was a rough time for me; I had been with only two bands in seventeen years and was kind of out on a limb health-wise, drinking too much, and career-wise, nothing in the pipeline."

LAWFIRM

Music is another planet

-Alphonse Daudet

Paul Rodgers has a short fuse. If the music does not touch him in a deep place, he seeks new palettes upon which to paint his sounds. After the self-assembled *Cut Loose*, he opened communications with Jimmy Page and was slowly drawn in to a project to be dubbed the ARMS benefit. Ronnie Lane had become afflicted with Multiple Sclerosis and in light of the courageous spirit he'd shown in the shadow of this crippling disease, friends had amassed around him in order to assemble a benefit in his honor.

"We got a call from Clapton's management about the ARMS tour," Paul recalls. "They said Jeff Beck would be out there and Joe Cocker and Clapton and a few people and they'd heard we [Paul and Jimmy Page] had been doing something together, I don't know how, and wanted to know if we could put a band together and come and support this thing. We were a little unsure because we thought, 'Wow, have we even got enough material?' We only needed half an hour because there were so many bands on, like the old days and the package tours, so we decided to go for it. Just for the experience. We weren't The Firm then, we were just Jimmy Page and Paul Rodgers, and that was the birth of The Firm."

Both artists had their roots in the blues and this is where they connected. The undoing of Bad Company happened around the same time Led Zeppelin came off the road because of Bonham's death. Jimmy and Paul began kicking around the idea of working together.

"At this time (circa 1981-1982), Jimmy came around to my studio that I'd put together for *Cut Loose*, just to see what I was up to really. We started to play, we started to write some songs, he played me some ideas and the first thing we put together was 'Midnight Moonlight Lady' which I thought was an incredible piece of music that he had written. He gave me a cassette of it which was often the way we worked in those days because I really needed to re-wind and work on it. And I wrote the lyrics to it and he came back and was really knocked out – it was really great."

The song would eventually wind up on the collaborative unit they assembled, a band called The Firm. The song title was later amended to "Midnight Moonlight."

Prior to the coupling of singer and guitarist, Page appeared with Jeff Beck and Eric Clapton and rallied around the former Small Faces bassist – the first time these three classic players had performed together. Glyn Johns undertook technical duties and with him on board, enlistees could not sign on fast enough. Joe Cocker, Charlie Watts, Simon Phillips, Bill Wyman, Jan Hammer, Andy Fairweather Low, Fernando Saunders, Ray Cooper, Kenny Jones, Steve Winwood and a host of other luminaries participated in the benefit. And of course Paul Rodgers and Jimmy Page were brought into this flamboyant fold.

Rolling Stone, in its 19 January 1984 issue, dedicated the cover story to these philanthropic performances and titled the project *Concert Of The Year*. ARMS stood for "Action Research into Multiple Sclerosis". There were only a few dates actually realized, one at the Royal Albert Hall and shows in Los Angeles and New York. But it was enough to sow the seeds of an idea resulting in the merging of Page and Paul to form The Firm.

"The ARMS show was absolutely the first time I'd played with Paul," elaborates Page. "There was no intention at that time to put a band together but I didn't have one and it was like an SOS really. Because Steve Winwood was singing at the Royal Albert Hall show in England but he wasn't coming to the States. So there I was without me fig leaf, so to speak. I had played with Paul a few times at his house; we had a couple of jams. I had been to his house and there were these bits and pieces but that was well prior, six or nine months prior, to the ARMS thing.

"I was terrified but I wanted to do the whole thing. It was funny because I said, 'Yeah, I'll do it, I'll do it, yeah, great!' but at the last moment I thought, 'Oh God, what am I gonna do?' It's the truth. Everyone else had notable solo careers. Like Stevie Winwood – fuck, he's had enough solo albums, and Eric, and Jeff [Beck]. But the fact was everyone was working so tightly together. Not for themselves but for the cause of it which was great. I'll tell you, I don't think any promoter could get those three guitarists doing that. Do you know what I mean? But for the right reason they're there.

"It felt good playing together, the three of us have never played together. We've never played together as the three of us. I've played with Jeff and Jeff has played with Eric and I've played with Eric but never the three of us."

Jimmy embodied bits and pieces from the Zeppelin days in establishing The Firm's sound.

"Oh, of course, everything. You're still pushing yourself onward, but you're still identifiable as yourself. "The only thing I can do in life is play guitar. It's a commitment to the guitar."

This benefit package opened Paul's eyes to the possibilities of pursuing different projects and would be the spark for what would become a lengthy solo journey.

"I wanted to move on and find other things," declares Rodgers about his desertion of Bad Company. Though he had been part of an ensemble situation since he initially made his southward trek from Middlesbrough to London, none of his collaborations really prepared him for what it might take to pursue a career as a soloist. In a band, he was able to bounce ideas off of other like-minded thinkers but out there as a lone voice all the decisions would fall on him. This did come as "a shock" and required a ramping-up period in order to prepare himself for life alone. And it also took his new audience time to accept a Paul Rodgers on his own, without Mick Ralphs or Andy Fraser or any of those other personalities the world had come to associate with him.

"They did accept me but they didn't know me. One of the things I had done was buried myself in the bands and not really featured the name Paul Rodgers. So people said, 'Well who's Paul Rodgers?' and when they said, 'He's the singer from Free and Bad Company,' they'd go, 'Oh, yeah, I know.' So it wasn't an instant recognition thing and that was a problem for a while, having to explain who I was all the time and which band I came from. But that's much easier now."

After going through a trial-by-fire period during the ARMS shows, Page and Rodgers continued the relationship. Working on new material and unearthing the peculiarities unique to each of them, they made a decision to work together and brought in the drums/bass duo of Chris Slade and Tony Franklin. Jimmy had a concrete concept in mind when choosing his backing band.

"I wanted to get a couple of hooligans, yeah. They're good guys and damn fine musicians. Tony is amazing."

Tony Franklin had been a mainstay with Roy Harper for the previous three years and it was during this time the pair met. Drummer Slade was a stickman for several bands and in another one of those rare coincidences, on the day the Zep guitarist contacted him, David Gilmour rang him for his own solo outing. A workaholic, Chris managed to fit both ventures into his schedule. But securing Paul as his frontman was Page's main priority.

"He was certainly good for me and I've been good for him, too," muses Page. The band would record the 1985 debut *The Firm* – they'd originally knocked around the moniker The Royal Court Of China but that was vetoed – followed a year later with *Mean Business*.

"After you've been with someone, Zeppelin and Robert [Plant], for that amount of years, you get to know each other as a band very, very well.

It can almost be an ESP type of thing. With Paul, his phrasing is totally different. I would think that Robert was like a vocal gymnast. And Paul, he's such a technical singer. He really is. And yet he has a quality within his voice that on the ballads he does is really caressing. And yet it's really vibrant in a way."

These two albums by The Firm represented a homogenized version of all the worst elements of both Bad Company and Led Zeppelin. The commercial songs were far too pop-oriented, far too FM-directed, and the ballads bore none of the mystique or intelligence inherent in both of the mother groups' material. Still, there were moments.

"We did a lot of different things; 'Radioactive' was strangely unique," reflects Rodgers. "I played the guitar solo on that. 'Live In Peace' (from an earlier Rodgers record) and 'All The King's Horses' and 'Satisfaction Guaranteed' were good ones. We did actually do some interesting things, I think.

"But I don't know if it ever totally gelled. We put a lot of our creative input into it, but it didn't quite work. Jimmy had been off the road and was very keen to get back onto the road which was partly the reason why I got talked into doing the ARMS tour. So we kind of compromised and said we'll make two albums and tour with them and see how we feel at the end of that time. And I agreed with that and that's what we did. At the end of that two years, it was, 'OK, well, that was great, let's move on.'"

Following The Firm's second album, *Mean Business*, the band embarked on an extensive tour of America, but ticket sales and audience reaction was poor. Paul then assembled The Law, centered on Who/Faces drummer Kenny Jones and a supporting cast including bassist John McIvers, keyboardist Albhy Galuten and guitarist Steve Acker. *The Law* was an attempt to expand on the basic guitar/bass/drums foundation and was supplemented with the Memphis Horns, layered synth textures (Ronnie Lee Cunningham) and percussion (Joe Lala). The result was lightweight and lacked poignancy. Ron Albert tended to over-produce this one-off. They did play a single show at The Milton Keynes Bowl where they opened for ZZ Top. Save for re-formatted versions of "Can't Get Enough" and "All Right Now", the concert was soon forgotten. And so was the band.

But The Law was a serious attempt to construct a durable partnership with fellow players. Rodgers secured ZZ Top's manager, Bill Ham, and in many ways, this was a similar situation to the one he'd experienced with Bad Company. Strong players, strong management and a singular vision were all pieces deftly assembled. But the winds of change were blowing and the industry, in 1991, was undergoing a Renaissance. Vinyl had been phased out and a new cult of players – metal bands with attitude – had become the norm. And The Law was hardly amongst the most wanted.

NOW IT'S ALL RIGHT

Following The Law, Rodgers took a different tack and decided to insti-
gate the beginnings of a true solo career by recording *Muddy Water Blues*,
released in 1993. This was a tribute to the great bluesman and for the
project Paul called on some guitar whizzes to flesh it out. Amongst those
involved were David Gilmour, Buddy Guy, Ritchie Sambora, Brian Setzer,
Brian May, Slash, Steve Miller, Neal Schon and Jeff Beck.

Pino Palladino and Jason Bonham made up the rhythm section. The
album generated a Grammy nomination (he'd earlier won a Grammy for
"Feel Like Makin' Love") and revealed the Rodgers so long missing in
music circles. His voice tugged at the heart with that urgency pumping
through the early Free songs and the vocal cat-and-mouse techniques presented were again reminiscent of that magical give-and-take he and Kossoff so artfully nurtured.

Though there are a host of keen players here, the album is really highlighted by the Beck tracks. Jeff, notorious for changing vocalists like the
proverbial socks, lights up the night with his performances on "Rolling
Stone", "I Just Wanna Make Love To you" and "Good Morning Little
Schoolgirl – Part I". In fact the ex-Yardbirds player was the only musician
guesting on more than two cuts. The pair had met briefly during the
ARMS stops but they never had a real chance to perform together. Even
this album was created via long-distance recording magic – basic tracks
were mailed to Jeff and on top of these he'd record solos, guitar fills and
various rhythm parts.

Beck, in Annette Carson's *Crazy Fingers*, a wonderfully researched biography on the legendary pickmaster, said, "It was real gung-ho, powerhouse
blues – more English, like *Truth* or *Beck-Ola* and the old band I had with
Rod Stewart. I think this has more balls than *Truth*: it's how I would have
wanted the Jeff Beck Group to sound."

Having realized a hit album in this return to his roots, Paul assembled a
band to take on the road. Neal Schon was chosen as guitarist (ex-Journey),
someone the singer met during the Muddy sessions, and the former Santana player brought in fellow Hardline (the group he assembled following
Journey) bassist Todd Jensen. They rehearsed, along with one-time Little
Feat drummer Richie Hayward, at Hollywood's S.I.R. Studios for about
a week and then began the voyage. Paul was not happy with Hayward's

performances and a week into the tour Richie was dismissed. Dean Castronovo, another Hardline member, was brought into the fold.

Following the tour, Rodgers re-entered the studio to record *The Hendrix Set*, another tribute album. After these sessions, Paul worked with a series of musicians including Tony Thompson, Tony Franklin and Reeves Gabrels. He eventually cemented a backing band comprising Geoff Whitehorn (ex-Crawler) on guitar, Jim Copley (Jeff Beck, Upp, Tears For Fears) on drums, and Jaz Lochrie (Tears For Fears, Go West) on bass. This quartet went on to tour extensively and record the *Paul Rodgers Live* album (1996), *Now* (1997) and his most recent, *Electric* (2000).

In the fall of 1997, Paul also recorded four tracks on Voices In the Wind, an album by guitarist Tim Donahue. With Jaz Lochrie on bass, the album features Rodgers on "How Long", "Another Day", "Sharing the Same Dream" and the title track.

David Evans, executive producer of the project as well as the visionary for the cutting edge Spirit Nation project (on Triloka Records), recalls his experiences. Keep in mind that Paul Rodgers had not contacted his ex-Bad Company mates for years. He is an extremely soft-spoken person but as has been evidenced earlier, his moods may strike fear in even the mightiest of men.

"I was hired to put the album together," details Evans. "Since the album featured a lot of instrumental guitar work, I wanted to hire the best guitar producer in the business. I called Eddie Kramer. In our discussions about the album, Eddie suggested we bring in a vocalist on a few songs. He thought his friend, Paul Rodgers (from the *Running With the Pack* sessions), would be the right choice.

"I flew Paul to L.A. from London, along with his manger. First class. The day after they arrived, I received a call from the manager telling me that Paul would like me to take them out for dinner – Tony Roma's on the Universal City Walk. I agreed. It was a little pushy but I figured this was just the price you pay when dealing with rock stars. So I thought I'd break the ice by giving Paul $10,000 in cash at the dinner. A portion of his fee. Money talks, right?

"As I was about to leave for dinner, I receive a fax from his lawyer informing me that the terms of our agreement were unacceptable, and that Paul would not sing unless I agreed to major changes. I couldn't deal with it at the moment. I arrived at Tony Roma's before my guests. I really had no idea what Paul looked like but when he walked through the door the rock star air was thick – and it was obvious.

"Paul was very distant and acted as though I wasn't in the room. But I figured we'd get friendly during our meal. Nothing could have been further from the truth. He and his manager sat across from me mumbling and acting amused, completely ignoring me. When I tried to make polite conversation, they looked at me as though I had just walked over for an autograph that he wasn't going to give. This went on for two hours and several beers later it was, thankfully, time to leave.

"And the $10,000? It stayed right in my pocket until the next morning when I laid it on my attorney's desk to deal with Paul's new demands – which he didn't get.

"During the sessions, I was instructed by Eddie never to talk to Paul during recording, and never to enter or leave the room. Paul was going to sing in the control room, not behind the glass in the normal fashion. To my amazement, Paul delivered one of the finest vocal performances I have ever seen or heard – in one take. An hour later he was off and that was the last time I saw him."

SAD COMPANY

Bad Company MK2 bore little resemblance to its predecessor.

-Simon Kirke

The mist had cleared and in the distance Paul Rodgers was now riding herd over a new group of musicians. Left in his wake were the skeletal remains of Bad Company – Simon Kirke, Boz Burrell and Mick Ralphs. Realizing that the singer was not returning, at least not any time soon, they all undertook various projects.

Then in 1986, when the opportunity arose to re-form the band, the remaining trio jumped at the opportunity. Ahmet Ertegun, head of Atlantic Records, had approached Mick Ralphs about putting the group back together. The guitarist phoned Simon and the hunt was on for a singer.

"When we were approached to start the band up again I thought, 'Well, why not?'" explains Kirke. "Just because one of the players in a team decides to leave, should that whole team roll over and die? We had nurtured the band for nearly eight years so we thought we'd give it a go. Mick was keen and Boz was sort of OK about it."

Mick Jones of Foreigner fame recommended Brian Howe, a vocalist from Portsmouth, England. The guitarist had been eyeing Brian as a replacement for Lou Gramm but sacrificed him to Bad Company.

Bad Company sans Paul Rodgers was like Deep Purple without Ritchie Blackmore, The Who without Keith Moon, Led Zeppelin without John Bonham. Sure, Joe Satriani and Steve Morse knew very well how to play "Smoke On the Water", Jason Bonham knew all of his father's drum fills and Kenny Jones could fake "My Generation", but these bands with these new players bore the distinct aroma of mediocrity. Bad Company suffered the same fate.

The Mark II version of Bad Company had its moments but very few of them. They recorded *Fame and Fortune, Dangerous Age, Holy Water, Here Comes Trouble* and *What You Hear Is What You Get*.

Mick Ralphs left around the time of Holy Water and was replaced by Geoff Whitehorn. The band expanded its sound to incorporate second guitarist Dave Colwell.

Brian Howe departed after the release of the 1993 live album and pursued a solo career. Mark Spiro, an established songwriter who has worked with Bad English, Heart and Julian Lennon, collaborated with the vocalist on several tracks.

"He was one of the funniest guys I've ever worked with. He had a positive work ethic and was a blast. He had great blond hair and a great tan."

For all of Spiro's spirited observations, Kirke and crew were less than forthcoming with the shining adjectives. Also, when Paul Rodgers' management was first contacted regarding this book, his handlers mentioned that if the name *Brian Howe* even appeared in print, there would be no access allowed to Rodgers.

Kirke found in Howe a strong singer – but certainly no replacement for Paul.

"Brian came down to the audition and so began a period which I ultimately regret. Howe was more a hard rock singer than a soulful one but Mick and myself thought we would try him out because he did have a good voice. He was inexperienced and we thought we could mold him to our way. He was very eager to work and he was good with a crowd. A sort of people pleaser really. Paul had become more and more withdrawn and sometimes barely acknowledged the crowd at all.

"Brian seemed to be more clued in to the sounds of that day and we thought why not take Bad Company down a more contemporary road?

"We had severed connections with Peter Grant (who would pass away several years later) and Swan Song, and we were free to go with who we wanted. Foreigner's manager Bud Prager and Phil Carson, who had worked for Atlantic as vice-president, became our managers and off we went."

Indeed. They toured and recorded but hardly made a splash. After Howe's leaving, the band recruited Robert Hart and bassist Rick Wills (late of Foreigner). This third lineup recorded *Company Of Strangers* and *Stories Told & Untold*.

In 1999 the original quartet re-convened for a tour. They undertook a 31-date cross-country run and in support of the reformation released the double-CD *Anthology* set commemorating the band's 25th anniversary. But it was not a particularly happy reunion, Boz Burrell and Mick Ralphs rented a separate tour bus so they would not have to travel with the singer. After two weeks of riding on the same bus as Paul, they leased their own mini-van – paid for with their own money – because they refused to ride with him. Some of these between-show legs took up to ten hours or more and since a mid-sized van is not appointed with the luxuries of a professional touring bus – private bunks, kitchen, and entertainment facilities – they'd often arrive at a show exhausted and infuriated. They eventually rented their own private bus.

This animosity coursed through the entire tour, with threats of physical violence arising whenever Paul's name was mentioned.

But now, in 2001, the band has reunited once again to tour. There is talk of a new album – but only talk.

EPILOGUE

Let me die to the sounds of delicious music.

-Conte de Mirabeau

Free and Bad Company have had undeniable influence on the contours of contemporary rock music. In fact these bands so excelled in capturing the essence of electric guitar and blues-meets-rock 'n' roll vocals, that bands are still defined and compared to them. The Black Crowes, Lynyrd Skynyrd, Aerosmith and others cite them as heroes and main influences.

Record buyers were so desperate for new material that the original quartet returned to the studios to record four new songs – "Tracking Down A Runaway", "Ain't It Good", "Hammer Of Love" and "Hey Hey" – for 1999's *The 'Original' Bad Co. Anthology.* This was the first time the crew had recorded together since the 1981 sessions for *Rough Diamonds,* their farewell project.

Bad Company, a band so inspired and articulate in the fashion in which they presented their music, have not been allowed to slip quietly into the long night. In 1999 they returned for a reunion and here in 2001, they are touring once again, co-headlining with Styx, Billy Squier and Joe Stark.

Paul Rodgers, the man who was the main focus of both bands, is a difficult person to understand. This writer has met him several times, sat and talked with him for hours at a time, and yet still has difficultly in trying to fully explain what he is about – his temperament, his temper and his vicious mood changes.

All those many years ago, the day after I wrote that story for *Rolling Stone* magazine, I invited Paul to an Elvis Presley concert at the mammoth Inglewood Forum. He jumped at the opportunity and I picked him up that day in my beat up Triumph Herald, the ugliest car ever built but one that made the singer feel at home when he saw me drive up.

Our tickets were not front row but that didn't lessen his feelings of attraction. Every time the King shook a hip or tossed a scarf into the audience, he'd mutter, "Did you see that? That was amazing! I can't believe what he did." No one around him seemed to recognize who he was. It was as if he was a young boy attending his first concert. Paul was absolutely mesmerized. He would grab me at various points, so entranced by what he was experiencing that he could barely control himself. Watching him, I was overjoyed by his reactions. Here I was, a rock scribe attending a Presley show, with arguably one of the most critically acclaimed singers in the world. Heady stuff for a young man.

Following the set, we made our way to the backstage area. I knew we'd be able to gain access to the inner sanctum and we simply approached the head bouncer. I told him I was with Paul Rodgers, the singer from Bad Company, and would it be possible to cross the velvet rope so Paul and Presley might meet? Again, another extraordinary coincidence reared its head when it turned out that Led Zeppelin, with Peter Grant, were also in attendance at the show and had already crossed the golden threshold to the backstage area. When we ventured down to the guarded entryway, we saw several Zeppeliners already cruising the sacred territory. "No problem," we thought.

The main security giant, though sympathetic, would not allow us entry. I explained who Paul was, that his manager and label representatives were already back there, and that, if he permitted us to pass through his watch, he would be facilitating a truly historical moment.

"Clive Coulson was our tour manager and he was with Peter backstage," recalls Rodgers. "And they actually met Elvis and I was originally supposed to be with them. They mentioned me to Elvis and he said for them to tell me, 'Take time to live.' That was his message to me. Clive came back to me and said, 'Yeah, I met Elvis and he's got a message for you: Take time to live.' And I thought, 'Wow, what does that mean?' Of course, he died not too long after that. It makes you wonder, doesn't it? It did make me think actually because I thought, 'Well, I'm living, aren't I?' And then you begin to realize being out of control and whoosshhh, you're on this roller coaster thing.

"And in some regards that's what success can be, but I measure success in different ways than other people. I don't really measure it in how many swimming pools and yachts and houses in the country and all that. I measure it in how happy I am and how happy am I making the people around me. So eventually I do step back from what I'm doing and stop."

There is an interesting wrinkle here: Grant and Zeppelin knew Paul desperately wanted to gain entry through the golden gates and it's almost impossible to fathom why they were not able to pull the singer backstage.

On the ride back to the Hyatt House, Paul was babbling and singing Elvis songs – absolutely elated. This cemented a relationship that has lasted over two-and-a-half decades.

That was one side of the man, the vulnerable and big-hearted traits. But every pendulum swings in the opposite direction and certain tales reveal a character with a somewhat more mean-spirited and heartless side.

His 1993 tour in support of the Muddy Waters honorarium in particular, revealed a dark underbelly. This cavalcade was a major operation and an entire summer was spent as support act on Steve Miller's American tour

Because the album was defined by the pageantry of guest attendees – Jeff Beck, Brian Setzer, Trevor Rabin, Slash and others – many of the shows were crowned when these various pickers came on stage. In spite of these once-in-a-lifetime combinations, the band was soon made aware that "you didn't want to be drinking with Paul." At the time, he was imbibing regularly and when fueled by alcohol, Rodgers was a transformed man. (He has since cleaned up entirely and now spends hours each day at the gym, working his body, and eating nutritiously).

But back then, slurred speech, loss of balance and a generally dark-spirited persona were revealed when alcohol was in his system. Paul the drinker was an angry man and his ego became uncontrollable. Woe-is-me tales abounded about a lackadaisical solo career and even when Free and Bad Company were mentioned in his presence, he responded as if those bands amounted to less than nothing. Presented with the possibility of a Bad Company reunion, he sneered at the mere suggestion.

Two laps around America, an extensive tour of Japan, and finally a scheduled tour covering Europe would mark the road trip's conclusion. But then an accident happened on a German autobahn and the final leg was scrapped.

The band was traveling in a separate rented van than Paul and his assistants were riding in another vehicle. En-route to Hamburg, a roadie driving the instrument truck had taken his eyes off the autobahn for a split second while loading in a cassette. During that instant, the crew's van ahead had reduced speed and the truck, unable to swerve around the crew's vehicle, ended up rear-ending it. The van was turned on its side and slid down the highway at a speed in excess of 70 miles per hour.

According to hospital records and local press, a member of the band had shattered his leg in three places and one of the roadies in the van broke several ribs. With the tour effectively ended, the band flew home. Upon his release from hospital, the musician was met by Paul's road manager who proceeded to pay for the five-day hospital stay.

This was the band member's last contact with Paul Rodgers. Management did not compensate the injured musician for additional medical expenses. Attempts were made to communicate with Rodgers' business managers but they turned a deaf ear. Not to mention that when the tour ended, this particalur instrumentalist was left handicapped and unable to find other gainful employment.

There is a closer to the German autobahn debacle. During the 1999 reunion tour, David Lee Roth was chosen as opening act. The injured musician who had been a part of Paul's band was now a member of the ex-Van Halen singer's group.

The musician and Paul only encountered each other two times during an entire summer tour. The shows had been running for about three weeks and backstage one afternoon the two parties were heading towards each other. The injured musician seeing the singer approaching, extended his hand, and said, "Hey, Paul?" Rodgers eyed him and continued on, without missing a step, not uttering a word. They met again several weeks later, amongst a crowd of people – their eyes locked and again Paul went mute.

On the other side, it must be mentioned that Paul is known to compliment his musicians on their abilities and can go out of his way to extend his gratitude. During first weeks of rehearsal, Paul tends to be very supportive but once a tour has begun, slaps on the back become a rarity.

Still, there is no denying what Paul Rodgers and Free and Bad Company have brought to the plate. "All Right Now" remains a classic in the same mold as "Stairway To Heaven", "Smoke On the Water" and "Johnny B. Goode". With dozens of tours and albums behind him, Paul, to this day, is touched by his creation.

"Hearing your own music on the radio has always been a thrill for me, even from day one. There is a lot of magic in music, there are a lot of moments when it's great. When you write a song, when you come up with a really good idea and you're completely absorbed in it and you completely forget time and space and surroundings, and you're completely involved in painting this musical picture, that's great. And then when you can go out and play that on stage and share that kind of musical landscape with other people, that's always a buzz."

Free and Bad Company were true artistes, creators of a pastiche that became the background for so many music fanatics and vinyl junkies. Though they obviously borrowed from the blues and R&B, what they committed to plastic seems unadulterated, as if the sound and style had just been invented. Certainly these various ingredients became more apparent in Paul's own solo work and for that matter in Paul Kossoff's as well.

Had Kossoff pulled through his nightmarish addictions, he would have certainly been regarded as one of the reigning string kings. What seems so fairytale-esque about his life is the fact that he entranced anyone and everyone who met him. Anger did not seem to be part of his emotional vocabulary. Frustration, disappointment, and insecurity, yes, but malice was not in him.

When I interviewed him for *Guitar Player*, just months before his final flight, it was only too obvious that he was intoxicated and high. When he opened the hotel room door, Koss had to hang on to the door handle to keep from keeling over. But from the moment I walked in, he completely enchanted me with his honesty and genuine love for the music he played and the musicians with whom he worked. He adored Paul Rodgers and many times during our conversation, the fact that Free had ended seemed still to be a concept impossible for him to grasp.

After speaking with him for most of the afternoon, I asked him if he had a guitar around. He said he had his Les Paul. "Would you like to see it?" he asked. I nodded vigorously and he said, to my utter amazement, "Are you sure?" As if he was imposing on me, as if cradling the Gibson he coaxed the most delicate sounds from, was an act I wouldn't be interested in. He watched as I fingered the chords to "All Right Now" and muttered something positive. Taking the pristine Les Paul from me, he played the chords and gave me that utterly disarming and innocent smile with which he'd charmed everyone he met and everyone who saw and heard him play.

Through the music of Free and Back Street Crawler and his various side projects, his soul will live forever. And Rodgers, now sober for years and the very picture of positivism, keeps that memory alive by including Free songs in his own solo set.

"I go my own way and I'm grooving, you know? When I go on stage I put the best of all my music across the years: music from Free, songs I wrote with Bad Company, songs from The Firm, solo songs, blues songs, and I put it all together. And it all equals a lot of music and a lot of good times."

When it is all over how would Paul Rodgers like to be remembered?

"It's hard to sum yourself up in a nutshell because it's not over yet. You know what I mean? Not for a long time. I still have a great deal of music I want to make, new material, and I have a lot of playing to do. I suppose it is a bit of a rock 'n' roll fantasy. I leave it for others to say – I leave that up to you.

"Whenever I hear a record I made twenty or thirty years ago, it's always a bit of a surprise to me. Because they're only ever that take of that moment. They become cast in stone by virtue of the fact that they're on tape and that's the record that goes out, that's the version of events that goes out. I listen to it and go, 'Wow, I did it that way then.'"

The recent box sets on both bands provide additional chronicling of the momentous steps taken by these groups. In particular, the *Songs Of Yesterday* Free set is an expansive cross-section of all the work the quartet managed to create in a period of just over four years. Young at the time, inexperienced and happy just for the opportunity to record, Free early on signed away the publishing rights to most of these songs, compositions that yearly generate hundreds of thousands of dollars in revenue.

"They [Universal Music] were gracious enough to call the band members and ask us for our input. Not whether or not we'd like to do it mind you. I was very wary at first because they were going to be digging into the archives of unreleased material which can mean junk if you're not careful. I have mixed feelings about it. I think it's interesting listening for hardcore Free fans, it gives you a little bit of the inside story. It was interesting for me because there were some outtakes that I'd completely forgotten. I hear myself singing things and I go, 'Good Lord, what the hell is that?' I know it's me but I don't remember doing it. There were things I never thought would see the light of day. I did a reggae thing out in Jamaica when I was there with Chris Blackwell, and that was quite refreshing to hear. And a song from Peace as well – so it's mixed feelings."

Andy Fraser was particularly displeased with the entire project. He told Rodgers, "Christ, I'm singing and it sounds like I'm twelve years old. Give me a break."

Fraser, for all his natural instinct and experience, has remained a mystery. Basking in the California desert, he has become the Howard Hughes of music.

"I speak to Andy – he doesn't talk back but I speak to him," chides Rodgers. "He's a difficult chap at the best of times."

Free and Bad Company has become part of our vocabulary. Television is replete with band references. On an edgy comedy skit program called *The Kids In the Hall*, a routine revolving around the disappearance of rock music is based on the line, "Rock 'n' roll has been on the wane since the release of the first Bad Company album in 1974." In a cheap horror flick called *Bordello Of Blood*, "All Right Now" is played in its entirely and acts as the film's opening musical sequence. In the film *The Castle*, "All Right Now" is also used as the introductory segment. In the broadcast version of Roddy Doyle's *The Commitments*, a debate arises about rock casualties and the line "So did your man from Free" is uttered in reference.

Most recently, Oklahoma bomber Timothy McVeigh is cited in *American Terrorist*, a biography written by Lou Michel and Dan Herbeck, as being infatuated with Bad Company. The authors write, "He called it [a Bradley fighting tank] 'Bad Company' after the 1970s rock group of the same name. The song's lyrics were tailor-made for McVeigh who related to the song, and not only because it mentioned guns. He loved the last few lines [actually the fade] including the phrase 'dirty for dirty' – giving back to people what they give to you."

Katie Couric, a nationally-syndicated television anchor, interviewed Michel and Herbeck and when they mentioned the slang "dirty for dirty," the hostess immediately responded by saying, "Oh, yeah, like in the Bad Company song." Instant recognition.

"Lots of people name their bikes, cats, jet skis and fuckin' snakes after our band," bemoans a not too amused Simon Kirke. "And this scum has to name a tank. Oh well, publicity like this we don't need."

Indeed they don't. Free and Bad Company managed to express emotion and edginess and anger and love without the overblown gimmicks so currently popular – vulgarity, violent imagery, and the now-so-standard big budget video with skimpily-clad ladies.

Many of the principals in this historic and personal narrative are now gone. Alexis Korner died on New Years Day, 1984. Guy Stevens was silenced forever when, on 29 August 1981, he overdosed on prescription medication. Peter Grant succumbed in 1997.

But their participation in the histories of these two bands will be long remembered. With a Bad Company reunion in full swing, an entirely new generation of rockers will be sucked into the fold. Even Paul Rodgers' children, Jasmine and Stephen, have taken up the cause with their own band called Boa.

In a recent conversation I had with Paul Rodgers, he looked back at his body of work – all the triumphs and traumas, the long winding road from Middlesbrough to London. From a boy with a dream, he became a man widely recognized as one of the most expressive and original singers of a generation. Simon Kirke, Paul Kossoff, Andy Fraser, Boz Burrell and Mick Ralphs were giants, the likes of which we may never see again. Over 30 years later, the music Rodgers and company has created still causes the spine to tingle.

They screamed to the heavens with cries of sheer electric freedom that many have tried to copy but few have been able to emulate. When they were mediocre, they were still more inventive and soulful than just about anybody around. And when they spoke that perfect language, a dialect based on extracting sounds from wood and wires and stretched animal skins and the infinitesimal grunts and groans of the human voice, they took us to new places. And Paul Rodgers, with his fellow guardians, may have never quite understood how they did it. But when it did happen, the music touched people like the sweetest kiss of rain. We didn't question it, and we never asked why. We just shut our eyes and let the serenade wash over us and when the rhapsody was complete, we simply turned over the record – and began again…

BIBLIOGRAPHY

Baker, Glenn A. and Stuart Coupe. *The New Music*. Harmony Books, 1980.

Benson, Joe. *Uncle Joe's Record Guide: Hard Rock – The First Two Generations*. J. Benson Unlimited, 1988.

Carson, Annette. *Jeff Beck: Crazy Fingers*. Creda Communications, 1998.

Charlesworth, Chris. *A-Z of Rock Guitarists*. Proteus Publishing Co., Inc., 1982.

Christgau, Robert. *Christgau's Record Guide*. Pantheon Books, 1990.

Clayson, Alan. *The Best of Rock: The Essential CD Guide*. Collins Publishers, 1993.

Clayton, David and Todd K. Smith. *Heavy Load: Free*. Moonshine Publishing, 2000.

Clifford, Mike. *The Harmony Illustrated Encyclopedia of Rock – Fifth Edition*. Harmony Books, 1986.

Cole, Richard and Richard Trubo. *Stairway To Heaven*. Harper Collins, 1992.

Collis, John. *The Blues: Roots and Inspiration*. Salamander Books Limited, 1997.

Downey, Pat. *Top 40 Music on Compact Disc: 1955 – 1997*. Pat Downey Enterprises, 1998.

Eddy, Chuck. *Stairway To Hell: The 500 Best Heavy Metal Albums In the Universe*. Harmony Books, 1991.

Erlewine, Michael and Vladimir Bogdanov and Chris Woodstra and Stephen Thomas Erlewine. *All Music guide – 3rd Edition*. Miller Freeman Books, 1997.

Frame, Pete. *The Complete Rock Family Trees*. Omnibus Press, 1993.

Free: Songs From Their A&M Recordings. North American Publishers Group.

Gillan, Ian and David Cohen. *Child In time: The Life Story Of the Singer From Deep Purple*. MBS Corporation, 1993.

Heatley, Michael. *The Ultimate Encylopedia Of Rock.* HarperPerennial, 1993.

Henke, James and Ron Van Der Meer. *The Rock Pack. Rock and Roll Hall Of Fame & Museum.* St. Martin's Press.

Hinton, Brian. *Message To Love: The Isle of Wight Festival 1968 – 1969 – 1970.* Castle Communications, 1995.

Jahn, Mike. *The Story of Rock – From Elvis Presley to the Rolling Stones.* Quadrangle/The New York Times Book Co., 1973.

Logan, Nick and Bob Woffinden. *New Musical Express Book of Rock.* IPC Magazines Ltd., 1973.

Miller, Jim. *The Rolling Stone Illustrated History Of Rock & Roll.* A Random House/Rolling Stone Press Book, 1980.

Pareles, Jon and Patricia Romanowski. *The Rolling Stone Encyclopedia Of Rock & Roll.* A Rolling Stone Press Book, 1983.

Rees, Dafydd and Luke Crampton. *Rock Movers & Shakers.* Billboard Books, 1991.

Russell, Tony. *The Encyclopedia of Rock.* Crescent Books, 1983.

Schaffner, Nicholas. *The British Invasion.* McGraw-Hill Paperbacks, 1983.

Shapiro, Harry. *Lost In the Blues.* Da Capo Press Inc., 1992.

Stone, Rolling editors. *The Rolling Stone Record Review.* Pocket Books, 1971.

Strong, M.C. *The Great Rock Discography.* Canongate Books, Ltd., 1995.

Tobler, John. *The Rock 'N' Roll Years.* Crescent Books, 1990.

Various authors. *Guinness Rockopedia: The Ultimate A-Z Of Rock and Pop.* Guinness Publishing, Ltd., 1998.

Various authors. *Rock Guitarists Volume II.* Guitar Player Books, 1977.

Various authors. *Rolling Stone Rock Almanac: The Chronicles of Rock & Roll.* A Rolling Stone Press Book, 1983.

Various authors. *The Rolling Stone Record Review.* Pocket Books, 1971.

White, Timothy. *Rock Lives: Profiles and Interviews.* Henry Holt and Company, 1990.

Young, Jean and Michael Lang. *Woodstock Festival Remembered.* Ballantine Books, 1979

Discography of major release Free and Bad Company albums in the US and UK

Part 1: Releases by FREE

Tons of Sobs

Released: November 1968
A&M SP-4198 (US LP)
Island ILPS 9089 (UK LP)
Island IMCD 62 (UK CD reissued June, 1988)
Highest chart position: #197 (US)
Produced by: Guy Stevens
Recording engineer: Andy Johns

Side One Over the Green Hills Pt. I
Worry
Walk In My Shadow
Wild Indian Woman
Goin' Down Slow

Side Two I'm A Mover
The Hunter
Moonshine
Sweet Tooth
Over The Green Hills Pt. II
Extra piano: Steve Miller

Singles released from the album:
I'm A Mover/Worry (March 1969)

Free

Released: October 1969
A&M SP-4204 (US LP released 1970)
Island ILPS 9014 (UK LP)
Island CID 9104 (UKCD reissued June, 1988)
Highest chart position: #22 (UK)
Produced by: Chris Blackwell

Side One
I'll Be Creeping
Songs Of Yesterday
Lying In The Sunshine

Trouble On Double Time
Mouthful Of Grass

Side Two
Woman
Free Me
Broad Daylight
Mourning Sad Morning

Singles released from the album:
Broad Daylight/The Worm (Island WIP 6054 -
March 1969)
I'll Be Creeping/Sugar For Mr Morrison
(Island WIP 6062 - June 1969)
I'll Be Creeping/Mouthful Of Grass (August
1969)

*Fire and Water

Released: June 26, 1970
A&M SP-4268 (US LP) – later version A&M
SP-3126 – released June 1970
A&M CD 3126 (US CD)
Island ILPS 9120 (UK LP)
Island 842 556-2 (UK CD reissued September, 1986)
Highest chart position: #17 (US)
Highest chart position: #2 (UK)
Produced by: Free and John Kelly

Side One
Fire and Water
Oh I Wept
Remember
Heavy Load

Side Two
Mr Big
Don't Say You Love Me
All Right Now

Singles released from the album:
All Right Now/Mouthful Of Grass (Island WIP 6082 - May 1970)
All Right Now/Lying In the Sunshine (Summer 1970)

Fire and Water was originally recorded on eight-track equipment. Upon completion, the album was presented to the label that felt additional recording was required. Tapes were transferred to sixteen-track where changes were made. In the meantime, the original version was released in the US and UK. When the sixteen-track remix was completed, this version replaced all prior recordings in the UK (including the CD re-issue). Inexplicably, the original tapes were never replaced in America. Original eight-track mix of album is still available on CD in the US.

Highway

Released December 1970
A&M SP-4287 (US LP released February, 1971)
Island ILPS 9138 (UK LP)
Island IMCD 63 (UK CD reissued June, 1988)
Highest chart position: #190 (US)
Highest chart position: #41 (UK)
Produced by: Free

Side One
The Highway Song
The Stealer
On My Way
Be My Friend

Side Two
Sunny Day
Ride On a Pony
Love You So
Bodie
Soon I Will Be Gone

Singles released from the album:
Stealer/Lying In the Sunshine (Island WIP 6093 - October 1970)
Stealer/Broad Daylight (November 1970)
The Highway Song/Love You So (January 1971)

*Free Live!

Released: June 1971
Released A&M August, 1971
Island ILPS 9160 (UK LP)
Island 842 359-2 (UK CD reissued June, 1988)
Highest chart position: #89 (US)
Highest chart position: #4 (UK)
Produced by: Free and Andy Johns
(+) Recorded live at Sunderland and Croydon
"Get Where I Belong" recorded at Island Studios

Side One
+All Right Now
I'm A Mover
Be My Friend
Fire and Water

Side Two
Ride On Pony
Mr Big
+The Hunter
Get Where I Belong

Singles released from the album:
I'll Be Creeping/Mr Big (March 1971)
My Brother Jake/Only My Soul (Island WIP 6100 - U.K. -April 1971)
My Brother Jake/Only My Soul (U.S. – April 1971)
*US version of album includes "My Brother Jake," not appearing on UK release.

Kossoff Kirke Tetsu Rabbit

Released: November 1971
Reissued: June 1994 U.K. CD

Side One
Blue Grass
Sammy's Alright
Anna
Just For the Box
Hold On

Side Two
Fool's Life
Yellow House
Dying Fire
I'm On the Run
Colours

Free At Last

Released: June 9, 1972
A&M SP-4349 (US LP released June, 1972)
Island ILPS 9192 (UK LP)
Island IMCD 82 (842 360-2) (UK CD reissued June, 1988)
Highest chart position: #69 (US)
Highest chart position: #9 (UK)
Produced by: Free

Side One
Catch A Train
Soldier Boy
Magic Ship
Sail On
Travelling Man

Side Two
Little Bit Of Love
Guardian of the Universe
Child
Universe

Singles released from the album:
Little Bit Of Love/Sail On (Island WIP 6129 - U.K. -May 1972)
Little Bit Of Love/Sail On (A&M 88170 - U.S. – May 1972)

Heartbreaker

Released: January 19, 1973
Island ILPS 9217 (US LP) later version Island SW-9324
Island ILPS 9217 (UK LP)
Island 422-842 361 (US CD)
Island (UK CD reissued September, 1986)
Highest chart position: #47 (US)
Highest chart position: #9 (UK)
Produced by: Free and Andy Johns

Side One
Wishing Well
Come Together in the Morning
Travellin' in Style
Heartbreaker

Side Two
Muddy Water
Common Mortal Man
Easy on My Soul
Seven Angels

Singles released from the album:
Wishing Well/Let Me Show you (Island WIP

6146 - November 1972)
Travellin' In Style/Easy On My Soul (March 1973)
Travellin' In Style/Come Together In the Morning (March 1973)
All Right Now/Mouthful Of Grass (U.K. re-release: July 1973)

The Free Story

Released: March 1974
Island ISLD 4 (UK LP) later version ISL D3
Island CID 9945 (UK CD reissued 1989)
Various producers

Side One
I'm A Mover (*Tons of Sobs*)
I'll Be Creepin' (*Free*)
Mourning Sad Morning (*Free*)
All Right Now (*Fire and Water*)
Heavy Load (*Fire and Water*)

Side Two
Fire and Water (*Fire and Water*)
Be My Friend (*Highway*)
The Stealer (*Highway*)
Soon I Will Be Gone (*Highway*)
Mr Big (*Free Live!*)

Side Three
The Hunter (*Free Live!*)
Get Where I Belong (*Free Live!*)
Travelling Man (*Free At Last*)
Just For the Box (*Kossoff/Kirke/Tetsu/Rabbit*)
Lady (previously unreleased)

Side Four
My Brother Jake (*Free Live!*)
Little Bit of Love (*Free At Last*)
Sail On (*Free At Last*)
Heartbreaker (originally on *Hearbreaker* but unreleased in this live version)
Come Together in the Morning (*Heartbreaker*)

Best of Free

Released: May 1975
A&M SP-3663 (US LP)
A&M CD-3663 (US CD)
Highest chart position: #120 (US)
Album never released in UK
Various producers

Side One
Fire and Water (*Fire and Water*)
The Highway Song (*Highway*)
Little Bit of Love (*Free At Last*)
Mouthful of Grass (*Free*)
My Brother Jake (*Free Live!*)
The Hunter (*Free Live!*)

Side Two
All Right Now (*Fire and Water*)
Woman (*Free*)
Catch A Train (*Free At Last*)
I'm A Mover (*Tons of Sobs*)
The Stealer (*Highway)*
Goodbye (*Free At Last*)

The Best of Free: All Right Now

Released: February 1992
A&M released 1972
Island ILPTV 2 (UK CD reissued 1988)
Highest chart position: not available
Remixed by Bob Clearmountain

Side One
Wishing Well (*Heartbreaker*)
All Right Now (*Fire and Water*)
Little Bit of Love (*Free At Last*)
Come Together in the Morning (*Heart-breaker*)
The Stealer (*Highway*)
Sail On (*Free At Last*)
Mr Big (*Fire and Water*)

Side Two
My Brother Jake (*Free Live!*)
The Hunter (*Tons of Sobs*)
Be My Friend (*Highway*)
Travellin' in Style (*Heartbreaker*)
Fire and Water (*Fire and Water*)
Travelling Man (*Free At Last*)
Don't Say You Love Me (*Fire and Water*)

Molten Gold: The Anthology

Released: 1993
A&M CD 31451 8456-2 (US CD)
Various producers

Disc One
I'm A Mover
The Hunter
Walk in my Shadow (from the album *Tons of Sobs*)
I'll Be Creepin'
Songs of Yesterday
Woman
Broad Daylight
Mouthful of Grass (from the album *Free*)
All Right Now
Oh I Wept
Heavy Load
Don't Say You Love Me (from the album *Fire and Water*)
The Stealer
The Highway Song
Be My Friend
Soon I Will Be Gone (from the album *Highway*)

Disc Two
My Brother Jake
Fire and Water
Ride On Pony
Mr Big (from the album *Free Live!*)
Time Away
Molten Gold (from the album *Paul Kossoff-Back Street Crawler*. 1973)
Catch A Train
Travelling Man
Little Bit of Love
Sail On (from the album *Free At Last*)
Wishing Well
Come Together in the Morning
Travelling in Style
Heartbreaker (from the album *Heartbreaker*)

Songs of Yesterday

Released: 2000
Highest chart position: not available
Various producers

Disc One
Over the Green Hills (new stereo mix)
Walk in My Shadow (alternative stereo mix)
Wild Indian Woman (new stereo mix)
Guy Stevens Blues (version previously unreleased)

Visions of Hell (version previously unre-
leased)
I'm A Mover (unused 7" mono mix)
Moonshine (alternative stereo mix)
Woman By the Sea (version previously
unreleased)
Free Me (version previously unreleased)
Long Tall Sally (version previously unre-
leased)
Broad Daylight (original 7'" mono mix)
The Worm (original 7" B-side)
Trouble On Double Time (version previously
unreleased)
Spring Dawn (version previously unreleased)
I'll Be Creepin' (version previously unre-
leased)
Sugar For Mr Morrison (new stereo mix)
Songs of Yesterday (new stereo mix)
Woman (version previously unreleased)
Mourning Sad Morning (alternative stereo
mix)
Fire and Water (alternative stereo mix)

Disc Two
All Right Now (version previously unreleased)
Oh I Wept (new stereo mix)
Remember (new stereo mix)
Don't Say You Love Me (new stereo mix)
The Stealer (full version)
The Highway Song (alternative stereo mix)
On My Way (alternative stereo mix)
Sunny Day (new stereo mix with different
vocals)
Ride On A Pony (alternative stereo mix)
Love You So (new stereo mix with alternative
vocals)
Soon I Will Be Gone (version previously
unreleased)
My Brother Jake (new stereo mix)
Makin' Love (Only My Soul) (previously
unreleased)
Rain (previously unreleased)
Get Where I Belong (version previously
unreleased)
Only My Soul (original 7" B-side)
Molten Gold (version previously unreleased)

Disc Three
Little Bit of Love (alternative mix)
Soldier Boy (alternative mix)
Sail On (version previously unreleased)
Guardian of the Universe (version previously
unreleased)
Child (alternative mix)
Honky Tonk Women (previously unreleased)

Lady (previously unreleased)
Muddy Water (version previously unreleased)
Heartbreaker (live from the mixing desk)
Wishing Well (version previously unreleased)
Let Me Show You (previously unreleased
jam)
Let Me Show You (original B-side)
Muddy Water (alternative mix)
Common Mortal Man (alternative mix)
Heartbreaker (alternative mix)
Seven Angels (alternative mix)

Disc Four
(live)
Ride On A Pony
Be My Friend
Fire and Water
The Stealer
Don't Say You Love Me
Mr Big
I'll Be Creepin'
Free Me
Woman
I'm A Mover
Walk In My Shadow
Songs of Yesterday
All Right Now
Crossroads

Disc 5
(associated recordings)
(I Just Wanna) See You Smile (Paul Rodgers
and The Maytals – previously unreleased)
Like Water (Peace – previously unreleased)
Zero (Peace – previously unreleased)
Ol' Jelly Roll (Sharks – alternative 7" mix)
Follow Me (Sharks – alternative 7" mix)
Fool's Life (KKTR –version previously
unreleased)
I'm On the Run (KKTR – version previously
unreleased)
Sammy's Alright (KKTR – version previously
unreleased)
Hold On (KKTR – new stereo mix)
Tuesday Williamsburg (Rabbit – previously
unreleased)
Unseen Love (Rabbit – previously unre-
leased)
Time Spent (Time Away) (Paul Kossoff/John
Martyn – full 18-minute version; previously
unreleased)

Part 2: Releases by BAD COMPANY

Bad Company

Released: June 8, 1974
Swan Song/Atlantic 7567-92441-2
Island ILPS 9279
Highest chart position: #1 (US)
Highest chart position: #3 (UK)
Produced by: Bad Company

Side One
Can't Get Enough
Rock Steady
Ready For Love
Don't Let Me Down

Side Two
Bad Company
The Way I Choose
Movin' On
Seagull

Singles released from the album:
Can't Get Enough/Little Miss Fortune (June 1974)
Movin' On/Easy On My Soul (March 1975)

Straight Shooter

Released: April 17, 1975
Swan Song/Atlantic 7567-92436-2
Island ILPS 9304
Highest chart position: #3 (US)
Highest chart position: #3 (UK)
Produced by: Bad Company

Side One
Good Lovin' Gone Bad
Feel Like Makin' Love
Weep No More
Shooting Star

Side Two
Deal With the Preacher
Wild Fire Woman
Anna
Call On Me

Singles released from the album:
Good Lovin' Gone Bad/Whisky Bottle (May 1975)

Feel Like Makin' Love/Wild Fire Woman (September 1975)

Run With the Pack

Released: February 7, 1976
Swan Song/Atlantic 7567-92435-2
Island ILPS 9346
Highest chart position: #5 (US)
Highest chart position: #4 (UK)
Produced by: Bad Company

Side One
Live For the Music
Simple Man
Honey Child
Love Me Somebody
Run With the Pack

Side Two
Silver, Blue and Gold
Youngblood
Do Right By Your woman
Sweet Little Sister
Fade Away

Singles released from the album:
Run With the Pack/Do Right By Your Woman (February 1976)
Youngblood/Do Right By Your Woman (May 1976)
Honey Child/Fade Away (August 1976)

Burnin' Sky

Released: March 12, 1977
Swan Song/Atlantic 7567-92450-2
Island ILPS 9441
Highest chart position: #15 (US)
Highest chart position: #17 (UK)
Produced by Bad Company

Side One
Burnin' Sky
Morning Sun
Leaving You
Like Water
Everything I Need

Side Two
Knapsack

Heartbeat
Peace of Mind
Passing Time
Too Bad
Man Needs A Woman
Master of Ceremony

Singles released from the album:
Burnin' Sky/Everything I Need (April 1977)

Desolation Angels

Released: March 10, 1979
Swan Song/Atlantic 7567-92451-2
Island SSK 59408
Highest chart position: #3 (US)
Highest chart position: #10 (UK)
Produced by: Bad Company

Side One
Rock 'N' Roll Fantasy
Crazy Circles
Gone, Gone, Gone
Evil Wind
Early In the Morning

Side Two
Lonely For Your Love
Oh, Atlanta
Take the Time
Rhythm Machine
She Brings Me Love

Singles released from the album:
Rock 'n' Roll Fantasy/Crazy Circles (June 1979)
Gone, Gone, Gone/Take the Time (August 1979)

Rough Diamonds

Released: August 28, 1982
Swan Song/Atlantic 7567-92452-2
Highest chart position: #26 (US)
Highest chart position: #15 (UK)
Produced by: Bad Company

Side One
Electricland
Untie the Knot
Nuthin' On the TV
Painted Face
Kickdown

Side Two
Ballad Of the Band

Cross Country boy
Old Mexico
Downhill Ryder
Race Track

Singles released from the album:
Electricland/Untie the Knot (October 1982)

10 From 6

Released: January 1986
Swan Song/Atlantic 7567-81625-2
Highest chart position: #137 (US)
Produced by: Bad Company

Side One
Can't Get Enough
Feel Like Makin' Love
Runnin' With the Pack
Shooting Star
Movin' On

Side Two
Bad Company
Rock 'N' Roll Fantasy
Electricland
Ready For Love
Live For the Music

Singles released from the album:
This Love/Tell It Like It Is (November 1986)

Fame And Fortune

Released: November 1986
Swan Song/Atlantic CD 81684-2
Swan Song/Atlantic LP 69
Swan Song/Atlantic CS 816844
Highest chart position: #106 (US)
Produced by: Bad Company

Side One
Burning Up
This Love
Fame and Fortune
That Girl
Tell It Like It Is

Side Two
Long Walk
Hold On My Heart
Valerie
When We Made Love
If I'm Sleeping

Singles released from the album:

Fame and Fortune/When We Made Love
(1987)

Dangerous Age

Released: October 1988
Atco CD 81884-2
Swan Song/Atlantic CD 81884-2
Swan Song/Atlantic LP 7818841
Swan Song/Atlantic CS 818844
Highest position reached: #58 (US)
Produced by: Bad Company

Side One
One Night
Shake It Up
No Smoke Without Fire
Bad Man
Dangerous Age

Side Two
Dirty Boy
Rock of America
Something About You
The Way That It Goes
Love Attack

Singles released from the album:
Shake It Up/Dangerous Age (April 1989)
No Smoke Without Fire/Love Attack (1989)

Holy Water

Released: June 1990
Atco CD 91371-2
Atco CS 91371-4
Atlantic/Swan Song CD 91371
Atlantic/Swan Song LP 91371
Produced by: Terry Thomas

Side One
Holy Water
Walk Through Fire
Stranger Stranger
If You Needed Somebody
Fearless
Lay Your Love On Me

Side Two
Boys Cry Tough
With You In A Heartbeat
I Don't Care
Never Too Late
Dead Of the Night
I Can't Live Without You
100 Miles

Singles released from the album:
Holy Water/I Can't Live Without You (August 1990)
If You Needed Somebody/Dead Of the Night (1990)
Walk Through Fire/Lay Your Love On Me (1990)

Here Comes Trouble

Released: September 1992
Atco CD 91759-2
Atco CS 91759-4
Produced by: Bad Company

Side One
How About That
Stranger Than Fiction
Here Comes Trouble
This Could Be the One
Both Feet In the Water

Side Two
Take This Town
What About You
Little Angel
Hold On To My Heart
Brokenhearted
My Only One

Singles released from the album:
How About That/Brokenhearted (1992)
This Could Be the One/How About That (1992)

The Best of Bad Company Live...
What You Hear Is What You Get

Released: 1993
Atlantic CD 92307
Atlantic CS 92307
Side One
How About That
Holy Water
Rock 'n' Roll Fantasy
If You Needed Somebody
Here Comes Trouble
Ready For Love
Shooting Star

Side Two
No Smoke Without A Fire
Feel Like Makin' Love
Take This Town
Movin' On
Good Lovin' Gone Bad

Fist Full Of Blisters
Can't Get Enough

Company Of Strangers

Released: 1995
East West CD 61808
East West CS 61808
Elektra/Asylum CD 61808
Elektra/Asylum CD 61808
Produced by: Bad Company

Side One
Company Of Strangers
Clearwater Highway
Judas my Brother
Little Martha
Gimme Gimme
Where I Belong

Side Two
Down Down Down
Abandoned And Alone
Down And Dirty
Pretty Woman
You're the Only Reason
Dance With the Devil
Loving You Out Loud

Stories Told & Untold

Released: October 15, 1996
Elektra/Asylum CD 61976
Elektra/Asylum CS 61976

Side One
One On One
Oh, Atlanta
You're Never Alone
I Still Believe In You
Ready For Love
Waiting On Love
Can't Get Enough

Side Two
Is That All There Is To Love
Love So Strong
Silver, Blue And Gold
Downpour In Cairo
Shooting Star
Simple Man
Weep No More

The 'Original' Bad Co. Anthology

Released: 1999
Elektra/Asylum 62349-2 (2 CD set)

Disc One
Can't Get Enough
Rock Steady
Ready For Love
Bad Company
Movin' On
Seagull
Superstar Woman
Little Miss Fortune
Good Lovin' Gone Bad
Feel Like Makin' Love
Shooting Star
Deal With The Preacher
Wild Fire Woman
Easy On My Soul
Whiskey Bottle

Disc Two
Honey Child
Run With The Pack
Silver, Blue And Gold
Do Right By Your Woman
Burnin' Sky
Heartbeat
Too Bad
Smokin' 45
Rock And Roll Fantasy
Evil Wind
Oh Atlanta
Rhythm Machine
Untie the Knot
Downhill Ryder
Tracking Down A Runaway
Ain't It Good
Hammer Of Love
Hey, Hey

Buy Online

All SAF and Firefly titles are available from the SAF Publishing website. You can also browse the full range of rock, pop, jazz and experimental music titles we have available. You can also keep up with our latest releases and special offers, contact us, and request a catalogue.

www.safpublishing.com

You can also write to us at:
SAF Publishing Ltd, Unit 7, Shaftesbury Centre,
85 Barlby Road, London, W10 6BN. England

Mail Order

All SAF and Firefly titles are also available by mail order from the world famous Helter Skelter bookshop.

You can either phone or fax your order to Helter Skelter on these numbers:

Telephone: +44 (0)20 7836 1151 or Fax: +44 (0)20 7240 9880
Office hours: Mon-Fri 10:00am - 7:00pm,
Sat: 10:00am - 6:00pm, Sun: closed.

Helter Skelter Bookshop,
4 Denmark Street, London, WC2H 8LL, United Kingdom.
If you are in London come and visit us, and browse the titles in person!!

Email: helter@skelter.demon.co.uk
Website: http://www.skelter.demon.co.uk

www.safpublishing.com

saf publishing

www.safpublishing.com